THE PALACE GUARD

THE

★

PALACE

★

GUARD

★

Dan Rather
and Gary Paul Gates

HARPER & ROW, PUBLISHERS

NEW YORK, EVANSTON, SAN FRANCISCO, LONDON

For Jean, Robin and Daniel
D.R.

For Linda, Christopher and my mother
G.P.G.

Grateful acknowledgment is made to Macmillan Publishing Co., Inc., for permission to reprint the excerpt from "The Second Coming" by William Butler Yeats as published in *Collected Poems*. Copyright 1924 by Macmillan Publishing Co., Inc., renewed 1952 by Bertha Georgie Yeats.

Designed by Sidney Feinberg

Library of Congress Cataloging in Publication Data

Rather, Dan.
  The palace guard.
  1. United States—Politics and government—1969—
2. Presidents—United States—Staff. 3. Cabinet
officers—United States. I. Gates, Gary Paul, joint
author. II. Title.
E855.R37   320.9'73'0924   74–4855
ISBN 0–06–013514–X

75 76 77 78 16 15 14 13 12 11

CONTENTS

ILLUSTRATIONS

Except where noted, all photographs are from Wide World Photos.

PREFACE

A number of other books proved to be of invaluable assistance in the conception and writing of this book. It is unfair, perhaps, to mention only a few of them, but the following works, we feel, are deserving of our special thanks. In our efforts to place the Nixon Presidency in perspective, against the background of its more recent predecessors, we are especially indebted to *The President's Men,* Patrick Anderson's 1968 study of the White House staff system from the Roosevelt era down to Lyndon Johnson's years in office. The two Nixon biographies we found most helpful in dealing with the pre-Presidential years were *Nixon Agonistes* by Garry Wills and *The Resurrection of Richard Nixon* by Jules Witcover. We are also grateful to Theodore H. White for the cumulative portrait of Richard Nixon that emerges from his four campaign books, starting with *The Making of the President 1960,* and to Richard Whalen for *Catch the Falling Flag,* his insider's account of the 1968 campaign. In terms of the Presidential years themselves, our task was immeasurably aided by the reporting of Rowland Evans, Jr., and Robert D. Novak in *Nixon in the White House: The Frustration of Power.* Their account of the early years of Richard Nixon's Presidency helped to remind us of many events that might otherwise have been forgotten in the attempt to give shape and focus to our own view of the period leading up to Watergate.

Also of immense value were the hundreds of newspaper and magazine articles that have been published since January 20, 1969. In this area, we are especially conscious of our competitors on the firing line itself: the men and women who have covered the Nixon White House during these years. Again, at the risk of being unfair to the others, we would like to pay special tribute to the following members of the White House press corps whose articles helped to chart some of the paths taken in this book: John Osborne of *The New Republic,* James Deakin of the St. Louis *Post-Dispatch,* Hugh Sidey of Time-Life, Martin F. Nolan of the Boston *Globe* and Marty Schram of *Newsday.*

We are deeply indebted to our colleagues at *CBS News,* so many of whom have given us the benefit of their journalistic judgment and wisdom. Beyond that, in a more personal sense, their warm words of encouragement came as a much-needed boost at times when our own spirits had begun to flag. In working on this project, we have done our best—in another form—to live up to the high standards that are so much a part of the *CBS News* tradition. Whatever strengths there are in this book reflect that effort, while its defects are entirely our own.

A special word of thanks must go to Donald R. Murdoch, who worked at the White House during these years. Although he does not agree with everything we have said in this book, he was kind enough to review the manuscript and offer his comments.

It is customary in such acknowledgments for writers to mention the help they received from their editor and publisher, but our sense of gratitude requires much more than a perfunctory "thank you" for editorial assistance. Our editor, Kitty Benedict, and her colleagues at Harper & Row salvaged this project at a time when it seemed to be drifting toward imminent extinction. At a time when others gave us little cause for hope, they saw relevance in our conception and re-mained steadfast in their confidence that we could somehow get it down on paper. For that, we are forever in their debt.

Finally, it must be said that this book could not have been written without the gallant contribution of various men and women who have been a part of the Nixon Administration. In the chapters ahead, we are often critical of those who were engaged in the pursuit and exercise of power during the years of Richard Nixon's Presidency. But the primary source of these criticisms is not the "media" or alleged "enemies" of the Nixon White House, but rather dedicated government officials who came to Washington because they believed in Richard Nixon and were later saddened by what they saw unfold deep within the catacombs of power. In hundreds of confidential interviews over the past five and a half years, they disclosed information that was often painful for them to disclose, and they did so at great personal risk to their own careers. Even now, it would not be appropriate to identify them by name. They wanted the Nixon Presidency to succeed, but they did not let that loyalty corrupt their belief in a free and vigorous press and the public's right to know. In our view, they are the unsung heroes of this book.

June 10, 1974

The first impression that one gets of a ruler
and of his brains is from seeing the men that he has about him.

—MACHIAVELLI

PART I

The Age of Nixon

One

RICHARD NIXON came into office as a minority President. Then as he set out to govern the country, he had to endure taunts that he was nothing more than an accidental President who, in effect, had slipped into the White House through the back door. According to this view, the Presidency had come to Nixon not so much as a result of his own efforts, or those of his party, but rather because of everything that had happened to the Democrats. To hear his opponents tell it, his squeak-through victory in 1968 was like that of Fortinbras, another shrewd opportunist, who got his hands on Elsinore only because the best of the Danes lay slaughtered, having chosen to destroy each other instead of joining forces against a common enemy.

In disparaging Nixon's '68 triumph, Democrats would recall the incredible sequence of events that overwhelmed them during Lyndon Johnson's last year in the White House. First, there was the war in Vietnam, which touched off a bitter revolt within their own party. Then came LBJ's dramatic abdication, which only deepened the existing chaos since it sent the Democrats into that election year with a President who, suddenly, was no longer a candidate. Then, just when it looked as if everything might coalesce around a new leader, the crown prince of Camelot, a second Kennedy, was cut down by an assassin's bullet. And, finally, there were the riots on the streets of Chicago, which destroyed any hope of bringing order and harmony to the party's national convention. Having suffered through all that, there was hardly a Democrat in the land who had any stomach left for the main event. But, as in *Hamlet,* one of the few survivors with a recognizable name was Horatio (*Hubert* Horatio), and he agreed to lead the exhausted troops into battle. It promised to be a real massacre.

But it wasn't. Even in their battered condition, the Democrats came close to pulling it out. True, much of the credit for that belonged to candidate Nixon, who revived his old 1960 trick of taking a big early lead and driving it to the edge of the cliff. (Many Democrats at the time shuddered at the thought of what would have happened if they had been thrown into the ring against a real hitter, like Rockefeller.) Yet the nature of the opposition was only part of it. Even a great many dispassionate observers, who felt no allegiance to the Democratic cause, were convinced that the closeness of the 1968 election revealed a deeper truth: that, despite Vietnam and the Chicago convention and all the rest of it, the old coalition put together by Franklin D. Roosevelt was still viable, and the Democratic party continued to speak for the majority of Americans. The party's victories in the Senate and Congressional races that fall were cited to buttress the argument. To many, the conclusion was indisputable: had it not been for the extraordinary circumstances of that curse-ridden year, there would have been no Nixon victory.

At the heart of this view of the '68 election was the belief that Richard Nixon was out of tune with the times, those times being the sixties. For example, early in 1968, just a few weeks before he was killed, Martin Luther King was asked to comment on Nixon and his then-emerging candidacy for President. The civil-rights leader promptly dismissed both man and candidacy as "a total irrelevance." It was noted that Nixon's point of identity was somewhere back in the forties, when he was defending the Free World against the likes of Alger Hiss and Helen Gahagan Douglas; or, if you prefer, the fifties, when he spent eight years carrying the father figure's golf clubs. All this served to reinforce the notion that the Nixon Presidency would be an anachronistic interlude, a one-term exercise in treading water, and that's all. Then, in 1973, somebody more "relevant"—no way of avoiding that word, for it was the operative cliché of the sixties—would move in and take up the slack.

But what so many people failed to grasp at the time was that the sixties were coming to an end—not only on the calendar, but in other important ways as well. The various political and social forces that swept across America during the Kennedy-Johnson years may have seemed robust and still full of life in 1968, but in reality they were a dying volcano, going through its last spasms. Richard Nixon was one man who understood this, and during his first term in the White House he presided over the death of the era that preceded his election. In the course of his early Presidential years, it was the sixties that came to seem irrelevant—not Nixon. To cite some of the more significant examples:

—*The Kennedy Cult.* It may be said that the opening gong of the sixties was sounded in the summer of 1960 when, in his first speech as the Democratic Presidential nominee, John Kennedy summoned his countrymen to join him in the adventurous journey across the New Frontier. By the time Nixon entered the White House, two Kennedys lay buried in Arlington, yet the torch—once again—had been passed, this time to the last of the brothers. And the many Americans who still yearned for a return to Camelot now centered their hopes on Edward Kennedy. Then in the first year of Nixon's Presidency—and nine years to the month after JFK's "New Frontier" speech—came Chappaquiddick. While that tragedy did not eliminate Ted Kennedy as a future Presidential aspirant, it sullied the mystique. The romantic aura that surrounded the Kennedys all through the sixties has never been the same since.

—*The Great Society.* When first introduced, the sweeping legislation of the early Johnson years, aimed at improving the economic and social life of the country's less fortunate citizens, seemed to have the support of a majority of Americans.

Johnson went to his grave believing that his social-welfare program was what people voted for in the 1964 landslide. Nixon, however, viewed the '64 results as a case of Americans voting *against* something, namely Barry Goldwater and his image as a far-right extremist. Whichever view deserves the most weight, it is true that time and, perhaps, the Vietnam war brought a change in the public mood about Great Society legislation.

After Nixon became President, the change accelerated. What once had been called the "war on poverty" became known as the "welfare mess," giving "cheap handouts" to "chiselers" and "loafers." And the cry of "We Shall Overcome," which Johnson once borrowed to dramatize his commitment to civil rights, became lost in a maze of code words, like "law and order," "low-income housing," and the most emotional of them all, "school busing."

—*Black Militancy.* Out of the civil-rights struggle of the early sixties came the "black power" movement and the angry rhetoric of Stokely Carmichael and H. Rap Brown. By the time Nixon was elected, this movement was reaching its crest with the emergence of the Black Panthers. With upraised fists clenched in defiance, the revolutionary Panthers sounded the battle cry "Right On!" and called on their "brothers" to stand up against the "evils" of America's "white power structure." Yet, long before Nixon's first term was over, the Panthers found themselves in disarray. Their most articulate spokesman, Eldridge Cleaver, was living in exile in Algeria, and other leaders of the group, such as Bobby Seale and Huey Newton, had returned to "straight" lives within the system. And the disintegration of the Black Panthers marked the end of violent black protest as a sustained and organized movement.

—*The New Left.* The white, middle-class cousins of the black militants also were riding high as the sixties drew to a close, and they had even persuaded themselves that the tide of history was flowing in their direction. A number of middle-class liberals, they contended, already had been "radicalized" by the war in Vietnam. Now they were counting on Nixon to be an inept and inflexible ruler, whose policies would force still more fence-straddling liberals to head for the barricades, there to rally around the flag of radical protest. But it wasn't long before the campus-oriented apostles of the New Left discovered an important truth: that, in order to have any chance of success, radical movements need in the seat of power a government that is at least somewhat sympathetic to their concerns. The relatively tolerant officials of the Kennedy-Johnson years were now gone, and in their stead were men who, for the most part, viewed protest demonstrations not as expressions of dissent to be controlled, but as criminal acts to be suppressed. So, faced with an iron resistance they had not encountered before, the white radical groups also began falling apart. Some of their leaders wound up in jail, or went underground; still others, buckling under the pressure, turned their attention to less-threatening issues, like ecology. If it is true that the radical politics of the sixties began with the sit-in movements in 1960 and the issuing of the SDS manifesto at the Port Huron meeting in 1962, then the last hurrah was sounded on the campus of Kent State in

1970 and, one year later, at the massive May Day bust in Washington.

—*The Counter-Culture.* The music and values of the rock and drug culture had built up big steam during the mid-sixties. Around this time the Beatles became the leading minstrels of the drug scene, celebrating the joys of acid in songs like "Lucy in the Sky with Diamonds." And not long after that came the popular musical *Hair,* in which the new breed of "flower children" conjured up a psychedelic vision of the good vibes and groovy trips that would come to all of us with the dawning of the Age of Aquarius. Yet, even as that message was being proclaimed, the Age of Aquarius was fading into the sunset. By the early Nixon years, the Beatles had lost the magic that held them together, and *The Yellow Submarine* never surfaced again. Other voices were stilled in a more tragic way. The demands of a life style that revolved around hard rock and hard drugs proved to be too much for Janis Joplin and Jimi Hendrix. Their deaths, in the opinion of Ellen Willis, the rock critic for *The New Yorker,* symbolized the end of the sixties "as a cultural unit."

The death of the sixties represented a fundamental change in the nation's view of itself, a turning-away from the upheavals that had so transformed America during the Kennedy-Johnson years. And this change was responsible, as much as any other single factor, for Richard Nixon's obtaining, in 1972, the huge victory that had eluded him four years earlier. (This is not to overlook the impressive contributions made by George McGovern and Thomas Eagleton; or, for that matter, the criminal contributions made by Arthur Bremer and the Watergate saboteurs.) Nixon's first term, then, was a period of transition, a time of uncertain passage, but in the immediate aftermath of the '72 election there seemed little doubt that we had entered into a new era—the Age of Nixon.

For by 1972 Richard Nixon's Presidency had become the dominant reality for all Americans: for Ted Kennedy as well as Ted Agnew; for Bob Dylan as well as Bob Hope; for Jane Fonda as well as John Wayne; for the Berrigan brothers as well as Billy Graham; for Daniel Ellsberg as well as Warren Burger. For black and white, for left and right, for war protester and POW, for pot smoker and hard hat. For all of them and for all of us. By 1972, Nixon already had made significant strides toward redefining his age and giving it a new identity more in keeping with his own beliefs and aspirations. And, when he became only the fourth man in this century to get himself elected to two full terms in the White House, he seemed destined to make of his tenure a watershed Presidency, one that would so influence the course of events that its effects would be felt, in a variety of ways, in years and even decades to come.

This was the mood, the sense of epochal milestone, that permeated Washington in 1972 on the eve of the second term as Richard Nixon stood on a pinnacle seldom reached in American politics. No longer could carping critics dismiss him as a caretaker President whose presence in the White House was just an irritating interruption in the natural flow of history. Now looming ahead were the much-heralded "four more years," and in the course of that interval, with a sweeping landslide serving as his mandate, Nixon fully intended to alter the flow of history, to leave a legacy that his successors could ignore only at their peril. In foreign policy, this meant that the initiatives of the first term would be carried further toward lowering Cold War intensity, an enduring peace and a reordering of the world's power structure along new lines of stability. At home, the effort would continue, with far more zeal and purpose, to steer the country away, not just from the Great Society, but from the deeper liberal-Democratic tradition it represented, which had dominated American government since Roosevelt's time.

The goal was nothing less than to push America as definitively to the right as FDR had pushed it to the left forty years earlier; and, in the process, to build a new conservative majority as strong and enduring as the old Roosevelt coalition, which now lay in ashes on George McGovern's funeral pyre. As one White House official put it at the time of the second inaugural: "During the first term, we stopped their revolution. Now we can move forward with our own." Clearly, there was every reason to believe that the Age of Nixon, as he and those close around him had dreamed of it, was for better or for worse upon us.

Yet, within a few weeks after the second inaugural, the great dream began dissolving into nightmare. For, in the spring of 1973, there came the Watergate deluge. And, once the dam broke, there was no stopping its fury. Over the months that followed, the flood waters raged on and on, washing up over the bobbing heads of the highest officials in the Nixon government, and finally seeping through the cracks and into the Oval Office itself. Yet, even before the scandal escalated to the level of impeachment proceedings, it was obvious that the damage was done. Regardless of what happened to Nixon himself, the ambitious hopes and aspirations of his Presidency already lay in ruin. What had been envisioned as a New Rome, complete with law-and-order efficiency at home and Pax Romana abroad, was spread out like the wreckage of Carthage after the third Punic War. And by then there could no longer be any doubt that the Age of Nixon would be chiefly remembered as an era which left an indelible moral stain on the American Presidency.

Two

IN many respects, the Presidency that Richard M. Nixon inherited is a relatively new institution, one that began with Franklin D. Roosevelt. For it was during Roosevelt's twelve years in the White House that the colossus we call the *modern* Presidency came into existence. What brought it into being was nothing less than a governmental revolution carried out on three distinct levels:

—On the international stage, there was the challenge of global war, which compelled the nation to assume a commanding role in the forefront of world affairs. Since World War II when GIs were dispatched to fight in Europe, Asia, and Africa, the sun has yet to set on what some historical revisionists like to call the American Empire. Some Americans perhaps prefer to think of it as a defense perimeter; nevertheless, one of the major tasks of all Presidents since Roosevelt has been to try to keep the Empire, or defense perimeter, in order.

—The second revolution took place on the national level. Faced with the crisis of depression, Roosevelt made the federal government the chief instrument of relief and recovery; in doing so, he completely reversed the policy of his predecessor. It wasn't that Hoover enjoyed watching people lose their jobs and go hungry, but that he believed, on firm philosophic principle, that it was up to the state and local agencies to provide the solutions. In his defense, this was very much the traditional view. Even during the Progressive Era, which spawned the activist Presidencies of Teddy Roosevelt and Wilson, it was the state governments that were regarded as the best sources of innovation—"the laboratories of reform," as they were called. (Worth noting is the fact that Wilson and the two Roosevelts all cut their pre-Presidential teeth as Governors of progressive states; for them especially the states served as laboratories where they carried out experiments they later developed more fully in the national sphere.) But all that changed with the New Deal. Since FDR's time, the federal government has been the center of action and creativity and experience. It is no accident that since Roosevelt no man has gone from a statehouse to the White House; except for the special case of War Hero Eisenhower, Congress has been, and continues to be, the principal breeding ground of Presidents and Presidential candidates.

—Third, there was the revolution within the federal government, in which the executive branch assumed more and more power as opposed to the Congress. To meet the emergency of the depression, Roosevelt had seized command. The barrage of programs that he and his lieutenants rammed through Congress during the early weeks of the New Deal—the famous Hundred Days—established the President's role as Chief Legislator.

This supremacy over Congress grew so much, so quickly, that by the middle 1960s, when Lyndon Johnson put together *his* version of the Hundred Days, up to 90 percent of all laws passed by Congress originated within the executive branch. This development represented a major reversal, for throughout most of our history, especially during the nineteenth century (but also as recently as the 1920s), it had been the legislative branch which dictated the course of national policy.

With all this new power flowing into the Presidency from all directions, the job soon became far too much for one man to handle. In a sense, of course, this has always been true; even in the past, when it was a comparatively modest operation, there were few Presidents who wanted, or were bold enough, to assume that Chief Executive meant sole executive. But, for the modern President, there simply has been little choice in the matter. Given the size, strength, and complexity of the office, as it is now constituted, he *must* delegate large chunks of authority if he hopes to stay afloat. As the late Clinton Rossiter put it in his excellent book about the office: "The Presidency has been converted into an institution, and we can never again talk about it sensibly without accounting for *the men around the President.*" (Our italics.)

The traditional place for a President to delegate power has been in the Cabinet. Ever since Alexander Hamilton put together his virtuoso act as Secretary of the Treasury in the first years of the Republic, the Cabinet has been recognized as a center of influence and prestige. The first four Presidents of the nineteenth century all groomed themselves for the top job by serving as Secretary of State. The last of them, John Quincy Adams, was the chief architect of the hemispheric doctrine bearing the name of the President he served, James Monroe. In our own century, we've had the ironic experience of William Howard Taft and Herbert Hoover: two men who succeeded so well on the Cabinet level that in their next stop—the White House—in each case their performance fell far short of expectation. Still others—John Marshall, Roger Taney, Salmon Chase, and Charles Evans Hughes—went directly from Cabinet posts to the second most eminent office our political system has to offer, Chief Justice of the Supreme Court.

Only the President can appoint or dismiss a Cabinet member. But his selections require consent from the Senate. And, once approved, Cabinet members can be required to answer for their actions and policies to the House and Senate. This way of keeping powerful Presidential appointees answerable to the American people through other elected representatives has been an integral part of our government's system of checks and balances.

It was at the base of the tradition of allowing men chosen by a President to wield power. The first impulse of the modern Presidency was to carry this tradition forward. FDR delegated vast authority to his Cabinet officers, and not just to those in the "glamour" posts, State and Treasury. With the coming of the New Deal, people such as Henry Wallace at Agriculture, Frances Perkins at Labor, and Harold Ickes at Interior found themselves charged with responsibilities far greater than anything known by their predecessors. Roosevelt depended upon them for initiatives, advice, and criticism. In his first inaugural, Roosevelt had sounded the call "for action, and action now," and insofar as this meant relief for the farmer, jobs for the unemployed and putting the nation's land and waterways to better use, it meant that Wallace, Perkins, and Ickes were expected to come up with new ideas and develop them into concrete programs. They did.

But Roosevelt, who was frantically moving on as many fronts as possible in his push to get the country back on its feet, did not rely solely on his Cabinet. Beginning with the original "Brain Trust"—the Columbia University professors he brought with him to Washington at the start of his Presidency—FDR gathered around him a special corps of advisers who were an essential part of what he himself often described as his "inner cabinet." This in itself was not exactly new. (Bear in mind as we go along that Presidential staff members, unlike Cabinet officers, do not require Senate consent for approval, and are not required to answer publicly to Congress.) Some earlier Presidents had chosen to lean on advisers outside of government. Andrew Jackson, for example, had his famous "Kitchen Cabinet," and during Wilson's Presidency few men inside the government wielded as much influence as the esteemed Colonel Edward M. House. Roosevelt, however, refined this technique in at least one very important way. He made certain that the members of *his* kitchen cabinet were put on the payroll and given official duties.

Notable among this cast of influential characters were two of the early Brain Trusters, Raymond Moley and Rexford Tugwell, who helped shape many of the programs of the first term, especially in the economic field. Later, as Roosevelt moved away from the formulation of New Deal policies (for which he needed heavy thinkers of the professorial stripe), and toward the spirited defense of those policies in open political warfare, the Brain Trust lapsed into eclipse. The man of the hour became the peppery Tom Corcoran, a tough, political in-fighter, whom FDR adroitly used as a lightning rod in the battles with Congress that erupted during his second term. ("The way to get ahead," Corcoran liked to tell his friends, "is to fish in troubled waters.") Finally, there was Harry Hopkins.

Hopkins had been, from the beginning, a Presidential adviser on many things, a member of the "inner cabinet," yet throughout the first two terms he took on a number of official jobs as well. During the early years, he ran WPA and other relief agencies; later, he put in a few months as Secretary of Commerce. In fact, this had been the pattern with the other special advisers. For example, when the New Deal opened for business, Moley was officially appointed Assistant Secretary of State, and Tugwell was given a similar post at Agriculture—even though the *real* assignment, for both men, was to serve as counselors to the President on a broad range of issues. The problem was that when Roosevelt assumed office there were no precedents for naming high-level policy men to the White House staff. That practice became established during FDR's Presidency, and it was Harry Hopkins, more than any other man, who became the model for it. Thus in the fall of 1940, as the war clouds in Europe began edging out over the Atlantic, Hopkins gave up all pretense of justifying his existence in the performance of other "official" duties, and moved into the White House. (Literally, that is: he was one of the few Presidential aides who was ever allowed to live there.) From then until the end, he served as Roosevelt's right-hand man, his number-one adviser and trouble-shooter during the war years. Thus, in historical terms, Hopkins could well be described as the first "superstar" of the White House staff, though he was by no means the last.

Bearing in mind the three developments which helped to create the modern Presidency—the emergence of the United States into the forefront of international affairs, the growth of federal power in relation to the states, and the increased domination of Congress by the executive branch—let us now add a fourth development. That is, the trend inside the executive branch itself to increase the power of the White House by drawing power and responsibility away from the Cabinet. While the three other revolutions matured during the course of FDR's Presidency, this one did not. Roosevelt, to be sure, planted the seeds with his use of the Brain Trust and Harry Hopkins, but full growth did not come until later. Although Roosevelt's special advisers played vital roles in the policy-making process, their power was shared extensively with the Cabinet.

FDR simply was not that systematic. His goal was to widen, not reduce, his circles of advice. If a Cabinet officer such as Frances Perkins had a viable plan for helping people through the anguish of unemployment, Roosevelt would grab it; the eventual result would be Social Security. If a Tommy Corcoran knew how to draft New Deal legislation in language that satisfied the constitutional qualms of the Supreme Court, then the job was his. What Roosevelt wanted was ideas and solutions that could be made to work, and he didn't especially care where they came from. Nor did he care at all about having a neatly-structured hierarchy with a rigid chain-of-command.

Many critics, then and since, have deplored his lack of organizational ability, but FDR himself thrived on the chaos, and enjoyed reaching out in all directions at once—toward Cabinet members and non-members alike. Which was why he brought the outside advisers on board in the first place: to get that many more ideas into the mix. In short, Roosevelt's intent, in creating the special White House advisory system, was *not* that it be used as a club to downgrade and humiliate the Cabinet or control and dominate Congress. It remained for his successors to use it for that purpose.

Not his immediate successors, however, for the trend was slow to develop. Truman expanded the size of his White House staff, but there was no corresponding increase in the power and prestige they enjoyed. Quite the contrary. Since he believed in administering the government through a strong Cabinet ("I propose to get Cabinet officers I can depend on, and have them run their affairs," he said shortly after his accession), Truman made little effort to bring top-quality aides into the White House. Instead, he stocked the place mostly with bungling incompetents; old cronies from Missouri like the raffish Harry Vaughan, his Army buddy from World War I days. The White House cronies were, in the words of Truman's AEC Chairman David Lilienthal, "as sorry a bunch of third-raters as I have ever seen in many a moon." Yet in fairness it should be pointed out that Truman never intended that they take part in the serious business of the Presidency. They were put on the payroll to perform certain mundane chores, and beyond that to serve—during off-duty hours—as poker and drinking companions. That was all. The fact that some of them, like Vaughan, got into trouble by becoming involved in graft and two-bit corruptions was a source of embarrassment to Truman. But their shoddy misdeeds had little or no effect on the true purpose of his Presidency.

The one member of his White House staff who did have an effect —who was in no way a "third-rater"—was Clark Clifford. A young lawyer from St. Louis, Clifford, ironically enough, was himself a product of the crony system, having been brought into the White House by one of Truman's Missouri friends. Like most of the others, he was at first hired on as a modest functionary (Naval aide), but once Truman became aware of Clifford's qualities—his quick intellect and shrewd political judgment—the President upgraded him into an

Oval Office regular. In time, Clifford became one of the President's top advisers, especially in domestic affairs, where his influence helped to strengthen Truman's wavering commitment to the then-emerging programs of the Fair Deal.

Yet even Clifford's role must be viewed in perspective. For most of the landmark decisions of the Truman Presidency were in foreign policy. And in this area Clifford was clearly overshadowed by the top dogs at the State Department: a group that included not only the two great Secretaries, George Marshall and Dean Acheson, but also some of the brilliant second-echelon men at Foggy Bottom, like Robert Lovett and George Kennan. These were the men most responsible for such achievements as the Marshall Plan, the Truman Doctrine, and the formation of NATO. Hence, they were the ones who left the strongest imprint on the Truman years.

Under Eisenhower, the White House staff system, as dominated by the autocratic presence of Sherman Adams, grew in both size and importance; yet, at the same time, never was the Cabinet more powerful than during those years. This paradox is perhaps best explained by the fact that Ike was so generous in his delegation of authority that *everyone* benefited. Eisenhower's commitment to a strong Cabinet was a direct result of his determination to structure his administration along military lines. He envisioned the various departments as separate "divisions." Each division commander was given autonomy to carry out his mission within the vague guidelines of overall strategy. This point was driven home to Defense Secretary Charles Wilson when, in the early months of Eisenhower's Presidency, he made the mistake of bouncing into the Oval Office a little too often for advice on routine details. Finally, an exasperated Ike told him: "Look here, Charlie, I want *you* to run Defense. We *both* can't run it. And I *won't* run it." This was the kind of independence he expected from all his Cabinet officers.

Within this structure, the White House was command headquarters, and Sherman Adams was its chief adjutant. As such, he wielded considerable power in the day-to-day operation of Eisenhower's Presidency. Seldom before, if ever, had a White House aide been given so much authority in administrative affairs. Adams was put in complete charge of Eisenhower's daily schedule, which meant, among other things, that he determined priorities. It was Eisenhower's belief that, while many matters required his personal attention, most did not—and it was up to Adams to know the difference: to know, for example, who should get in to see the President, and who should not. Moreover, Ike relied on his adjutant to handle the grubbier side of Presidential politics. With his high-school civics-class conception of the office, Eisenhower didn't even like to acknowledge that such things as patronage existed, and he depended on Adams to spare him any direct involvement in the dispensing of judgeships or dealing with other unsavory realities that came with the job.

Because of the authority Adams was given in administrative and political matters, he enjoyed an awesome reputation during the Eisenhower years. In 1955, when Ike suffered his heart attack, this morbid joke began making the rounds: Straight Man: "Wouldn't it be terrible if Ike died and Nixon became President?" Quipster's reply: "Yes, but what if Adams died and Ike became President?"

Yet, for all his operational power, Adams had comparatively little to do with the shaping of policy. In this respect, he differed from a Harry Hopkins or a Clark Clifford, whose major contributions to their Presidents were as policy advisers. The overriding concerns of the Eisenhower years were in foreign affairs and domestic economy— and in these areas Adams's influence was minimal. As in Truman's time, foreign policy was largely the private preserve of the State Department; the office of Secretary of State, already glowing with eminence from the Marshall and Acheson years, took on an almost theological grandeur in the hands of the zealous John Foster Dulles, who seemed at times to imbue his role with the stern solemnity of Presbyterian dogma. (In those days the enemy wasn't just Communism, but *atheistic* Communism.) Similarly, in economic matters: there, neither Adams nor anyone else dared to challenge the authority of Treasury Secretary George Humphrey, who, with his dogmatically conservative approach, saw to it that there were periodic recessions. Unlike "Engine Charlie" Wilson, neither Dulles nor Humphrey needed any lectures from the boss on how to exert power; they both grabbed the ball right at the start, and never stopped running.

It is true that some of the less-prestigious Cabinet officers sometimes grumbled that when they appeared at the White House, uninvited, Sherman Adams would often deny them access to the President. But such complaints were never very loud or sustained.

Division commanders under Ike knew that they could count on having their say when they felt strongly about it. This was because Eisenhower was a great believer in Cabinet meetings. He insisted on getting together frequently with his ranking officers, to hear their grievances, to settle interdepartmental disputes, and to reassure them, one and all, that they had free rein to run their programs. The men who attended these meetings were, in a sense, an endangered species. For in succeeding years no President's Cabinet enjoyed such status.

John Kennedy had little use for Cabinet meetings; he regarded them as a bore, a waste of time. That, as much as anything, points up the difference between his approach to the Presidency and that of his predecessor. For it was under Kennedy that the first significant steps in the shift of executive power from the Cabinet to the White House staff were taken, with the most dramatic changes taking place in the handling of foreign policy. In the weeks following Kennedy's election in 1960, the big question was: Whom would he pick as Secretary of State? The list of prominent Democrats included names such as Adlai Stevenson and J. William Fulbright, as well as others whose credentials in international affairs were similarly impressive. But Kennedy passed over the big names, choosing instead Dean Rusk, who, although he had served in the State Department during the Truman years, was a man of modest reputation. That, coupled with his unobtrusive manner, made him the perfect choice for Kennedy; it was JFK's intention from the beginning to run foreign policy from the White House. Thus, in the hands of the acquiescent Rusk, the office of Secretary of State came tumbling down from the heights of the Marshall-Acheson-Dulles era and settled into a position where it was frequently overshadowed by the energetic but mostly inexperienced New Frontiersmen who hovered over Kennedy's desk in the Oval Office.

Kennedy brought into the White House a whole slew of ambitious would-be star performers. They included Ted Sorensen, the self-proclaimed alter ego; the two godfathers of the Irish Mafia, Kenny O'Donnell and Larry O'Brien; and from Harvard, in the greatest infusion of academic clout seen at the White House since the days of FDR's Brain Trust, a parade of professors led by McGeorge Bundy. (The Cambridge influence, in fact, was so manifest in the overall

formation of the Kennedy administration that when Orville Free-
man, then Governor of Minnesota, was asked why Kennedy had
appointed him Secretary of Agriculture, he replied: "I'm not really
sure, but I think it has something to do with the fact that Harvard
does not have a school of agriculture.")

Kennedy's White House staff did not have a major domo, one man
who stood out as the dominant force, the way Clifford did in Truman's White House or Adams in Eisenhower's. Sorensen, though
primarily a speechwriter, came the closest to being an all-around
adviser who roamed across a broad landscape of issues. Bundy concentrated on foreign policy, where he proceeded to make spectacular end runs around Dean Rusk, while the Mafiosi devoted their
attention to political and domestic affairs. The essential point, however, is that between the four of them, they elevated the White
House staff system to new levels of power and prestige.

Yet to leave it at that would be misleading. Kennedy did not
completely abandon the Rooseveltian balance between Cabinet
members and in-house advisers; not all of JFK's Cabinet officers
shared Rusk's misfortune. True, Kennedy steered clear of the Eisenhower method of running things at the leisurely pace of regularly-
scheduled Cabinet meetings, but those in his Cabinet who could
adjust to his crisp, give-it-to-me-in-a-hurry ways made their presence
felt. Robert McNamara, for example, may have been the most assertive Secretary of Defense since the creation of that post in 1947
(critics said of him, "Frequently in error but never in doubt"). And
as such he was as great an influence as Bundy. It is worth remembering that in the early days of the Vietnam conflict it was fashionable
to refer to it as "McNamara's War," a designation that McNamara
himself accepted, almost with relish. Kennedy, political slyboots that
he was, must have been only too happy to let him accept it. Finally,
there was the Attorney General—admittedly a special case. For it
goes without saying that if Robert Kennedy's official title had been
Custodian of the White House Men's Room he still would have
ranked, next to the President himself, as the most influential voice
on the New Frontier. Nevertheless, by naming his brother Attorney
General, Kennedy made certain that at least one Cabinet department would become a center of action, prestige, and power in his
administration.

The appointment also furthered the tendency toward politicizing the Department of Justice, a fact about which Kennedyites do not like to be reminded. After all, they argue, Eisenhower had appointed *his* political campaign manager, Herbert Brownell, Attorney General. But this doesn't address itself to the danger, in appearance if nothing else, of any President having his chief political operator double as chief law-enforcement officer. This danger, however, would not be fully perceived until the misdeeds of Nixon's first Attorney General, John Mitchell, were exposed.

Lyndon Johnson somehow resisted the temptation to appoint his brother, Sam Houston Johnson, to a Cabinet post; but he did take other steps to give his departments a shot in the arm. First of all, he brought Dean Rusk out of the shadows, and encouraged him to speak up at policy meetings. In gratitude, Rusk was one of the few Johnson men to remain steadfastly loyal right to the end, even when it became obvious that all was lost. Other holdovers from the Kennedy Cabinet also flourished. McNamara's influence, if anything, increased under Johnson; that is, until the latter years when he finally came to disbelieve in what had started out as "his war."

But, as McNamara and some of the other Kennedy people left the Cabinet, Johnson came up with outstanding replacements. Indeed, his best appointments—Republican John Gardner at HEW and the veteran Clark Clifford at Defense (back for a return engagement in the exercise of power)—were among the most distinguished of any recent President's. Unfortunately, because of the war, there were disappointments here as well, a notable one coming in 1967 when Gardner resigned, with Vietnam his main reason. Still, whatever the setbacks, there was no question of Johnson's intent: both in his use of the Kennedy holdovers and in his own appointments, he made a determined effort to restore to the Cabinet some of the luster it had lost during the Kennedy years.

Johnson's White House staff was also a mixture of Kennedy transitionists and fresh blood. Bundy stayed on for a couple of years, accepting with grace the odd notion that Rusk might actually have something constructive to say about foreign policy. But by 1966, as the situation in Vietnam grew darker and darker, he decided that— even though he had played a major role in creating that situation— a prominent seat on Lyndon Johnson's war council was no longer a suitable place for a proper Bostonian who had once been dean of

Harvard. So he "skedaddled," as LBJ put it, taking a job as head of the Ford Foundation. Johnson replaced Bundy with another Kennedy import from academe: Walt Rostow, the MIT professor who, as Bundy's deputy under Kennedy, helped originate the Vietnam policy and, from beginning to end, was its most ardent true believer. More than any of the others, more even than Rusk or Johnson himself, Rostow never flagged in his devotion to the Quagmire. Even when it was all over for Johnson, Rostow accompanied him to his St. Helena, as if to make certain that in his long hours of reflection down there on the ranch LBJ would never falter in his belief that he had been the great patriot-warrior of his age—and that Rostow's advice had been right.

But for the most part Johnson filled his staff with his own people, and in recruiting them he reached deep into his native Texas. At the top, Bill Moyers was to Johnson much of what Clark Clifford had been to Truman: personal protégé and all-around adviser, whose influence overshadowed that of the other Texans. Like Clifford, Moyers' greatest contribution was in domestic affairs, where he was a major force in getting the ambitious programs of the Great Society off the ground. At the other end of the scale was Jack Valenti, who was a sycophantic crony in the Harry Vaughan tradition. A decent and likable man, Valenti stamped himself as an unabashed hero worshiper when he confided in a famous speech: "I sleep each night a little better . . . because Lyndon Johnson is my President."

Valenti is of interest not because he exerted influence—on the contrary, he seldom had effect on Johnsonian policy—but because he stands out as a symbol of LBJ's fundamental problem in dealing with people and power. More than any other President of recent memory, Johnson needed sycophants, adoring courtiers, to keep his batteries charged. In his constant, fury-driven demands for loyalty, loyalty, and still more loyalty, he so devoured those around him that many of them reached the point where they just couldn't take it any longer.

It is too easy to say that everyone who fled his administration did so because of the war. Just as important a factor was Johnson himself; he often was kind, but the scalding abuse that flowed from him (and often over some trifling matter) was simply too much. Recalling Truman's famous remark, the level of heat in LBJ's kitchen was so intense that many decided they had to get out in order to survive as self-respecting human beings. Nor was it just Kennedy holdovers like Bundy and outside mavericks like John Gardner who left. Long before his Presidency came to an end, Johnson lost some of his most intimate aides: his prize pupil, Moyers, and even the hero-worshiping Valenti himself decided they were better off living and working outside of Lyndon Johnson's orbit. And those who escaped were the lucky ones. As Richard Rovere wrote, in commenting on Hubert Humphrey's melancholy experience as LBJ's Vice President: "For four years he was a slave to a master who destroys his slaves."

Which brings us back to Johnson's successor. What Franklin Roosevelt began with his Brain Trust, what John Kennedy expanded with his New Frontiersmen—that is, the idea of a large, private staff accountable to no one but the President, and the centering of power in that staff—was further expanded, solidified, and aggrandized by Richard Nixon. Ironically, he came into office promising to reduce the size of the White House staff, yet its size increased dramatically. He promised to reduce the cost of White House staff operations, but the costs multiplied. Nixon's staff assumed more authority by far than that of any previous President. And, in setting up rigid lines of authority inside the White House, he created a system of personal power in which a kind of palace guard became nearly as isolated as he was. And—in excesses of zeal and devotion—men who were supposed to have been *his* slaves opened the gates to criminal actions that disgraced their master.

Three

THE salient point to remember is that in the course of his first term in office Richard M. Nixon gathered around himself the most powerful White House staff ever assembled. Never before had so much authority with so little accountability been delegated to so few. Throughout those years and into the early months of the second term —up to the moment the Watergate affair exploded in everyone's face —the great power brokers of the Nixon White House were Henry

Kissinger, John Ehrlichman, and H. R. (Bob) Haldeman, known in their prime by such endearments as the Teutonic Trio, the Berlin Wall, and All the King's Krauts.

Each man had his own special province, and within it each wielded an authority that earlier White House aides could only have regarded with awe and envy. A Harry Hopkins might have acquired a large measure of renown as FDR's personal envoy during World War II, but none of us realized what a Presidential envoy could be —or do—until Kissinger began embarking on his secret missions to the far corners of the earth. And, while McGeorge Bundy had made sharp inroads into the authority of the Secretary of State, Dean Rusk's discomfort was the height of self-esteem compared to the humiliation endured by William Rogers, Nixon's friend at Foggy Bottom. Nor was the Secretary of State Kissinger's only victim. As he eventually assumed exclusive control of the Vietnam peace talks, he became not only Nixon's chief diplomatic officer but his top military strategist as well, with the authority to make fundamental decisions on troop withdrawals and other matters that normally would have been the prerogative of the Pentagon and Defense Secretary Melvin Laird.

Similarly with Ehrlichman, who was Kissinger's counterpart in domestic affairs. In terms of shaping policy, his influence on Nixon may not have been any greater than that exerted by Clark Clifford on Truman or Bill Moyers on Johnson; but in the operational details Ehrlichman was given far more authority than either of these men to place the key domestic departments directly under his control. Once his position at the White House was clearly established, Cabinet officers like Elliot Richardson, then in charge of HEW, and Housing Secretary George Romney came to realize that they were answerable to Ehrlichman; although they weren't especially happy about the arrangement, they accepted it. That is, most of them accepted it. A man like Interior Secretary Wally Hickel was unable to rid himself of the old-fashioned notion that as a Cabinet officer he had every right to deal with the President directly; hence, when he persisted in his efforts to go over Ehrlichman's head—to pole-vault the Berlin Wall—he became, in Mafia jargon, "a walking corpse." (Ehrlichman, in fact, was the man poised at Nixon's side the day Hickel was finally summoned to the Oval Office to be presented with his head on a plate.)

As for Haldeman, he, like Sherman Adams, was delegated extremely broad authority in administrative affairs, including running the President's daily schedule and literally standing guard at his door to decide who should—and who should not—be admitted into the Oval Office. But, as we've noted, access was never that serious a problem with Eisenhower. Ike preferred to see people at the appropriate time and in the appropriate setting, which had less to do with personal aloofness than with his determination to run things in an orderly manner—or "by the numbers," as he had been taught at West Point. Sherman Adams's job was to run a taut ship, not a closed shop. As for Kennedy and Johnson, their White House operations were so loosely structured there never did emerge, in either man's Presidency, a discipline-conscious chief of staff on the order of Adams or Haldeman; and in the case of both men accessibility was rarely, if ever, a problem.

What gave Haldeman such overwhelming power was that he served as sentinel for a President who chose to sequester himself behind a wall of "Do Not Disturb" signs. Of all the characteristics that define Richard Nixon, none perhaps is more striking than his celebrated sense of privacy, a trait that he personally attributes to his Quaker heritage. Nixon's obsessive desire to spend long hours by himself, insulated from all contact with his fellow man, would hardly be worth mentioning if he were a theoretical physicist given to pondering the mysteries of the universe. But for a consummate politician like Nixon, such behavior is nothing short of extraordinary. Politicians, regardless of party, race, or creed, tend to be compulsive extroverts (Hubert Humphrey and Nelson Rockefeller are two names that spring to mind), and if you spend any time at all around them, you soon learn that in a real sense their very identities are shaped by their need to interact with people—whether voters, journalists, other politicians, or financial backers. As Murray Kempton once observed, after years of studying the breed up close: "To respect a politician's privacy is almost to deny him his existence."

But in this regard, Nixon has always been an anomaly among his lodge brothers. And once inside the White House, where all kinds of barriers were available to seal him off, he retreated even deeper into his natural cocoon of solitude. Thus Bob Haldeman, as the go-between, stood not only as the chief line of resistance, but also as the chief line of communication—the person that all those frustrated petitioners gathered at the White House door had to deal with. If, in response to their questions, he seemed to offer guidelines, the supplicants had no choice but to assume that such guidelines had Presidential authority written all over them.

The introverted tone of Nixon's White House was further enhanced by the way Haldeman and Ehrlichman themselves chose to operate. Hopkins, Clifford, Adams, Sorensen, and Moyers all acquired celebrity status of sorts during their years in the White House. But of the top men in Nixon's shop only Kissinger followed the path of his predecessors into the limelight. It might even be argued that Kissinger monopolized the limelight, leaving only a sliver around the edges for anyone else to squeeze in.

There is no denying that once Kissinger got going he earned for himself a world-wide reputation of awesome proportions. On a staff dominated by advertising men and lawyers of limited experience, the bespectacled professor with the German accent was the closest thing to a figure of real distinction and glamour.

Haldeman and Ehrlichman, on the other hand, took great pains to stay out of the limelight. Throughout the first term, their spectral movements deep within the shadows of the White House served to conceal from general scrutiny the enormous impact they were having on the life and direction of Nixon's Presidency. Only in the last year of his White House service did Ehrlichman become a visible spokesman for the domestic policies he had long been responsible for overseeing. As for Haldeman, he remained cloistered until the very end, and it was not until then, when the two men became impaled on the prongs of Watergate, that the depth and breadth of their influence were recognized.

During their years of power, we as reporters often had occasion to appreciate just how little Haldeman and Ehrlichman were known to the general public. In traveling around the country meeting normal people—i.e., people who are not obliged to clutter up their minds with the day-to-day whirl of the Washington merry-go-round —we were often asked about Richard Nixon and his various cohorts. The questions usually centered on the more familiar names like Kissinger, John Mitchell, Spiro Agnew, et al., but if, in illustrating a particular point, we referred to Haldeman and/or Ehrlichman, the response invariably was a puzzled frown, a scratch of the chin or a tentative reply to the effect: "Well, yes, I've heard of those two guys, I guess, but they're not all that important, are they?"

Even in Washington, where there is really only one year-around topic of conversation (the Redskins being a seasonal obsession), Haldeman and Ehrlichman succeeded, to a remarkable degree, in keeping themselves out of focus. In general, Washingtonians knew about them, knew they were ensconced in the White House, and were aware that they figured prominently in the Nixonian scheme of things. Yet even many otherwise in-the-know local folk had only vague notions of who the two were and what they did. As late as 1972, a famous American journalist, a man generally knowledgeable in the affairs of Washington (although neither government nor politics is his field), was under the impression that Haldeman was the real-estate lawyer from Seattle, and Ehrlichman, the Los Angeles advertising executive, instead of the other way around.

His confusion was understandable, for the two men were inextricably linked. In fact, they were so closely identified with each other that most White House observers fell into the habit of referring to them in tandem: Haldeman-and-Ehrlichman, a pair of naturals like Huntley-Brinkley, Laurel-and-Hardy, or those other two wily contributors to intra-palace intrigue, Rosencrantz-and-Guildenstern. (Sad as it was in human terms, it surprised no insiders that, when Watergate finally came crashing down on the pair, their resignations were announced on the same day and in the same White House bulletin—Siamese twins to the end, as it were.) They were indeed bosom buddies, and had been ever since their days as classmates at UCLA in the middle 1940s. Often overlooked, however, was the fact that Haldeman was very much the senior partner and, insofar as they did work in combo, Ehrlichman was more likely to do Haldeman's bidding, rather than the other way around. For Ehrlichman was never one to forget that it was Haldeman who delivered him into the world of Richard Nixon, carefully nurtured him through the ranks, and adroitly maneuvered him into his position of power. While Ehrlichman held sway over Nixon's domestic policy, Haldeman held sway over Ehrlichman. And between them they kept piling brick after brick onto the Berlin Wall, until it became the greatest barrier ever to stand between an American President and his Cabinet, the Congress, and the citizenry that put him in office.

Every now and then, a Cabinet officer did succeed in breaking through the Wall. For example, when John Connally came in as Treasury Secretary early in 1971, he promptly forced a showdown and—for a few months, anyway—was granted the rare privilege of easy access to the President. But Connally was a meteor that blazed across the sky of Nixon's first term—a dazzling but brief distraction. And, even before he left the Cabinet to organize the Democrats-for-Nixon operation, there were clear signs indicating that he too had been brought to heel. (Significantly, his brief reincarnation in the second term, as an unofficial adviser and overeager aspirant for the post vacated by Spiro Agnew, was a post-Watergate happening, which took place only after Haldeman and Ehrlichman were gone.)

A far more complex example of personal power and access to the President from outside the White House was John Mitchell. Like Robert Kennedy in his brother's administration, Mitchell's power had almost nothing to do with his Cabinet status as Attorney General, and everything to do with the special relationship he had with the President, developed from his position as personal confidant and campaign manager in Nixon's 1968 victory over Humphrey. (As often noted, Mitchell was the muscle behind the famed "Southern Strategy.")

During the very early stages of the first term, Mitchell ranked above the top White House aides in overall power and influence—certainly well above Ehrlichman. But it didn't last long. Even so, for most of the first three years, he ranked no less than on a par with the two. During much of this time, in fact, he served, in relation to Haldeman and Ehrlichman, as a kind of senior partner—a patient, pipe-smoking front man who absorbed much of the public heat for unpopular policies. From all appearances, the three of them were united in their dedication to Nixon and to the values and the law-abiding virtues of "middle America."

Yet, as time went on, there crept into the relationship an element of strain. By the end of 1970, Haldeman was privately boasting, with an unmistakable edge in his voice, that "even Mitchell has to go through me" to get to the President. The signs of discord were always fairly subtle, but to seasoned observers they were definitely there. Then in February, 1972, Mitchell began his rapid descent from the peaks of power, stepping down first as Attorney General, and four months later quitting his post as campaign manager for Nixon's re-election. As the Watergate testimony later revealed, he continued, during the summer and fall of 1972, to work for Nixon behind the scenes—as undercover man in keeping the public believing that

Watergate was nothing more than an insignificant burglary. Yet by then he was clearly on the defensive, reduced to playing the part of the little Dutch boy jamming his fingers in the dike in an effort to plug up leaks that could only lead to deluge and disaster. (He suspected but apparently did not know, as tape recordings later revealed, that the President, Haldeman, and Ehrlichman were secretly trying to drown him as a possible way of saving themselves.) When the deluge finally came full force, he was one of the first to be engulfed by it. But, for all his one-time prominence, by then he had been out of the administration for over a year, almost a forgotten figure, a man whose influence had been confined to the early Presidential years. Well before Watergate indictments brought about his official exile, he had ceased to be a high prince of the court.

With Mitchell gone, Haldeman, Ehrlichman, and Kissinger reigned supreme. For there is no question that the three aides reached the apex of their power during the final months of the first term and the early weeks of the second, when a mood of smug euphoria permeated the Nixon White House. Just a few days after the second inaugural, Kissinger added the jewel of a Vietnam truce agreement to his crown of earlier triumphs in Peking and Moscow. With the November landslide spurring them on, Haldeman and Ehrlichman began exerting more aggressive authority than ever before, moving full steam ahead to expand their power base into an empire that would reach into every corner of the federal bureaucracy. Whatever their private fears may have been about the Watergate period, they did not betray a trace of public concern. With customary arrogance, they rode the crest right up until that April morning in 1973 when they were forced to resign.

One scene, in particular, remains etched in memory, a scene witnessed time and again by journalists covering Nixon. Envision, if you will, the setting: It is twilight, and reporters are waiting at a military airport. It could be El Toro Marine Base in southern California, near the President's home in San Clemente. Or it might be Homestead Air Force Base, near the President's winter home in Key Biscayne, Florida. Or a third possibility is the heliport at still another Presidential retreat, Camp David in rural Maryland, which Nixon has fondly described as "my mountain top," and which was called by low-echelon staff support personnel "Mount Sinai." In other words, one of the three sites from which the man has chosen to conduct so much of his Presidency. (From the beginning, he spent remarkably little time in the White House itself. In 1969, for example, he was away from 1600 Pennsylvania Avenue nearly as many days as he was there. Haldeman once explained this by saying, "The man knows the value of contrasts, and he's entitled to be wherever he chooses. Besides, he likes to be left alone, and getting out of Washington sometimes is the only way he can be alone, really alone.")

The Presidential helicopter has just landed, and reporters are waiting now for the President and his party to disembark. Finally, the hatch opens and out they come. First, the President walking alone. That is typical; for unlike his more recent predecessors, this President is seldom seen emerging from a helicopter or an airplane or even a drawing room in the midst of conversation. Now, as always, Nixon stands out as a solitary figure, moving through his own private world, as though his head were encased in an invisible bubbletop. Walking a few steps behind the President is his personal secretary, Rose Mary Woods, who has served Richard Nixon faithfully since she first joined his Senate staff in 1951; in many ways, she is as close to Nixon as anyone who has ever worked for him. The stately procession continues in single file. Behind Miss Woods there is the tall, lean figure of Haldeman, who, with his ramrod-straight posture and assertive crew cut, gives the appearance of a military man in mufti. A few steps behind him strolls Ehrlichman; but the mark of his efficiency comes less from his physical makeup (balding, portly, round-shouldered) than from the ever-present briefcase, the lawyer's security blanket, clutched tightly at his side. And finally, if he happens to be around—if he happens, that is, to be in the hemisphere and not switching planes at that moment on some remote air strip in the Himalayas—there is Kissinger, looking rather bemused, as though he is secretly embarrassed by the company he's obliged to keep in order to bring his Metternichian dreams to reality. And that's it: in that silent procession, silhouetted against the early evening shadows, were the people who mattered, really mattered in the days before Watergate.

Visually, that image of arrival is a cameo of the Nixon Presidency; verbally, Lyndon Johnson gave us a telling glimpse. A few weeks before he died, Johnson flew to New York on business, and while there he had a meal with some comrades-in-arms from his White House years. Already by then Johnson was dying, and in recent

weeks he had worked at husbanding his strength, trying to be sub-
dued, soft-spoken. But on this day he was in one of his old expansive
moods, and as the luncheon progressed he began flashing some of the
old fire—fire that the others had no trouble recognizing, for their
memories were still vivid.

At one point, Johnson leaned back in his chair and observed that
a former aide who was there was probably "damn glad" to be rid of
the old days, "when I was getting your ass out of bed at five o'clock
in the morning to find out what kind of war we were fighting that
day."

The ex-adviser, ever courteous, was quick to assure Johnson that
just the opposite was true ("oh no, Mr. President"), that actually those
had been the best, "the most productive" years of his life.

To this Johnson responded with a kind of dubious snort (he had
always been a little leery of this particular man, as he had been of
most of Kennedy's Harvard crowd), but he had a point to make, so
he moved on, delving into a long reminiscence of how he had run
the Presidency. He talked, among other things, about his desk in the
Oval Office and the impressive display of phones he had stretching
across it; how each phone had all kinds of buttons on it so that, on
a moment's whim, he could send his voice crackling not only through
the main arteries of government but through its capillaries as well.
Or, as he put it: "If I needed to get hold of somebody, all I had to do
was mash a button." (In dealing with television sets, telephones, and
other gadgetry, LBJ never merely pressed the appropriate switch or
button. To make sure it would work, he *mashed* the mother, and you
better believe it, sonny.)

"And I mean anybody," he went on, emphasizing. "Even some
little fella tucked away in one of the agencies. If I thought he should
have the answer to something, I'd just get him on the horn."

Johnson paused to smile, perhaps in recollection of a particularly
memorable ass chewing he had inflicted on some trembling bureaucrat—some "little fella"—who did *not* have the answer, and who
had been jolted into the early stages of cardiac arrest by the mind-
blowing realization that this was the voice of the President—*the
President*—saying these awful things to him over the phone. But
soon the smile vanished, and Johnson picked up the thread of his
theme, which was that his way was *the* way to run the government.
He kept hammering away at the point that a President must keep

in contact with the sprawling bureaucracies around him, that he must reach out, day and night, and grab hold of the government. Because if he didn't, if he let it slide away from him, "then the day will come when you wake up and discover that the damn thing is running *you.*"

Again he paused, this time for several moments, but since everyone at the table was familiar with his monologic approach to conversation, nobody interpreted the interlude as a cue for someone else to speak. Instead, they watched with a sense of nostalgic dread as there crept across Johnson's face an expression, a hard-eyed gaze, that all of them had seen many times before, especially during his most troubled months in the White House, whenever anyone dared to mention names like Fulbright or Bobby Kennedy in his presence.

Finally, the taut facial muscles relaxed a bit, and he informed the group that during a recent visit to Washington he had stopped by the Oval Office to pay his respects. The office had changed, of course— "as you'd expect," he quickly added—and a number of details had caught his eye. Among them, and one that especially seemed to intrigue him, was the President's desk: the size, for one thing ("it's a lot smaller than the one *I* had, you know"), and the compulsive neatness ("there was hardly a damn thing on it"). And finally there was the matter of the phone, the *one* phone. He could hardly believe it: "Just *one* dinky little phone to keep in touch with his people." And on that phone there were three buttons. "That's all," he said, his voice rising to meet the point head-on. "Just three buttons, and *they* all go to Germans!"

He strung the story out in such a theatrical way that when he hit the end of the punch line—"Germans"—everyone at the table laughed. And Johnson, who always loved playing the showman, smiled along with them. But a moment later he became serious, and said it really was nothing to laugh at. Such isolation and such concentration of power in the hands of "these amateurs" was dangerous— dangerous for the President, and therefore dangerous for the country.

This conversation took place in December, 1972, and a little more than a month later he was dead. Had he lived just a few weeks longer —i.e., long enough to see Watergate erupt—he no doubt would have had a few choice comments as he sat back and watched the parade of chickens coming home to roost.

PART II

False Starts, Broken Promises

Four

At the beginning of his Presidency, Nixon gave no indication that he intended to delegate such enormous power to his White House advisers. Indeed, he went out of his way to convey the impression that this was *not* the original "game plan." In November, 1968, just one week after the American people finally said yes to Richard Nixon, a diverting little story appeared in the *New York Times*. Like so many articles published in the *Times* during that period, it carried the invisible dateline of the ornate Hotel Pierre, prominently situated along the millionaires' row of New York's Fifth Avenue; for it was there that the Nixon high command gathered after the election to chart its plans for the great adventure ahead. The story, based on public and private interviews with Nixon aides, began:

> Richard M. Nixon intends at this time not to allow his personal White House staff to dominate the functions or control the direction of the major agencies and bureaus of the Government. Sensitive to the possibility of empire building within his own small cadre of assistants, he plans instead to organize the White House staff in a way that will encourage and not inhibit direct communication between his Cabinet officers and the President. He is said to be firm in his view that his Cabinet officers should have the major responsibility for policymaking under the President and should be guaranteed regular access to the White House.

The piece went on in this vein for several paragraphs, and of course today stands as one of the more amusing relics from that pre-inaugural period when the Nixon camp was filling the air with earnest predictions of what the new Presidency would be like. But what gives it an especially piquant flavor, in view of subsequent history, is the fact that a prime source of the story was none other than H. R. Haldeman, who had just been appointed as a Presidential assistant. The announcement of *that*, in fact, was part of the *Times*'s story, but significantly enough it was buried several paragraphs down. The *Times* noted that Haldeman's major responsibility "would be to monitor and manage the activities of the entire White House staff," but in light of the information set down in the story's lead paragraphs—that there would be no "empire building" inside the Nixon White House—that didn't strike the *Times* reporter (or anyone else, for that matter) as much of a job.

In the months and years that followed, reporters covering the Nixon Presidency would come to appreciate Haldeman's subtle skill in playing down his role in the White House. Long after he acquired extraordinary power, he kept insisting, time and time again, that he was nothing more than an administrative detail man who regulated the President's appointments and kept his schedule in order; and that, as such, he had no real voice in the shaping of policy. In contrast to Kissinger, who rejoiced in his reputation as a big shaker and mover, Haldeman never wanted the press (and, therefore, the public) to get a fix on what he was really doing. From beginning to end he reveled in secrecy and deception.

So it is entirely possible that even on this early occasion, back in November, 1968, he was playing games in an effort to throw reporters off the scent; that would have been in character. But it seems far more likely that Haldeman was being sincere; that he truly believed his role in Nixon's White House would be a fairly modest one: glorified appointments secretary and general staff manager, as well as an adviser on Presidential image making. These were the duties he had performed for Nixon during the campaign just completed, and in earlier campaigns as well. Most matters of substance and policy were left to others.

Moreover, it is certainly true that the views he expressed the day of his appointment accurately reflected those of his boss. Nixon himself had been passing the word through other intermediaries besides Haldeman that he intended to get away from the Presidential styles of his immediate predecessors, Kennedy and Johnson, with their heavy dependence on powerful White House staffs. In keeping with his campaign pledge to give the American people an "open administration," he was determined, he said, to go back to the Eisenhower method of running the government through a strong Cabinet. To some extent, this was calculated to blend in with the "Eisenhower Revisited" theme that was being stressed at the time, a theme to be elaborated on later. But, in seeking to reverse the recent trend, Nixon and his people were prepared to go Ike one better. In discussing his new job that day at the Hotel Pierre, Haldeman made a point of saying that in the Nixon White House "there will be no Sherman Adams." It wasn't much more than a year later, when he was well on his way toward making Ike's chief of staff look like a piker by comparison, that the same man would be telling people, "I come closer to Sherman Adams than anyone else." The earlier "no Sherman Adams" line may well have been the first statement of the new era to be rendered "inoperative," if we may borrow the word that later was used in a more celebrated connection: to describe all those pious denials of White House involvement in the Watergate cover-up.

All the talk in the late fall of 1968 about restoring prestige and authority to the Cabinet naturally had the effect of stimulating interest in who would be on the new team. The atmosphere of expectation was further enhanced when Nixon agreed to go along with a public-relations stunt cooked up by Haldeman and television consultant Frank Shakespeare. Instead of announcing his choices in the traditional piecemeal fashion, Nixon tried to keep the lid on until one evening in mid-December when, in the full glare of prime time, he introduced his Cabinet nominees to the country, all in a bunch. As a theatrical event, the elaborately staged ceremony had little to recommend it. Most of the appointees and their wives appeared to be self-conscious, as who wouldn't be in such an awkward mass introduction before literally millions of eyes. As for the President-elect, the arrangement cast him in a role not unlike that of a TV game-show host. One reviewer likened the whole presentation to the kind that "an insecure Madison Avenue pitchman might make in trying to land a new account." But Haldeman thought the "Your President as Emcee" program was a big plus, and said so.

Aesthetics aside, the main interest was in the selections themselves, and what they told us about the incoming President—and the kind of people he apparently wished to have around him. First, he placed in strategic posts three of his closest and most-trusted friends. The biggest of the domestic departments—Health, Education, and Welfare—went to one of his oldest friends, fellow Californian Robert Finch, whose association with Nixon dates back to the early Congressional days in the 1940s. The top plum, Secretary of State, was given to Bill Rogers, his best friend in Washington during the middle years, when he was Senator and Vice President. And for Attorney General he turned to a friend from still a later stage in his life, the years of exile in New York, giving that post to his former Wall Street law partner and campaign manager, John Mitchell. In referring to Nixon's celebrated reputation as a "loner," someone once observed that in all his years of adult life, he probably has had no more than five close friends. That may or may not be an exaggeration, but, however small the circle of intimates, it is a group that would include these three men: Finch, Rogers, and Mitchell. So, in building his Cabinet around this trio, Nixon obviously was willing to risk the charges of "cronyism" he and others had leveled at Harry Truman twenty years earlier. It was a help that Finch and Rogers had deserved reputations as quality men with broad interests and experience.

Rogers also had another distinction going for him, one he shared with the new Commerce Secretary, Maurice Stans. Both men were graduates of the Eisenhower administration, Rogers having served as Ike's second Attorney General and Stans as Budget Director during the last two years; their presence on the new team did not exactly signal a return to the Eisenhower Era (or Ike Age), but between them they did provide a highly visible link.

Nor did Nixon ignore academe, though here he seemed to go out of his way to avoid drawing from the Ivy League campuses so heavily favored by such predecessors as Roosevelt and Kennedy. Instead, he reached into two Midwestern schools: the University of Chicago for his Secretary of Labor, George Shultz, and the University of Nebraska for his Agriculture man, Clifford Hardin. Significantly, both men had moved out of the classroom and into administrative duties by the time they were summoned to Washington. No blatant eggheads need apply, seemed to be the Nixon message even in these two academic appointments, though, as we shall see, he applied a much different criterion in picking his early White House staff.

What some observers found most encouraging about the new Cabinet was that it was heavily studded with men who had been tested in political combat. After a generation of turning the Pentagon over to auto magnates (Charlie Wilson, Bob McNamara) and a detergent tycoon (Neil McElroy), Nixon chose to put Defense in the hands of Congressman Melvin Laird, long regarded as one of Washington's most adroit politicians. And three other posts went to men who had been elected Republican Governors in normally Democratic states: Housing and Urban Development to George Romney of Michigan, Transportation to John Volpe of Massachusetts, and Interior to Wally Hickel of Alaska. Robert Finch also belongs in this category, for in 1966, while running for Lieutenant Governor in California, he demonstrated his political skill by polling over 100,000 votes more than the matinée idol at the top of the ticket, Ronald Reagan.

There also was evidence that, in some of his choices, Nixon was displaying his own political savvy, showing how adept he was at the art of the payoff. At least two of his appointments, Hickel and Stans, were payoffs in the most obvious sense. Hickel had served as Nixon's campaign coordinator in the Western states, and had delivered, while Stans had been the President-elect's top fund raiser. And, as a calculated bow to the blessings reaped from the campaign's "Southern Strategy," the patronage-rich job of Postmaster General, traditionally entrusted to a party politico, was given to Winton Blount, a Southern Republican of conservative bent.

A sense of gratitude may also have entered into Nixon's decision to give HUD to Romney. It was Romney, after all, who had been the early front runner for the 1968 GOP Presidential nomination, and who conducted a campaign of such glaring ineptitude (the high point of which was his confession that he had been "brainwashed" in Vietnam) that Nixon—dismissed as a "retread" when he first launched *his* comeback—began to look better and better by comparison. In politics as in pugilism, a contender for the crown needs a patsy or two along the way to build up his reputation; and in going down for the count in the tank towns of New Hampshire, Romney helped to put Nixon securely on the road back. Another reason Romney got the job is that no other Republican so well known was willing to take it. HUD is widely considered by many Republicans and Democrats to be a hopeless bureaucratic mess. Also, many sensed, correctly, that the new President wouldn't spend much of his own time worrying about housing policies or the plight of big cities.

Then there was Volpe, who was given Transportation to assuage his disappointment over not being picked as Nixon's running mate. For Volpe had been told that, at the Miami Beach convention that summer, the choice for the Vice Presidential nomination had been whittled down to two men—himself and Spiro Agnew—and, in the four months that had elapsed since then, he no doubt had been tormenting himself trying to figure out what qualities Nixon could possibly have perceived in the Governor of Maryland that he, the Governor of Massachusetts, did not possess. (If all of us had only known then what we would find out five years later!) In any event, the Transportation post was Nixon's way of saying it was nothing personal. Finally, there was the appointment to the Treasury post of Chicago banker David Kennedy, whose name rounds out the list of the original twelve Cabinet members. Kennedy, to be sure, was no relation to the you-know-who Kennedys, but with nation-wide sentiment running strong in the aftermath of the second assassination the previous June, it certainly didn't hurt to have that particular name on the roster. But, most importantly, this Kennedy had helped to raise big Midwestern and Western banking money for Nixon's just-completed campaign.

For the most part, Nixon's Cabinet selections met with approval, if not widespread enthusiasm. There was naturally some criticism, mainly focused on the new group's lack of diversity. ("Twelve gray-haired guys named George" was a popular description the day after the television presentation.) And it was true that, to a remarkable degree, the appointees appeared to be mirror images of each other.

It was, to begin with, an all-male cast. Not since Ike appointed Oveta Culp Hobby to be the first Secretary of HEW in 1953 had there been a woman named to the Cabinet, and there is no evidence to suggest that Nixon seriously considered putting a department in the hands of one. It is worth noting that there was scarcely a ripple of protest about this at the time, for the furies of Women's Lib had not yet been unleashed on the land. In 1968 Gloria Steinem was still writing about politics from a conventional left-wing point of view. She didn't care much for Nixon or Humphrey or even Eugene McCarthy for that matter, but her objections had little to do with their attitudes toward women. Basically, she didn't like them because they were poor replacements for the slain Bobby Kennedy; which is to say that, in her view, they could not relate to radical blacks or Cesar Chavez.

There is no question that the dominant hair color of the new Cabinet group was gray. At forty-three, Finch was the youngest of the appointees, while most of the others were in their fifties and sixties. In contrast, the team that Kennedy had put together eight years earlier had included three Cabinet officers who were under forty-three at the time of their appointments.

And of course they were all white. LBJ had been the first President to appoint a Negro to the Cabinet (Robert Weaver at HUD), and when Nixon failed to follow suit, Clarence Mitchell of the NAACP remarked that "Johnson, a President from Texas, desegregated the Cabinet, while Nixon, a President from California, resegregated the Cabinet." True, but in fairness Nixon had tried, however timidly, to get a black face into the mix. His first choice for HUD was Massachusetts Senator Edward Brooke (the Republicans' showcase Negro), but Brooke turned him down, in part because he felt uneasy about Nixon's approach to racial problems and also because he wished to remain in the Senate, where he continues to stand out as the only Negro elected to that body since Reconstruction. (Brooke, at the time, indicated he might consider appointment as Attorney General, but nothing less.) Blacks were not the only racial or ethnic minority group to be excluded from the new Cabinet. There also were no Jews, though Nixon would more than compensate for that with his major appointments to the White House staff; and no Irish Catholics, though some people may have been confused on that score by the David Kennedy finesse, not realizing, perhaps, that *this* Kennedy happened to be a Mormon. (Volpe and Stans were Catholic, but not Irish.) In short, the message conveyed by Nixon's Cabinet choices was a hearty "Let's hear it for white, male, middle-aged, and business-oriented Republicans."

Yet, on the matter of party affiliation too, as in his overture to Brooke, Nixon had tried for a touch of tokenism. Before calling upon Laird to run the Pentagon, he had offered the important Defense post to Senator Henry (Scoop) Jackson. And Jackson was all set to accept it, too, until Ted Kennedy, who was really feeling his oats at this time as the emerging new leader of the Democrats (he was about to unseat Russell Long as Senate majority whip, and Chappaquiddick was still several months off), went to Jackson and bluntly warned him that he'd be finished in his own party if he became Nixon's chief military spokesman. And, even if Kennedy hadn't intervened, Jackson's appointment would hardly have won the approval of Democratic liberals, who were quick to dismiss "the Senator from Boeing Aircraft" as an unreconstructed Cold Warrior who long has championed big spending for defense. Which is why he appealed to Nixon; he was one member of the opposition party who *would* fit in. And, as far as Nixon was concerned, the liberals should have understood that, instead of carping about Jackson being an "Uncle Tom" Democrat.

So Nixon went all the way with fellow Republicans. Yet, even in staying within the bounds of his own party, he was careful not to get too adventurous. Having captured the GOP nomination by adhering to a cautious, centrist course, threading his way between the Goldwater zealots on the right and the Rockefeller sellouts on the left, the President-elect chose not to stray far from the middle-of-the-road in picking his Cabinet. Some of the appointees were clearly conservatives of the old school (Mitchell, Stans, and Blount, for example), but Nixon purposely steered clear of anyone who had been prominently associated with the suicidal excesses of the Goldwater crusade four years earlier; there were no Bill Buckleys and no Ronald Reagans brought on board.

And, to make sure the other side was equally slighted, no Nelson Rockefeller. In New York Republican circles, where the name Rockefeller evokes the same kind of response that Allah gets on a good day in Mecca, the reaction was shock and dismay when Nixon somehow succeeded in forming a Cabinet without giving a post to the Governor, or some other member of The Family. In the weeks before the great TV unveiling, the more rabid Rockefeller buffs were touting no less than three of the brothers for Cabinet duty: Governor Nelson for State or Defense, banker David for Treasury, and conservationist Laurance for Interior—the theory, of course, being that since the family owns the country it should have a more direct say in running it.

In reality, however, Nixon never seriously considered appointing any of the Rockefellers to his Cabinet, and he said so privately to his aides on more than one occasion; he didn't give his reasons, but then he didn't have to. For, next to the Kennedys, no family had caused Richard Nixon more anxiety over the previous decade than the one whose political head is the former Governor of New York. In his first run for the Presidency, it was Nelson Rockefeller who had played the gadfly, who had dared to challenge Nixon's right to succession, and who had raised embarrassing questions about Eisenhower's leadership, questions which naturally reflected on the then Vice President, and which were ruthlessly exploited in the fall campaign by Kennedy and the Democrats. Now, in 1968, there had been more of the same. Again Rockefeller had kept up the pressure during the weeks leading up to the convention, traveling around the country telling Republican delegates that Nixon was a has-been, a loser, a man who might be able to get his party's nomination but who was sure to be repudiated in the general election, just as he had been eight years earlier. And so from the Nixon camp came the rhetorical question: Why should we reward a man like this with a post in our Cabinet? It was one thing to toss a Cabinet bone to someone like Romney, whose fluttering around in the early-primary states had actually helped the Nixon candidacy. But Rockefeller was different. He was formidable, dangerous, and not to be trusted. Bring him aboard, and he'd try to dominate, take over; maybe even try to set up a private government of his own over at State or Defense, to push his own White House ambitions from there.

Nor was this the extent of it, for Nixon's resentment went well beyond a natural concern over political rivalry. More than any other family, the Rockefellers represent the Republican elite of the East Coast establishment, those Ivy League bluebloods whose attitude toward Richard Nixon has always been tinged with contempt. These were the people who first spurned him when, fresh out of Duke University Law School, he came to New York in search of a job, but could not get into any of the better firms. Later, of course, when he seemed destined to become Ike's successor, they were obliged to put up with him, but that period of acceptance ended with the two shattering defeats of the early 1960s. (The disastrous first debate with Kennedy in the '60 campaign was dubbed by one critic as "a classic case of Harvard versus Duke," exactly the sort of remark Rockefeller and his friends would chortle at over cocktails at one of their private clubs, even though it was made at the expense of their own party's candidate.) And when, after the '62 defeat in California, Nixon came to New York to try to build a new life, the East Coast patricians completely snubbed him, treating him as an embarrassment from the past who was now beneath their notice.

Oh yes, Nixon knew all about these people, with their inherited

wealth, their prep-school backgrounds and their season tickets to the
opera. But now that the shoe was on the other foot, now that he was
at last victorious, he had a chance to do some snubbing of his own.
"Stick to your own kind," wailed the Puerto Rican girl in *West Side
Story*, and that's the advice Nixon followed in picking his Cabinet.
For as much as the twelve appointees seemed to be mirror images
of each other, even more so were they reflections of the President-
elect himself.

They had money, most of them. As one would expect in a Republican administration, the new Cabinet included at least seven millionaires: Blount, Hickel, Kennedy, Rogers, Romney, Stans, and
Volpe. Remarkably, however, not one of them was born to real
wealth; like Nixon, they had all come from middle-class backgrounds
and worked their way into big money. Thus the spirit of Horatio
Alger, which lured young Richard out of the California orange groves
thirty-five years earlier to begin the search for his destiny, also
guided the lives of these men toward their eventual fortunes in law
(Rogers), banking (Kennedy, Stans), auto manufacturing (Romney),
and the construction industry (Blount, Hickel, Volpe).

Shultz was the only member of the group who had been tainted
with an Ivy League education (Princeton), and he more than atoned
for that by pursuing his life's work in Chicago. Most of the others
went to the kind of solid, middle-echelon universities (like Colgate,
Northwestern, Fordham, and Purdue) where it is customary for students to be on a tight budget and take on odd jobs to help meet the
cost. Two of them were graduates of small private schools (Laird,
Carleton College in Minnesota, and Finch, Occidental College in
California), not at all unlike Whittier College, where Nixon went for
his bachelor's degree. And four of the others (Hickel, Romney, Stans,
and Volpe) had only skimmed around the edges of a formal college
education, choosing instead to graduate, in the honored tradition of
the self-made man, from the school of hard knocks.

Although Rogers, Mitchell, and Stans were living and working in
New York at the time of their appointments, all three of them came
to the city—as Nixon himself did—from that "other America," well
beyond the banks of the Hudson. Mitchell was raised in Detroit, Stans
in rural Minnesota, and Rogers grew up in a small town in upstate
New York, a region that always has had more in common with the
Great Lakes states of the Midwest than with the population centers

of the Atlantic Coast. All of the others were rooted in middle America, either by birth or by where they chose to settle down. In fact, the physical and social milieu from which they all seemed to emerge —*en masse,* as it were—is that of a country club in a Midwest suburb, with its lush fairways and locker-room camaraderie. To round out this image, two of them, Blount and Hardin, were bona-fide Rotarians, while two others, Volpe and Hickel, belonged to the Benevolent and Protective Order of Elks. But if, as a group, they seemed to reflect the style and attitudes of the well-manicured suburbs that spread across the country in the years following World War II, their spiritual fathers could easily be envisioned strolling down Sinclair Lewis's *Main Street;* or for that matter, walking through the Yorba Linda orange groves of Richard Nixon's childhood. For ultimately that's what they were: the sons of small-town America, now come of age.

As the passage of time would reveal, those who were left out in the cold—the blacks and the Democrats, the Jews and the Rockefellers—would have little cause for envy. A brief rundown on how the original twelve fared over the next four years is ample demonstration of that.

Postmaster General Blount, in some ways the most conservative member of the team, was given a rare opportunity to carry out a mission that has long been a cherished dream among right-wing Republicans: the removal of an unwieldy bureaucracy from the Cabinet. In the interest of efficiency, the Post Office Department was converted, in 1971, into the Postal Service, a quasi-private government corporation run by a board of directors; the idea being that as a corporation the vast operation would have a better chance of paying for itself. But, once his handiwork was completed, Blount left the administration and returned to Alabama, a happy man. Happy, that is, until the President he helped to elect refused to help him when he ran for the Senate in 1972. Instead Nixon wanted and got the re-election of conservative Democrat John Sparkman.

Happy is not at all the word to describe the mood Wally Hickel was in when *he* left his post at Interior in the fall of 1970, for he had just been fired. There were several reasons for Hickel's dismissal, the main one being that he tried to get pushy with the palace guard Haldeman and Ehrlichman had formed around the President.

What's worse, he committed the unforgivable sin of failing to prevent a staff employee from talking to the press about his problems with the White House staff.

Three other Cabinet officers—Finch, Kennedy, and Hardin—were eased out midway through the first term, and for similar reasons: their policies and attitudes clashed with those that had evolved within the White House. Their disagreements were far less dramatic than Hickel's, and so were their departures; unlike the troublemaker from Alaska, they agreed to go quietly. Kennedy and Hardin departed from the Washington scene, looking and sounding dazed by their first experience in the byzantine world of power politics. As for Finch, since he was an old and devoted friend of the President's, a cushion was provided for the blow that fell on him. When stripped of his HEW post in the spring of 1970, he was brought into the White House, and for a while an effort was made to dress up the move, to give the impression that he actually had been promoted to a position of more power. But anyone fooled by that did not remain fooled; for once inside the White House, Finch promptly vanished into the woodwork, where he languished, without influence or purpose, until the end of the first term, when he finally left to go back to California.

Four men—Romney, Volpe, Rogers, and Laird—held on to their portfolios to the end of the first term, but they all paid a price for their perseverance. Romney at HUD and Volpe at Transportation both enjoyed some early success in their respective fields, but once Haldeman and Ehrlichman moved into full command of domestic policy, the influence of the two former Governors rapidly waned. Volpe, blessed with the kind of easy disposition that knows how to roll with the punch, did not try to fight the trend, and therefore he kept himself in good odor. When he did leave the Cabinet at the end of the first term, he was appointed ambassador to Italy. Not an especially relevant job, perhaps, but still a most pleasant assignment. What is known in the Army as "good duty."

Romney, a more abrasive type like Hickel, was clearly out of favor by the time he resigned; so there was no cushy embassy plum tossed in his direction. Instead, the former president of American Motors indicated that he had become disillusioned with the whole tone of Nixon domestic policy, and that he now believed he could make a more lasting contribution toward building a "better America" by returning to the private sector. Translated from the evangelical gloss

Romney spreads over all his public utterances, this meant that he certainly couldn't be any less effective on the outside than he had been in Richard Nixon's Washington.

As for Rogers and Laird, they were destined to play Czechoslovakia and Poland to Henry Kissinger's blitzkrieg. In terms of having his authority usurped, no Nixon Cabinet officer was more openly humiliated than Rogers. Long before the first term came to an end, as Kissinger steadily tightened his grip on foreign policy, rumors began to circulate that Rogers would not put up with it much longer, and that he was planning to quit. Friends of Rogers were trying to help him drive home a message to Nixon: Rogers wasn't asking so much that Kissinger be downgraded, just that, please, couldn't Kissinger and the President bring Rogers into things a little more? When he stayed on, everyone assumed he was merely playing out the string, and that he surely would submit his resignation at the end of the first term. Yet, even then, Rogers did not choose to leave. An apparent glutton for humiliation, he was the only one of the original twelve to remain at his post into the second term, though by then, 1973, he had been completely reduced to such window-dressing assignments as a meaningless trip through Latin America (hemispheric matters ranking around ninety-seventh or so on Nixon's list of priorities), or showing up at summit ceremonies to sign agreements that had been negotiated by Kissinger. Then finally, in the summer of '73, what had been the reality for so long became official, as Kissinger replaced Rogers as Secretary of State. Rogers desperately wanted to stay on, but Kissinger was threatening to quit the whole administration if he wasn't given the title at State. Nixon wavered. Kissinger pressured. The President finally gave in while Kissinger smiled and Rogers swore. But even so, and right down to the "end," Rogers continued to give the President advice on such matters as what attorney Haldeman and Ehrlichman should hire for their and Nixon's Watergate defense. Rogers had no special liking for Haldeman or Ehrlichman, but he did for Nixon. He gave the President, all the way through, more loyalty and respect than he got in return.

By the time Laird resigned, at the end of the first term, his relations with the White House had sunk to their lowest ebb. For one thing, he claimed to friends in the press that he had opposed the 1972 Christmas bombing of North Vietnam, and that only added ice to an already chilled relationship. For his part, of course, Laird was deeply distressed by the fact that the entire Vietnam policy, including many basic military decisions, had been taken over by Kissinger. Thus he could hardly wait to get away from Washington and Nixon's White House. But what a difference a few months can make. For by the following summer, with the White House in a state of siege over Watergate, and Haldeman and Ehrlichman banished, Laird was back in a position of supposedly far more power than he had enjoyed at the Pentagon. Yielding to fervent pleas from Republican Senators as well as from Nixon himself, the pride of Marshfield, Wisconsin, after only six months out of the Cabinet, agreed to replace the fallen Ehrlichman as czar of the President's domestic program. But, despite what Laird thought were promises, Nixon did not heed much of Laird's advice, so his White House run lasted only briefly.

The cases of Mitchell and Stans were different. When they stepped down from the Cabinet early in 1972, it was to devote their energies to what, to them, was a more noble mission: the re-election of the President. As in the great comeback victory four years earlier, Mitchell was to serve as campaign manager and Stans as the President's chief fund raiser. This time, however, it led to their undoing. A year later, the two men stood indicted in federal court on charges related to the Watergate scandal. Not since Harding's Teapot Dome had two members of a President's Cabinet been formally charged, in a court of law, with violating the trust of their high office.

The biggest surprise of all was George Shultz. Scarcely known outside of academic circles when the group was first assembled, he was completely overshadowed by such prominent politicians as Romney and Laird, and by the trio of Nixon intimates—Finch, Rogers, and Mitchell. Yet, of the original twelve, Shultz was the only one who truly prospered at every step along the way. For one thing, he was a seasoned labor mediator who knew how to work out effective compromises. For another, Shultz, like Kissinger, knew how to hire and get work out of quality staff people. As Labor Secretary, he soon began extending his influence across a broad range of trouble spots, though it is significant that he did not take on real authority until the spring of 1970, when he left the Cabinet and moved into the White House as director of the newly created Office of Management and Budget. (Unlike the Finch move, which occurred at the same time, Shultz *was* stepping up to a bigger job.) As budget director, he became Nixon's top economic adviser, and when, early in

1972, he went back to the Cabinet (this time to the prestigious post of Treasury Secretary), the move represented still another advance. Indeed, with the earlier Cabinet strongmen Mitchell and John Connally now out of the picture, Shultz was visibly the most influential of Nixon's Cabinet officers, the only one who even approached the kind of power wielded by the Haldeman-Ehrlichman-Kissinger group. However good or bad his economic advice, Shultz was honest and principled. And, despite being that close to the center for that long a time, the Watergate mess left him *virgo intacta*.

None of this naturally could have been predicted on that morning in January, 1969, when the new Cabinet punched in at the White House for its first day on the job. Ever conscious of the work ethic so deeply ingrained in the American soul, the new President, having just been inaugurated the day before, summoned his department heads to the Oval Office to be sworn in at the spartan hour of 8 A.M., even though most of them had been up late celebrating at the inaugural balls. (Nixon had allowed himself only four hours' sleep.) Now it so happens that 8 A.M. is the hour that the NBC *Today Show* is beamed into homes across the country, and Haldeman arranged for live cameras to be there to record the event, giving the new team a chance to improve on its rather stiff television performance at the presentation ceremony a month earlier. Thus, as taxpayers from coast to coast roused themselves out of bed to begin their day's work, they could derive whatever satisfaction they might out of seeing their new leaders already shaved, dressed, breakfasted, and on the job. And Nixon, not content to let a point speak for itself, insisted on driving it home. Noting that some earlier administrations had acquired certain nicknames (e.g., Jackson's "kitchen cabinet" and Teddy Roosevelt's "tennis cabinet"), he suggested that morning that his group should properly be called "the working Cabinet."

Finally, before we leave the unconscious irony that characterized so many of these early promises, a note about Washington's socialites, who were hopeful that, in spite of the ominous start that first day, the new regime would not be all work and no play. It was agreed that with the Democrats out of power for the first time in eight years Georgetown, the local enclave made chic in the John Kennedy years, would go into a decline. But surely, they argued, since politicians' insatiable appetites for dinner parties and the spicy gossip that goes

with them must be served, some other part of the city would rise up
to fill the void. It was *Time* Magazine, in its post-inaugural issue, that
came closest to sensing the wave of the future:

"One center of social life in the Nixon Administration is obviously
going to be the Watergate apartments, a cooperative complex over-
looking the Potomac. Secretary Stans and his wife have taken an
apartment there, and Attorney General Mitchell and his wife have
just bought a $325,000 duplex in the building."

So at least there was one prediction that held up fairly well;
nothing "inoperative" in any of that.

Five

EVEN as the "working Cabinet" was getting all the fanfare,
it was apparent to those paying attention that despite what he said,
and what others said for him, Nixon had no intention of abandoning
the powerful White House staff system that had become a fixture of
the modern Presidency. The only real question, during the early
weeks and months of the first term, was just *how* powerful it would
be in relation to the Cabinet. As had been true in the Eisenhower
years, Nixon's two most pressing concerns on assuming office were
a foreign war (Korea in Ike's case, Vietnam in Nixon's) and inflation.
The question was, would the major initiatives and decisions in dealing with those problems come from the Secretary of State and Treasury Secretary, as they had under Eisenhower? Or would Nixon
choose, as Kennedy did, to downgrade the Secretary of State and
other top Cabinet officers, and encourage the making of policy decisions by advisers inside the White House? Or would he lean toward
the Johnson example of trying to strike a Rooseveltian balance between his Cabinet people and the White House staff? As Nixon
started out, the answer was not at all clear. What *was* clear was that
he had brought into the White House some rather heavy guns—three
men in particular who seemed ready to assume dominant roles in
shaping the course of Richard Nixon's Presidency.

This early trio of potential power brokers did not include Halde-man and Ehrlichman. Haldeman's position during these early weeks was basically what he had outlined the day of his appointment. In addition to being the President's top image man, entrusted with organizing trips and television appearances in ways designed to re-flect favorably on Nixon's popularity, he was in charge of the in-house administrative details, seeing to it that things were kept running as smoothly as possible. Although even at this stage he generally con-trolled access to the Oval Office, he did not yet feel secure enough to come down hard in this area; the Berlin Wall was nothing more than a vague, wishful notion far back in his mind—if indeed he had any notion of it at all.

During Haldeman's first days in the White House, he was suspi-cious of people, arrogant, and fiercely protective of Nixon. But he also seemed a bit unsure of himself, a little lost, and yes, a little awed by it all. He wasn't sure just how far he could go, how far he wanted to go, and most important how far Nixon would allow him to go. Only later, when Haldeman saw openings—some created by him, some not—and grasped their possibilities, did he move to expand his au-thority and begin to build his empire. As for Ehrlichman, he was even more obscure at this point. For he was first hired as White House counsel, a mundane job far down the line in the pecking order (though four years later it took on a certain notoriety in the hands of a young man named John Dean), and not until Haldeman made his move did Ehrlichman emerge as a power.

But the original trio did include Kissinger. As Special Assistant for National Security Affairs, the strategic and prestigious job held by Bundy and Rostow in the two previous administrations, Kissinger loomed as a prominent figure right from the start. Joining him at the top of the early power structure in Nixon's White House were two other professors: Arthur Burns and Daniel Patrick Moynihan. Be-tween them, these three men bore almost no resemblance, in politi-cal and cultural background, to the twelve Cabinet appointees. In-deed, it is almost as if Nixon had followed one rigid set of rules in selecting his Cabinet, and then, to throw everyone off balance, had completely reversed those guidelines in picking his top White House people.

Consider: In appointing Shultz and Hardin, his two academicians, to the Cabinet, he focused on Midwestern schools, steering clear of the Ivy League so deeply associated with the East Coast Establishment and the Democratic administrations of Roosevelt and Kennedy; moreover, both men had made their reputations as administrators rather than as heavy thinkers. In Burns (Columbia), Kissinger (Harvard), and Moynihan (Harvard), Nixon went for an Ivy League triple play to three men to whom the dread term "intellectual" could seriously be applied. Not "pointy-head intellectual," perhaps, although Moynihan, and even at times Kissinger, had come perilously close to that.

Consider: The Cabinet had a distinctly WASP character, with a Rotarian, Kiwanis Club sensibility, the roots of which could be traced to the Fourth of July picnics and church suppers of small-town America. But in Burns and Kissinger Nixon picked two first-generation Jews, disgorged from the Yiddish culture of central Europe, and in Moynihan, an Irish Catholic who grew up in the streets of a New York slum called Hell's Kitchen.

Consider: Nixon's Cabinet was completely Republican, almost defiantly so. But in Moynihan he chose a deep-dyed Democrat, an outspoken liberal. A *maverick* liberal, to be sure, one who had trouble getting along with other liberals (hence his appeal to Nixon), but nevertheless, from the viewpoint of most Republicans, a *real* liberal, a fellow whose main concerns were with poverty, the blacks, and saving the cities—i.e., all problems that generally evoked negative responses in the "middle American" suburbs that formed the basis of Nixon's constituency. (One of Moynihan's first comments on his new colleagues at the Nixon White House was that they "are very nice people with a perfectly dreadful constituency.")

Even Burns, while clearly no liberal, had dabbled in heresy. As a young man living in New York, he had been a registered Democrat, and during those years had voted for Roosevelt in Presidential elections. As for Kissinger, he seemed, at the very least, to be a *crypto-* Democrat, since he had served as key adviser to Nelson Rockefeller, and beyond that his social and intellectual base was the world of Harvard, up there rubbing elbows with the likes of John Kenneth Galbraith and Arthur Schlesinger.

So the overall contrast was dramatic to say the least—as though Nixon had been torn between the examples of two predecessors. His Cabinet, with its middle-age spread and board-of-directors mentality, resembled nothing so much as Eisenhower's original Cabinet—

the "eight millionaires and a plumber," as they were dubbed at the time. (That last reference should not be confused with Nixon's more recent "plumbers" of Watergate fame; Ike's plumber was his Secretary of Labor, trade unionist Martin Durkin, the only blue collar in amongst all those silk shirts.) But with the top dogs of his White House staff—two Jews and an Irishman, and all three of them professors steeped in the elitist ethos of the Ivy League—Nixon veered suspiciously close to Kennedyism. For, with their Harvard credentials and irreverent personalities, both Kissinger and Moynihan (though not Burns) would have been very much at home on the New Frontier. As a matter of fact, Moynihan had begun his Washington career in the Labor Department under Kennedy. Perhaps the best explanation for all this is that Nixon, exercising the poker-playing savvy of his Navy days, was simply hedging his bets. In race-track parlance, he put his big wad on the entry he knew and understood (the Ike-like Cabinet), and then decided to slap a deuce or two on a couple of long shots, as a "saver"—just in case.

As all the world now knows, his bet on Kissinger was the best one Nixon ever made—or at least the best one since his early days as a Congressman, when he put everything he owned on a horse named Whittaker Chambers in the celebrated match race against Alger Hiss. (That one, let's not forget, he managed to parlay into all that has followed, the long national career that is now nearing the end of its third decade.) But it should be emphasized that Kissinger's towering achievements did not come until the latter years of the first term, and that during the early months of 1969 there was no way of knowing he would deliver so big a payoff. It is true that he moved fast to stake out his position as Nixon's top foreign-policy man, but he was careful, in the beginning, not to move *too* fast. For Kissinger was fully aware that, compared to old friend Bill Rogers at State and long-time political ally Mel Laird at Defense, he was the "outsider," the Harvard man who had come into the White House directly from an intimate association with Rockefeller—not exactly the best set of credentials for establishing personal trust with Richard Nixon.

Kissinger's prudent, deferential approach was evident in the early strategy sessions on Vietnam, when Rogers and Laird began pushing hard for a policy of gradual troop withdrawal. Of the two, Rogers's position was clearly the more optimistic. He contended that unilateral troop reductions could serve as the "act of good faith" Hanoi apparently was looking for in the new administration, to distinguish *its* policy from the belligerence of the Johnson years; and that in response to this overture the North Vietnamese would be more likely to commit themselves to serious negotiations at the Paris peace talks, and thus bring about an early settlement of the war.

Laird had fewer illusions on that score (he wasn't counting that much on good news out of Paris), but, with more than 500,000 Americans bogged down in the Quagmire, he argued even more forcefully than Rogers that the most urgent priority was to start bringing them home, and to scale down U.S. involvement in the war to the point where, eventually, the South Vietnamese could take over the defense of their own country. His concern was essentially political.

Laird correctly sensed that the majority of Americans who had turned against the war had done so not out of an abstract regard for international morality but because their sons and brothers and husbands were being killed over there. Hence, the most pressing need, in order to prevent "Johnson's war" from becoming "Nixon's war," was to reduce the casualty figures which he, as Defense Secretary, was responsible for putting out every week. To Laird, the figures of Americans killed in action were the key. Let the Paris peace talks continue to flounder in stalemate if that's how the other side wanted it, and let the war drag on (and on and on), but as long as the U.S. role in the fighting steadily diminished, the American people would stand behind Nixon as they had not stood behind Johnson. Thus was born the policy of "Vietnamization," with Melvin Laird as its chief architect.

Kissinger was not an enthusiastic supporter of that policy. He could appreciate its value from Laird's political point of view, for there was no question that some kind of U.S. move toward disengagement would help calm the fires of dissent raging across the country. And he also understood (one crafty political operator to another) that a program of troop withdrawal would greatly ease the strain on Laird's enormous Pentagon budget; as the casualty figures went down, so would the cost—in short, good public relations for Laird all the way around.

But there were other, less promising factors. For one thing, Kissinger had no confidence at all in the South Vietnamese ever being able to take over the war themselves; all the training and assistance

in the world would never put General Thieu on an equal footing with
General Giap, or make Saigon's army a match for the North Vietnamese. No, he was well aware that at some point, either sooner or
later, there would have to be a negotiated settlement, and it was in
this area that he foresaw the real danger of unilateral withdrawal. To
Kissinger, Rogers's optimistic hope (a hope that Nixon himself
seemed at the time eager to grasp) that Hanoi would be impressed
by gradual withdrawal as a gesture of good intentions was wishful
thinking carried to the point of folly. Kissinger believed that, however leisurely its pace, withdrawal would be interpreted by the
North Vietnamese as signaling a desperate desire to get out of Vietnam. To follow such a course would be, in a paraphrase of Lyndon
Johnson's disdainful remark, to "cut and walk." Hanoi, knowing this,
would have everything to gain by playing a waiting game. Kissinger
himself was convinced that the only way to reach an agreement in
Paris short of "camouflaged surrender"—a solution everyone in the
Nixon camp regarded as unacceptable—was to negotiate from a position of strength; in other words, the bigger the gun put to Hanoi's
head, the better the chance of an early, satisfactory settlement.
Though the time would come when Kissinger would be gushed over
by liberals as the one voice of civilized sanity in Nixon's White House,
in truth the Nobel Peace Prize winner was, from beginning to end,
a hard-liner on Vietnam, more so than Laird and *much* more so than
Rogers.

But the important point, for our purpose here, is that he did not
push his own views hard in these early 1969 strategy meetings. As
Laird and Rogers prodded Nixon toward acceptance of the withdrawal policy, Kissinger adhered to a posture of seeming neutrality,
or something close to it. He did make a point of submitting alternatives, yet even these were clearly labeled as options to be considered
rather than as positions he himself was advocating. In essence, he was
not about to start off his new job by risking an open fight on the
critical issue of Vietnam with the two men who, officially at least,
were most responsible for shaping Nixon's foreign and military policies. He was more than willing to give Laird and Rogers their head,
for perhaps he believed even then that the day would come when
he, Kissinger, would be obliged to pull their chestnuts out of the fire.
That long after the soft-line approach to negotiations had proved a
failure, and long after Vietnamization was revealed to be, at best, a

limited expediency (there was no way, after all, for the Pentagon to withdraw, unilaterally, the POWs), he would be the one called on to wrestle, long and hard, with the North Vietnamese negotiators. And that even then, in early 1969, he wasn't ruling out the possibility that ultimately only shock-treatment displays of military muscle—up to and including the heavy bombing of population centers—might be necessary to convince Hanoi that its best interests lay in a negotiated settlement. But he was content to lie back and wait, to let the course of future events dictate the moves that would eventually send him into the arena where, at last, the long war would come down to a *mano a mano* chess match between himself and Hanoi's Le Duc Tho.

Next to Vietnam, the biggest foreign-policy challenge facing Nixon was the Middle East, and here Kissinger was especially intent on maintaining a low profile. For a long time, even after he became Nixon's top foreign-policy man but before he actually took over as Secretary of State, he gave the impression that he believed he could never assume the *official* duties of America's chief foreign-policy officer as long as the Middle East remained a prime trouble spot. "I doubt that I could ever be Secretary of State," he once said in a private interview, and when asked why, he replied with a diffident smile: "Well, for one thing, there's my heritage." If Kissinger truly did believe that, he was wrong; for not only would he go on to become the first Jew and foreign-born citizen to serve as Secretary of State, but the very first crisis to confront him in the Cabinet post would be the fourth Arab-Israeli war. Yet at the time such a view clearly reflected the conventional wisdom: that only a proper WASP like Bill Rogers could sip chicken soup with Golda Meir, then trot across the border and skewer lamb with the Arabs, and manage to convey, at both banquet tables, the necessary air of impartiality.

So the Middle East became Rogers's personal prerogative, the one area where he was assured complete command without having to worry about interference from Kissinger. The irony, however, is that this was probably the worst thing that could have happened to Rogers, for the savage desert politics of the Middle East soon became, for him, a giant sand trap, one he would spend the better part of two years hacking around in before finally blasting his way out.

Seeking to resolve the bitter antagonisms left over from the 1967 six-day war, Rogers made a determined effort to win Russian approval of a compromise agreement that both Israel and the Arab countries could accept. The idea was to go beyond the kind of fragile peace accords that had been hastily stitched together during earlier times of crisis, and strive for a comprehensive, long-term agreement, dealing with the basic questions of territorial rights and mutual recognition, that could bring permanent stability to the area; and a Middle East solution on that large a scale could not be achieved without Soviet help. Moreover, in terms of the broader sphere of Big Power politics, the Middle East was a fitting subject on which to commence the "era of negotiation" that Nixon had promised would be the hallmark of his foreign policy; for if Washington and Moscow could find common ground on this thorny issue, it could not help but open the door to further agreements. Indeed, if it had worked, with Rogers plotting the course, the Secretary of State almost certainly would have entrenched himself as Nixon's top global strategist, for that early success would have been his, and *he* would have been recognized as the man with the magic diplomatic touch.

But it did not work. Though later the Soviet Union would be all for détente, when it came to limiting nuclear weapons and coveting American computers (or, as in the case of Brezhnev's personal comfort, Cadillac Eldorados), the Middle East was one area where it chose—then and later—to remain intransigent. Yet all through 1969 Rogers persisted in making futile appeals to Moscow, and by the end of that time the Middle East situation had taken a critical turn for the worse. By 1970, the "mini-war" along the Suez Canal, the dividing line between Egypt and Israeli-occupied positions in the Sinai desert, had moved into a daily pattern of attack and counterattack; and these border raids soon threatened to escalate into another full-scale Arab-Israeli war, one which would pose the danger, however remote, of a nuclear showdown between the United States and Russia. Clearly, this was more like the "old era" of confrontation than the new one that had been heralded in Nixon's inaugural pledge. So, faced with this dilemma, Rogers was forced to lower his sights, to retreat from the ambitious goal of a long-term agreement, and instead concentrate all his energies on a Suez ceasefire, even if such a truce failed to resolve the larger questions that lay at the heart of the Arab-Israeli conflict.

By the summer of 1970, Rogers was able to induce Egypt and Israel to accept terms for a ceasefire, and since this helped to prevent another major war in the Middle East until 1973, it was no small achievement. Yet, compared to the grand design that had been envisioned a year earlier, of a far-reaching settlement backed up by a Washington-Moscow alliance, it was a rather modest success. More to the point, Rogers was destined to pay dearly for having taken so long to get the Arabs and Israelis off his back. For, while he was bogged down all those months in haggling disputes with Cairo and Jerusalem, Kissinger had moved solidly into the breach on the larger quest for Cold War détente; and already, by the summer of 1970, he was edging Nixon toward acceptance of his own daring blueprint for a *Realpolitik* breakthrough: namely, that the best way to reach Moscow and East-West accord was to follow the Marco Polo route—through Peking.

This, of course, was to become the dramatic triumph of Nixon's foreign policy. And the President himself deserves much credit for effecting it, despite the fact that it represented a reversal of what he had preached for so long before and what he had damned others for advocating. But the man who conceived most of it and put it all together was Kissinger. Rogers was sometimes—not always but sometimes—properly briefed, and even given a modest role to play, but for all practical purposes, the job of being number one in helping Nixon plot world strategy had been taken away from him. From that point on, Kissinger was in command.

But to reiterate, none of this could be foreseen with any clarity in the early months of the Nixon Presidency. During this period, Kissinger deferred to Laird and his elaborate charts, with their orderly timetables for winding down the war. And he did nothing to distract Rogers, as he trudged across the sands of the Sinai in search of that elusive oasis where Arab and Jew might pause to consider their mutual survival.

In the meantime, however, he was hardly idle. In his basement domain at the Nixon White House, he surrounded himself with a powerhouse staff of aides who, in their flair for innovative thinking and devotion to hard work, had to measure up to the exacting standards Kissinger imposed on himself. Then there were the daily visits to the Oval Office, where he proceeded, through a delicate balance of Prussian efficiency and Bavarian charm, to deepen the President's trust in his ability and judgment. And elsewhere, within the White House, on Capitol Hill, and even among the Washington press corps, he set about courting friends and supporters, many of whom would prove invaluable in the months ahead. In short, he was steadily moving his panzers into position so that when the time came to strike he would be ready.

Six

THIS period of courtship was essential for Kissinger, just as it was for one of the other professor appointees, Pat Moynihan. An immediate priority for both men, if they hoped to wield any real influence in the Nixon White House, was to ingratiate themselves with their new boss. It wasn't just a case of having to live down a dubious past, such as their associations with Harvard, that citadel of liberal academic chic, or their previous loyalties to Nixon's political enemies Rockefeller and Kennedy, although that was certainly part of it. More important was the fact that before becoming top-level advisers neither man had been in any way acquainted with Nixon, except by reputation. Kissinger met Nixon for the first time in 1967, at a party given in New York by Clare Boothe Luce. And, since he was then deeply enmeshed in the world of Nelson Rockefeller, he brought to this first encounter all the disdain that at the time still characterized the New York Establishment's attitude toward the man from Whittier. Nothing transpired in the few words they exchanged that evening to alter his opinion. As for Moynihan, he did not meet Nixon until a few weeks after the '68 election, when he was summoned to the Hotel Pierre for the series of discussions that led to his appointment as an Assistant to the President. Prior to that, it can be assumed that as a Kennedy Democrat his view of the man was similar to Kissinger's; we would doubt, for example, that his office at Harvard was adorned with pithy quotations from this Richard's almanac.

Even in retrospect, it is extraordinary that someone as sensitive to slights and as wary of rivals and outsiders as Nixon should have called on these particular men to serve as two of his closest advisers. Why pick two strangers who were members in good standing of cliques famous for their anti-Nixon bias? Well, he picked Kissinger and Moynihan because, even though they may have had a modest regard for him, he had come to admire them from a distance; he was impressed by the books and articles they had written. Ever since the publication in 1957 of Kissinger's major work, *Nuclear Weapons and Foreign Policy,* Nixon had been a fan of the professor's pragmatic, hard-nosed approach to world politics, with its adherence to the balance-of-power doctrine that evolved from the European state- craft of the nineteenth century. (Kissinger had written his Ph.D. thesis on Metternich and the Congress of Vienna.) With Moynihan, it was his unorthodox liberalism (a liberalism that irritated more than a few fellow Democrats, since it challenged some of the party's most cherished tenets) that won Nixon's respect. In fact, after reading some of his articles on the subject, Nixon even went out of his way to praise Moynihan in an early '68 campaign speech as a "thoughtful liberal," the most glowing adjective a Republican Presidential candi- date could apply to such a disreputable word and concept.

So it was that Nixon went after Kissinger and Moynihan because he was struck by the thrust of their ideas. He was willing to let that, and that alone, serve as the starting point for intimate working rela- tionships that, by definition, had to involve the spark and tension of personalities. These, therefore, were bold decisions that placed a great deal of faith on intellectual rapport, and it is rather amazing— and a credit to all three men—how well they worked out. Not only in Kissinger's case, but in Moynihan's too; for there was a fairly long stretch during that first year when no sun in Nixon's White House blazed more brightly than his.

But Moynihan's early success can only be appreciated if viewed against the experience that befell the third member of the profes- sorial trio. It has generally been forgotten, but of all the early appoin- tees to the White House staff it was Arthur Burns who first loomed as the man to watch. Given the imposing title of Counsellor to the President (the first time anyone had been designated *that*), Burns was the only one of the original bunch to be accorded Cabinet status, which automatically made him the ranking member of Nixon's staff. Nor did his position as *numero uno* stem entirely from his title and rank. For, unlike Kissinger and Moynihan, Burns did not start off with the handicap of being a stranger with a shady past. His record was

clean, unsullied by liaisons with the infidel. He had never been a
Rockefeller man, or a Kennedy man; in fact, for more than a decade,
he had been a loyal and dedicated Nixon man. In announcing Burns's
appointment, the President described him as "a long-time friend and
trusted adviser"—accurately summing up their relationship. Along
with Finch, Rogers, and Mitchell in the Cabinet, he was one of a
select few who could claim a "special relationship" with Richard
Nixon.

That relationship dates back to the early Eisenhower years, when
Burns served as chairman of Ike's Council of Economic Advisers. The
council had been established by Truman, but it wasn't until Burns
took over that it began to assume a prominent role in economic
policy making; and one of those who was most impressed by his
command of the subject was Vice President Nixon. Then as now it
was a rare politician who possessed a sure grasp of economics, and
Nixon, having spent most of his brief Congressional career chasing
Commies and headlines, was not one of them. But, to his credit, he
was eager to probe into the mysteries of the Dismal Science, so he
played up to Burns, who, in turn, readily agreed to tutor the young
Vice President. This was at a time when most members of Eisenhower's high command (including, in those days, Ike himself) looked
upon Nixon as a kind of necessary embarrassment; he was needed,
they allowed, during election years to cut up the Democrats while
the General, perched high above the battle, dispensed platitudes to
an adoring electorate. But, aside from that, aside from his skill with
the hatchet, there was no particular reason for him to be hanging
around at Cabinet meetings and such.

Arthur Burns did not share this view. He liked Nixon; what's
more, he respected him. Even before the Vice President came to
him for instruction, Burns had been impressed by the analytical
approach Nixon brought to complicated issues at White House meetings. (Years later, after his former pupil became President, Burns
would say of Nixon: "It's extraordinary that he's been so unpopular
over the years with intellectuals. He's really one of us—and I seem
to be one of the few who has been willing to take him for what he
is.") So, during the early Eisenhower years, there formed between
the two men an intellectual bond, a political alliance, and a formal
friendship. Very formal. Burns and Nixon have never been what
you'd call "pals" or "cronies." Lessons in Economics 101 simply do

not encourage that sort of camaraderie.

Burns resigned from the Council of Economic Advisers at the end of Ike's first term to return to his professorship at Columbia. But Nixon and Burns kept in touch, and in March, 1960, as Nixon was getting set to run for President on Eisenhower's record, Burns came to him with some disturbing news. The scholarly economist had made his reputation as an authority on business cycles—perceiving trends in the economy before they surface—and what he then saw on the horizon was recession: unless the government cut taxes or increased spending, Burns warned, the slump would come in the fall, just in time to influence the voters. Needless to say, the Vice President promptly rushed this information to Eisenhower's Cabinet, but it was no use. Ike's laissez-faire millionaires, suspicious of a plot to undermine their fiscal integrity, told Nixon, in effect, not to bother them with his election-year jitters: the answer was no. But Burns had it pegged exactly right. The recession (the third to occur under Eisenhower) arrived on schedule, and hit bottom in late October, just a few days before the country went to the polls.

For years afterward, Nixon would bitterly complain that the failure to act on Burns's warning cost him the 1960 election, though graduate students in Nixonology will recognize this as just one of twenty or so reasons given for that traumatic defeat. Some of the others were: the liberal press . . . his sore knee . . . the lousy makeup job he had for the first debate . . . the liberal press . . . narrow-minded Catholics who voted their prejudice . . . broad-minded Protestants who were overly conscientious about *not* voting their prejudice . . . the left-wing press (similar to the liberal press, only more virulent) . . . Mayor Daley's shoddy arithmetic . . . Lyndon Johnson's dead Mexicans . . . the liberal media (worse than the liberal press, since it includes television) . . . the patrician habits of his running mate, Boston Brahmin Henry Cabot Lodge, who insisted on taking afternoon naps during the height of the campaign, while his opposite number, LBJ, was out on the stump from dawn to dusk, spreading magnolia across every corner of the Old Confederacy . . . Jackie Kennedy's pregnancy . . . and so on. But let it be said that, of all the alibis, the recession that Arthur Burns tried to head off was among the more convincing.

And, during the lean years in New York, when so many Manhattan Republicans would have little or nothing to do with Nixon, Burns was one of the few who returned his telephone calls. In fact, their friendship, though still reserved and academic in tone, deepened during this period. The two men would get together fairly often for long, leisurely chats. On these occasions, they would reminisce about the old days, up to and including the 1960 misfortune ("if only . . ."). Or they would bemoan the present state of affairs, economic and otherwise, that had come to pass under Kennedy and Johnson ("if only . . ."). And, as 1968 drew near, and comeback suddenly loomed as a real possibility, they would speculate about the future ("if only . . ."). Thus, when the time finally came to translate "if only" conversations into Presidential action, it was hardly surprising that Nixon would summon his "long-time friend and trusted adviser" to serve at his side in the White House.

What did surprise many people, however, was the scope of Burns's assignment. He was put in charge not only of economic policy, but of the whole range of domestic affairs; to use the official White House term, he was to "coordinate" the new President's entire domestic program. Since this took him well beyond his acknowledged field of expertise, there were those who frankly wondered if he was qualified. The White House, of course, gave assurances that he was, and no one was more insistent on this point than Burns himself, who resented the suggestion that he was a *mere* economist. He argued that he too was concerned about such things as civil rights, the rising crime rate, quality education and the plight of the cities. In addition, he pointed out, rather stiffly, that in his undergraduate days at Columbia he first had been interested in architecture and the law before turning to economics. Like so many specialists, from brain surgeons to relief pitchers, he saw in himself the potential of a Renaissance man.

Yet within a matter of weeks it became obvious that Burns was not seizing control of Nixon's domestic program. Important policies on a number of fronts were taking shape without his involvement at all, as Cabinet officers like Romney and Volpe maneuvered skillfully around Burns to win direct approval from the President for their pet projects. (In those early days, before the Berlin Wall went up, Cabinet members who made the effort were getting into the Oval Office; and as a result, they influenced decisions.) Even more damaging to his special "Cabinet rank" status, Burns was steadily losing ground to his chief rival inside the White House, Pat Moynihan, who by early summer had completely supplanted him as Nixon's top domestic adviser. On those issues where Burns did take a stand, he suffered one rebuff after another. For example, he opposed sending any message extending funding for the Office of Economic Opportunity. But Moynihan was for it and Burns lost. He opposed the ill-fated SST project, but the President, yielding to Volpe's advice, chose to support it. And, in the most critical fight of all that first year, he argued long and hard against Moynihan's ambitious program for welfare reform, only to see Nixon give his blessing to that.

Nor was that the worst of it. By trying to live up to his billing as the "coordinator" of Nixon's entire domestic policy, Burns spread himself so thin that he relinquished leadership in the one area where his judgment and experience were most urgently needed: the fight against inflation. Yet nothing at the time was more important than that, for if the new administration failed to curb inflation then none of its other domestic programs would be worth a damn. That, after all, was the lesson to be learned from Johnson's Presidency: the war in Vietnam had brought on inflation, and inflation had wrecked the Great Society. Guns-and-butter had not worked then, and it would not work now. As long as so much money was needed to prosecute the war, massive cuts were required in other parts of the federal budget in order to slow down the runaway economy. To Burns this was so obvious that it never occurred to him that Nixon might be tempted to follow another tack.

So in the early weeks of 1969, when he was so anxious to prove himself a Renaissance man, Burns roamed across the full landscape of domestic issues, instead of immersing himself in the fight against inflation. He also was reluctant to muscle in on fiscal policy because the man who was then asserting himself as the President's top economist was Paul McCracken, the new chairman of the Council of Economic Advisers. Since Burns personally had recommended McCracken for his old post under Eisenhower, he didn't want to appear to be breathing down a colleague's neck—to be pulling rank, as it were. In no time at all, however, he would regret both the recommendation and the fact that he didn't keep closer tabs on McCracken.

For, as soon as Nixon's anti-inflationary measures began to emerge, Burns realized that they were woefully inadequate. True, there were some reductions in the budget, but the cuts were a pittance compared to what was needed to cool off the overheated economy. Once he grasped what was happening, he dropped everything else and rushed to intervene. But it was too late, for by then Nixon, following McCracken's advice, was committed to a policy of gradualism: he would attack inflation in bits and pieces. He would cut down spending, yes, but the cuts would be moderate so as not to be deep enough to cause a recession. To Burns, such talk was timorous prattle. What was all this nonsense about recession? The beast to be slain was *inflation* and if, in the process, there was a temporary rise in unemployment, that could be remedied once the economy was back on an even keel. But first things first. The way the President was talking, it was as if their former boss, General Eisenhower, had suddenly decided on the eve of D-Day to send only a handful of troops across the Channel because although he wanted to establish a Normandy beachhead he was also anxious to keep casualties down. (There was an even more contemporary military parallel, since Nixon's economic gradualism bore a striking resemblance to the strategy of piecemeal troop withdrawals from Vietnam.)

All through the spring and summer of 1969, Burns pleaded with the President to step up the attack on inflation, to take bolder and more decisive action. As a Republican economist, he had always been adamantly opposed to anything resembling wage and price controls, yet by midsummer he became so desperate that he reversed himself on that lifelong principle and urged Nixon to set up guidelines similar to those that had been imposed by the Kennedy administration. But all to no avail. Nixon would not budge from his cautious strategy, his economic game plan, as he called it. (It was this policy that the President first chose to honor with his favorite jock-strap image.) So there it was: even on his own special turf, Arthur Burns found his advice rejected at almost every turn. What had happened? Where was the Richard Nixon he had known and instructed over the past decade and a half? Where was the Veep of yesteryear, that earnest and eager young man who had come to him for guidance?

For one thing, he was now the leader of the Free World, as they say, and as Nixon took on the trappings and burdens of the Presidency, his attitude toward his "long-time friend and trusted adviser" underwent a subtle yet decisive change. When he joined the White House staff, Arthur Burns was sixty-four years old, and everything about him put one in mind of an old-style European professor, who properly belonged to another age and another culture. This was true even though his own ties with the "old country" had long since been severed. (Born in Austria in 1904, Burns came to this country at the age of ten. While the family of his fellow Jewish émigré, Kissinger, was driven out of Germany by the Nazis, Burns's parents settled here twenty years before Hitler's rise to power.)

His physical appearance seemed to place him in another time, in another world. His ample thatch of pewter-gray hair was precisely parted down the middle, as though to indulge the slightest deviation might make him look raffish. His old-fashioned rimless glasses, with small, wirelike runners that curled inconspicuously behind the ears, reflected a stern temperament, as did his conservatively-cut suits of somber blues and grays. And, finally, the ultimate cliché, the obligatory pipe, that time-honored prop so essential to the image of the contemplative man. Coincidentally, it was around this time that critics of another habitual pipe smoker, John Mitchell, became fond of saying that "just because he puffs on a pipe and grunts a lot doesn't mean he's intelligent." In the case of Burns, no one ever questioned his intelligence, but to many his nasal twang and ponderous speaking manner had all the appeal of a deep bass grunt.

"Ponderous," in fact, soon became everybody's favorite word for Arthur Burns, for in personality as in appearance he was insistently professorial. He did not engage in conversation, he lectured; he did not merely offer advice, he pontificated. The complete pedagogue, Burns viewed the world as one huge classroom, and in his role as White House Counsellor with Cabinet rank he took it upon himself to lecture everyone: Cabinet officers, Senators, Congressmen, other members of the White House staff, and the President himself. That, of course, was nothing new; he had been pontificating to Richard Nixon for years. But it was different then. It was one thing, after all, back in the days when he was Vice President (and therefore had nothing else to do) for Nixon to spend long hours curled up at Arthur Burns's knee; or even during the lawyer years in New York to devote an occasional evening listening to long and pedantic discourses. But now he was a busy man; a busy and important man.

And what a contrast he found between Burns and his other two professors. Kissinger was always concise and lucid, someone who moved directly to the point and presented his case with a certain style and charm. Moynihan was even more endowed with these qualities; articulate to the point of eloquence, his florid personality was buoyed by an Irish wit, which he used with telling shrewdness. He knew just when to employ the light touch, the irreverent remark. Moynihan had an uncanny sense of how and when to make contact with the President's funny bone, whereas many of Nixon's associates over the years didn't realize he had one. Even Moynihan's memos to the Oval Office were entertaining, spiced as they were with urbane epigrams and wry historical allusions. At the same time, both Kissinger and Moynihan were punctiliously deferential, ever respectful of the High Office.

Burns was another story. Though never in any way *dis*respectful, he often brought to his meetings with the President a certain patronizing air. Nixon actually might have been willing to overlook that (realizing, perhaps, how difficult it was for Burns to forsake his accustomed role as mentor) but oh, the rest of it: the dull, meandering, ponderous lectures; that droning voice with its mind-deadening cadences that went on and on and on, spelling out, in endless detail, the arid truths of economics. It was easy to imagine how his classes at Columbia might have served as miracle cures for insomniacs who had tried everything else.

In his trilogy on World War II, Evelyn Waugh describes one of his hapless characters as "a bore of international repute whose dread presence could empty the room in any center of civilization"—and that, alas, was how Burns came to be regarded in Nixon's White House. Which was no small achievement when you stop to consider that the place was something less than a haven for gifted raconteurs. (Moynihan, after all, was an exception in the other direction.) Yet, even in that atmosphere of buttoned-up admen and staid Cabinet officers, Arthur Burns stood out as a Super Bore whose "dread presence" at policy meetings caused heads to droop and eyes to glaze over.

The consequences of this were regrettable. As is so often the case with bores, Burns had a disconcerting habit of being right much of the time. His opposition to such projects as SST and welfare reform was vindicated when Congress, for reasons similar to his original objections, declined to approve either program. But, since his arguments were usually couched in such ponderous language, they failed to convince. Even on the issue that engaged his most intense commitment, inflation, the sense of urgency he sought to convey became lost in his tedious, long-winded manner of presentation. In fairness to Burns, it should be said that Paul McCracken, the man who persuaded Nixon to adopt a gradual course against inflation, was just as boring on the subject, but McCracken prevailed because he got to the President first, during the early weeks when Burns still had his gaze fixed on the big picture, the whole range of domestic policy. In fact, that may have been part of Nixon's motive in resisting Burns's later appeals to revamp the policy: having suffered through one long set of dreary arguments, he had no desire to go through all *that* again. Instead, let the agreed-upon game plan stand, and hope for the best.

The best, of course, is not what he got—far from it. Just as he lived to regret the fact that Eisenhower's economic advisers did not respond to Burns's warning of recession in 1960, so did he live to regret his own failure to heed the professor's arguments for stopping inflation in 1969. For, had he followed Burns's advice, he might have been spared the economic horrors that later plagued him, the twin curse of inflation *and* recession that took hold of the country simultaneously, an unprecedented mess that came to be known derisively as "Nixonomics." Yet, by the time all that happened, Burns was long gone from the White House, having moved on to a more independent job, one that allowed him openly to criticize Nixon's economic bungling—which he did.

In October, 1969, the President named Burns to succeed William McChesney Martin as chairman of the Federal Reserve Board, and shortly thereafter the word was leaked at the White House that this was what had been planned all along: that from the beginning, the two men had agreed that Burns would work in the White House for just a few months, then move on to the FRB. Whether this was a face-saving story cooked up to gloss over the fact that Burns had been a failure in his White House job is almost beside the point. For it goes without saying that if he had moved with vigor and authority to take charge of Nixon's overall domestic program, if he had proved himself as indispensable in that area as Kissinger became in foreign policy, then Nixon would have insisted on keeping him at the White House.

But Burns was clearly unsuited for the role of domestic czar. More than anything else, he lacked the temperament to become a power broker on the grand scale. No empire builder, no Renaissance man, his talents were precisely those of a specialist; and as a lifelong econo-mist, he had to welcome the opportunity to take over the country's central bank, since in his field the chairmanship of the Federal Re-serve Board offered the kind of prestige that a Supreme Court ap-pointment brings to a judge or lawyer. (He also had the further honor of becoming the first Jew to occupy a post that had long been the private preserve of Protestant bankers.) True, the power he would wield would be within the far more limited framework of monetary policy—controlling the flow of money and regulating interest rates —but this was in his domain, his area of expertise. And going to the FRB would liberate him from the intrigue and in-fighting and clash of personalities he had been unable to cope with at the White House; in his new post, there would be no flashy Pat Moynihans to challenge his judgment and usurp his authority. So if, in one sense, Burns was the first major casualty in the struggle for power within Nixon's White House, the knockout pill he was given was laced with sugar; in another sense, sending him to the Federal Reserve Board was an act of deliverance.

The real irony is that of the three professors it was Burns—the long-time friend—who failed to pass the critical test of personality; whereas the two outsiders, who were all but hired sight unseen on the strength of their ideas, went on to triumph in their personal relationships with Nixon. Moynihan's triumph, it is true, was not as long-lasting as Kissinger's, but for a while, at least, the flamboyant Irishman really shook up the place. Indeed, through most of 1969, when Dick spoke fondly of Pat, he was not necessarily referring to the First Lady.

Seven

ONE afternoon in the summer of 1969, Nixon allowed himself to be overheard saying: "My God, four minutes with Pat is worth four hours of Arthur Burns." The remark quickly spread through the White House grapevine, and when it reached the ears of Burns, it did little to ease the resentment that had been simmering inside him for the past several weeks. What especially rankled Burns was the fact that he had opposed Moynihan's appointment from the first: way back in the pre-inaugural days at the Hotel Pierre he had urged Nixon not to go through with it. But Nixon, still somewhat under the spell of his own campaign rhetoric about an "open administration," was intrigued by the prospect of pitting the liberal Democrat Moynihan against the conservative Republican Burns. It was his hope that such an adversary arrangement would generate ideas which, in turn, would act as a stimulus to his middle-of-the-road Cabinet. He hoped that out of the overall mix there would emerge a creative balance or synthesis in domestic policy. To some of his aides he made a point of referring to the notable success Roosevelt had managed with this clash-of-opposites approach.

Burns, however, was not impressed. To his way of thinking, the undisciplined free-for-all that prevailed under Roosevelt was hardly an appropriate model for a man whose temperament and working habits were as methodical as Nixon's. Furthermore, he argued, Moynihan was not just another Democrat; he was a committed *Kennedy* Democrat with a brash and abrasive personality, a man who had a reputation for inciting controversy wherever he went. Hence, Burns concluded, he could not help but be an alien presence and disruptive influence in the new administration. But, as a portent of future putdowns, all his objections to Moynihan's appointment were overruled, and the two men were set up as natural enemies in Nixon's White House. Burns, it is true, started off with all the advantages—the fancier title, the Cabinet rank, and the years of friendship with Nixon—but it didn't take his rival long to overcome that.

Moynihan came on like a hurricane. Right from the start he displayed the kind of shrewd instinct for power that Burns never seemed able to grasp. One of the first tasks, in setting up the new shop, was the assignment of office space. Haldeman was actually the man in charge of this operation, but since he had not yet launched his own drive for power, his main concern at this point was to make sure no important feathers were ruffled. As the ranking member of the White House staff, Burns could have demanded almost any location he wanted and Haldeman would have readily given it to him; yet he agreed to have his office and staff *not* in the White House itself, but next door in the Executive Office Building. He even said (and this was in character) that he preferred being in the EOB, since he would have a better chance to think and concentrate over there, away from the day-to-day bustle of the White House. But the daily bustle was exactly what Moynihan wanted to be in the midst of, so he insisted to Haldeman that *his* group be set up in the West Wing of the White House, close to the Oval Office. End of Round One, and a clear victory for Moynihan. Or as he later put it to a friend: "Never underestimate the importance of proximity."

The question of proximity settled, Moynihan promptly set out to win Nixon over with his captivating personality. As much as possible, this was done in conversation, but in between his talks with the President Moynihan bombarded the Oval Office with his lively, literate memos, which provided such a welcome contrast to the dreary bureaucratic prose Nixon was accustomed to reading.

It may be worth noting here that Burns's whole career style and mode of operation had been geared primarily toward academics, that is, study and teaching, as were those of his small staff. Moynihan's career had emphasized written production, even in his professorial jobs, and so had the careers of his sizable staff. Being able to produce many tightly-written, chock-full-of-substance papers quickly was no small asset in an operation as memo conscious as the one Haldeman was putting together for Nixon.

We mustn't make too much of Moynihan's flair and writing facility, however. It wasn't just a case of Nixon's falling prey to the man's wit and charm. Moynihan did not come into the White House to play court jester, and his early success with the President went well beyond an ability to make him laugh. Actually, the sense of mission that brought him to Washington could hardly have been more somber, since his overriding concern was to do what he could to help save America from the forces of anarchy he felt were tearing the country apart. For all his sprightly manner and seeming insouciance, the Pat Moynihan who went to work for Nixon in 1969 was a disillusioned and deeply troubled man.

This was a far cry from his mood eight years earlier. Then, just thirty-three years old, he was one of the many young liberal intellectuals who had flocked to Washington to join John Kennedy in the romantic endeavor to "get this country moving again." As Assistant

Secretary of Labor, Moynihan never quite advanced to the front
ranks of the New Frontier; in fact, his most prominent as well as his
most eloquent moment came at the very end of the Thousand Days.
During the long weekend from Friday's rifle shots in Dallas to Mon-
day's burial in Arlington, as millions of Americans sat paralyzed in
front of their television sets, Moynihan was one of several Washington officials who were asked to comment in a TV interview on Kennedy's life and death. He offered a poignant if somewhat ethnocentric observation: "You can't be Irish," he said, "without knowing that
eventually the world is going to break your heart. But in this case we
all thought we simply had more time."

Such a remark was haunting enough in the context of that weekend, but as time passed it became even more haunting—at least as
far as Moynihan was concerned. For he soon came to regard the
assassination of John Kennedy as something more than an isolated
tragedy, an aberrant nightmare that had briefly intruded on the
bright promise of the American Dream. To him, it stood out as a
decisive event in contemporary history, one which ushered in a new
age of violence, disorder, and sickness in America. Most obviously,
there was the fact that the first assassination was followed by others:
Martin Luther King, a second Kennedy, and the more extremist
figures such as Malcolm X and George Lincoln Rockwell. More than
ever before, the bullet had begun to compete with the ballot as a
means of political and social protest.

In a broader sense, Moynihan saw how the poisonous spirit of the
post-Kennedy years had perverted the best and most idealistic impulses of the JFK era. He saw, for example, how the noble aims of
the civil-rights movement degenerated into the strident excesses of
black militancy, which helped to foment, at least indirectly, the
ghetto riots that erupted in one major city after another. He saw
what had happened to Kennedy's lofty appeal to youth, that call to
action that brought into existence the Peace Corps, and in countless
other ways induced young Americans to forsake the too smug and
self-satisfied values of the "Silent Generation" fifties, and become
involved in service to their country and government. By the mid-
sixties, this call to service could no longer be heard above the din of
protest, as the spirit of the Peace Corps gave way to the angry challenge of SDS. Thus, with Vietnam serving as the catalyst, he saw
college campuses across the land become battlegrounds of protest

and insurrection, which soon spilled over into demonstrations in the streets, where the confrontations grew uglier and more menacing; and all of it spurred on by a mindless arrogance which found expression in the slogan "Never trust anyone over thirty."

The militants and radicals were bad enough, but even worse, from Moynihan's point of view, were the liberals who indulged them. Generally older and in positions of responsibility, they should have acted as a countervailing force against the storms that were building. But instead of speaking out in voices of moderation (suggesting more constructive ways to condemn the war in Vietnam, and pointing out that, despite the racial barriers that still existed in America, much had been accomplished over the past few years in the struggle for equal rights) scores of liberal politicians and professors lent their support to the extremists. Moynihan watched with mounting dismay as his liberal colleagues made heroes out of Stokely Carmichael and Rap Brown; he winced at the unseemly reversal of the Pied Piper story, as adults followed the siren song of their children to the barricades, beaming their approval as the students filled the air with chants of "Hey, hey, LBJ, how many kids did you kill today?" In one of his first memos to Nixon, Moynihan wrote that Johnson was "the first American President to be toppled by a mob. No matter that it was a mob of college professors, millionaires, flower children and Radcliffe girls."

As the rhetoric of protest and violence swelled in volume, Moynihan saw the inevitable backlash grow in size and strength, as fresh hordes rushed to the banner of George Wallace, whom Moynihan described (in that same memo to Nixon), as "a fourth-rate regional demagogue." By 1968 the divisions in American society seemed so deep that Moynihan seriously wondered if the country's democratic institutions could survive in their present form. It was as if the Republic had chosen to conform to Yeats's bleak vision of the modern age: "Things fall apart; the centre cannot hold; /Mere anarchy is loosed upon the world. . . ." And from the same poem: "The best lack all conviction, while the worst/Are full of passionate intensity."

This was the dark mood that Moynihan brought into Nixon's White House in January, 1969. Along with it he brought a message which, in a series of memos and conversations, he imparted to his new boss. He agreed with the other top advisers that Vietnam and inflation were the most urgent *specific* problems facing the new administration. But these concrete issues, he argued, were part of a larger, more philosophical challenge: to heal the wounds of the past few years and restore stability to American society. The country was deeply fragmented because the people, in their anger and confusion, had begun to lose faith in the authority of their social and political institutions—and this, indeed, was cause for alarm.

There is no evidence that Moynihan bothered to quote Yeats to Nixon, yet he had done enough homework on the new President to know that Nixon took himself seriously as a student of history. So he proceeded to chisel away at that lode.

To the President and others, Moynihan began to draw disturbing parallels between contemporary America and the chaotic years of the Weimar Republic. The sweep of inflation, with its destructive effects on emotional as well as economic stability . . . the breakdown of social and moral values . . . the drawing-away from the political center toward extremist positions on the left and the right . . . and, most ominously, the psychological need for scapegoats to be blamed for a foreign military adventure that went awry, resulting in humiliation abroad and disorder at home. These were the forces that brought about the collapse of democratic government in Germany forty years earlier, and in Moynihan's view similar forces were cutting into the body politic of America in 1969. With the felicity of phrasing that characterized his memos to Nixon, he wrote on the eve of the first inaugural that "freedom lives in the interstices of authority. When the structure collapses, freedom disappears." And a few paragraphs later, he exhorted: "Your task, then, is clear: To restore the authority of American institutions."

There is no way to exaggerate the positive impact all this was having on the man in the Oval Office. What Moynihan was doing was molding into an elaborate historical and intellectual framework the most visceral concerns Nixon himself felt in 1969. In fact, the new President's antipathy toward the disruptive sixties was greater than Moynihan's, since it extended well beyond the radicals and their more naïve liberal supporters. Though he usually took great pains to conceal it, Nixon had been at war with the whole crowd of national leaders that had dominated the decade. Dismissed by Martin Luther King as an irrelevancy and scorned by Lyndon Johnson two years earlier as a "chronic campaigner" (i.e., habitual bellyacher), Nixon let it be clearly known, in private, that he felt a similar disdain toward both these men, and toward others as well—including, of course, the Kennedys. As much as the bearded radicals, the long-haired hippies and the afro-wearing blacks, these men—the top political leaders of the era—were responsible for all the turmoil of the past eight years. From the exalted rhetoric of the Kennedy inaugural to the mob violence at the Chicago convention, the sixties had been, in his view, a hideous mistake which should never have happened; and he was determined, in the course of his Presidency, to move the country away from all that.

This was a large part of what lay behind the strenuous effort within the Nixon camp to promote the "Eisenhower Revisited" theme, to spread the word that the new regime would be a throwback to the moderate policies and placid tone of the Ike Age. Though fascinated by Moynihan's allusions to the Weimar Republic, the President was not especially eager to play up that analogy, since to do so would only draw attention to what *followed* Weimar. (No point giving ammunition to the smart alecks who would be quick to note that the author of *Mein Kampf* also ran on a strong law-and-order platform.) Instead, he chose to exploit a safer, more attractive historical parallel, and one in which he could claim a personal connection.

As Nixon saw it, many of the conditions facing him in 1969 were similar to those that existed when Eisenhower assumed office sixteen years earlier: an unpopular war in Asia . . . a rising tide of domestic unrest (though in Ike's day most of the hysteria came from the right, where Joe McCarthy was beating his tom-toms) . . . a sense of national exhaustion brought on by years of energetic social legislation . . . and a disturbing decline in the prestige of the Presidency (like LBJ, Truman was accused by Republicans of unseemly behavior in the White House, of partisan testiness and vulgarity not in keeping with the High Office).

Once Eisenhower took over, these conditions soon ceased to exist. He promptly ended the war in Korea. He used his calm demeanor to mollify domestic tensions, killing McCarthy with the kindness of his famous smile, while at the same time seeing to it that the Senator kept getting enough rope to hang himself. He applied gentle brakes to the New Deal and Fair Deal programs, yet took care to insure that they were not damaged in the process. And, by strictly adhering to an above-the-battle posture and acting at all times with decorum, Ike preserved his enormous popularity and restored dignity to the Office of President.

Ever since he first had latched on to the General's coattails in 1952, Nixon had never been shy about wrapping himself in leftover Ike jackets; as he began his own Presidency, he sensed that in the minds of many Americans the Eisenhower Era had begun to take on the nostalgic aura of the "good old days." This represented quite a departure from a few years earlier, when the crisp activism and sophisticated style of the New Frontier were all the rage. It had been fashionable then to scoff at the Ike Age as "eight years of drift and neglect" with "the bland leading the bland." But by 1969 even some of those who had led the sneering suddenly paused to reflect favorably on that tranquil period. Nixon, who was aware that this nostalgic mood was responsible in part for his own comeback and election, did not hesitate to make the most of his old ties. ("Let's win this one for Ike!" he shouted in his acceptance speech at the '68 convention.)

Nixon's general message to the country as he commenced his Presidency was that he too would end a Democratic war in Asia (though he never actually said he had a "plan" for doing so). He too would soothe the passions of domestic dissent. He too would curb the frenzied pace of Democratic legislation. And yes: he too would restore to the Office of President an appropriate dignity and respect. And he would accomplish all this in the manner of his mentor. He would adopt a moderate, centrist approach to policy matters—thus, his careful selection of a middle-of-the-road Cabinet, and the liberal-conservative balance he sought in his top advisers. And he would seek to establish, by his own personal conduct, a calm, conciliatory tone in the White House—thus the "bring-us-together" theme of the first inaugural, with its hands-across-the-barricades appeal to "stop shouting . . . so that our words can be heard as well as our voices." If there was indeed a national yearning for a return to the spirit of the Eisenhower Era, he tried to create the impression that it was fitting he should be the one in a position to gratify it.

We know from Garry Wills and other perceptive students of the Vice Presidential years that the Eisenhower-Nixon relationship was marked by numerous frictions and petty discords that belied the cheery togetherness both men sought to convey in public. For the most part, Ike treated Nixon with the undisguised contempt that so

many Presidents reserve for their Veeps; Nixon, so deeply sensitive
to slights from above, often lapsed into long bouts of brooding resentment. He was especially nettled by Eisenhower's lack of appreciation
for his earnest, good-soldier labors in the trenches of party politics.
It was no easy job keeping disgruntled Republicans in line, which was
one of Nixon's regular assignments during those years. But Ike didn't
seem to care, or even notice, and this did little to bolster his Vice
President's sagging self-esteem.

Yet on another level Eisenhower's utter indifference to politics
only deepened Nixon's admiration for the man's special kind of
power. As one who was convinced that he had to master every
political trick in the book in order to have any chance of success,
Nixon stood in absolute awe of Ike's ability to glide, serene and aloof,
far above the squalid tumult of partisan politics. One may not enjoy
working for a man who has such a cavalier disregard for the rules of
the game, but one learns to revere the qualities that allow him to get
away with it.

Toward the end of his Presidency, when the Democrats finally
worked up enough courage to criticize Eisenhower directly, instead
of focusing their attacks on the people around him (like Nixon), they
began referring to Ike as the father figure. The term had a deroga-
tory intent, meant to suggest an ineffectual old fogy who, to judge
from his syntax at news conferences, was no more than a five-iron
shot away from senility. To Nixon, this was stupid politics, since it hit
Eisenhower at his point of greatest strength. In Nixon's view, Ike was
indeed the father figure, and that's what accounted for his overwhelming popularity. He was the old warrior who had watched over
America's sons on the battlefields of Europe, and now, as President,
he was keeping his paternal eye on the country and the rest of the
Free World. Nixon himself thought of Eisenhower this way, which
was why he was so hurt by the frequent snubs and putdowns; he
wanted desperately to win the old man's approval, to be embraced
as the devoted political son in whom Ike the Father was well pleased.
To Nixon, then, the *pater noster* mystique was the special force of
Eisenhower's image, the towering strength of his personal stature.
With his age and experience, Ike stood out as a symbol of tradition
and authority, one who brought to the present some of the treasured
wisdom of America's past.

In fact, a reverence for age has been such an integral part of

Nixon's political personality that some of us were mildly startled when, as President, he himself quietly crossed over into the ranks of senior citizenship. For, even as he moved into his later years, he still seemed cast in the role of Telemachus, a man constantly yearning for fatherly counsel. This is not meant to suggest an image of eternal youth so much as one of eternal middle age. As a young Congressman, Nixon gave the impression of being older than he was—a man, say, in his middle to late forties. In an eerie sort of way, he has remained frozen in that bracket into his sixties, as though he had made some kind of Faustian bargain to give up the spark of youth in exchange for becoming forever forty-seven.

Ike's death two months after Nixon entered the White House deprived him of his model father figure, but there were still others around—De Gaulle, for example. Shortly after becoming President, Nixon made a fast, eight-day tour of European capitals. One of his main stops was Paris, where De Gaulle was nearing the end of his long reign. On his arrival at Orly Airport, Nixon approached the French leader in such an obsequious manner that a British journalist blurted out, "Good God, he's going to kneel!" As it turned out, he did not kneel, but for a few seconds there the bowing and scraping were so pronounced that a shudder of discomfort went through some of the Americans looking on. Yet neither of the principals seemed in any way embarrassed. De Gaulle had long ago decided that it was perfectly proper for an American President to tug at his forelock when ushered into the Gallic Presence, and he no doubt found Nixon's fawning approach a refreshing contrast to the youthful arrogance of Kennedy and the coarse behavior of Johnson. As for Nixon, he was paying his respects not just to another national leader but to *le grand Charles,* a living legend who, like Ike, was one of the great heroes of World War II; here also was a symbol of age and authority, who therefore belonged to a breed apart.

Ultimately then, some of Nixon's deep-in-the-gut loathing for the sixties is connected to his cherishing of the father image as model and ideal. More than anything else, he saw the decade as a period of youthful rebellion against age and authority, against the traditional values represented by men such as Ike and De Gaulle. Nixon needed no reminders that it was the student riots in Paris in 1968 that had led to De Gaulle's eventual resignation, just as, in Moynihan's words, it was the "flower children" who had toppled Lyndon Johnson from office. And, in Nixon's view, the roots of the rebellion could be traced to the Kennedy movement which launched the sixties.

The harsh note of challenge had been sounded in JFK's inaugural address: "Let the word go forth from this time and place, to friend and foe alike, that the torch has been passed to a new generation of Americans, born in this century." What was *that,* after all, but a slap at "old fogy" Ike? In fact, the quote underscores one of the basic differences between the 1960 Presidential candidates. Both Nixon and Kennedy had gone into politics as young men, after their war-time experiences as junior-grade Naval officers. In 1960, Nixon was still adhering to the old World War II lines of authority, or chain of command. He felt qualified for promotion to the White House be-cause the most honored officer of that war had plucked him from the ranks and elevated him to second-in-command; having carried out his duties in that post, he could present himself to the country as Ike's personal choice for the top job. And he deserved the promotion because he had spent eight years polishing the biggest apple of them all.

In contrast, the other junior-grade officer, Kennedy, was not seek-ing promotion so much as usurpation. He ran for President in the language of mutiny, exhorting his shipmates from coast to coast to reject the advice of their old commander and turn to the fresh blood of younger men to "get this country moving again." That in itself may have seemed innocent enough, but with its robust rhetoric (it was no accident that "vigor" became the byword of the New Fron-tier) Kennedy had set off darker impulses of rebellion in other young Americans. That at least is what Nixon saw happening in the sixties. Kennedy, of course, could not be held directly responsible for the gothic spectacles that later erupted, of hippies spaced out on drugs or radicals dancing around the pyres of their burning flags. Yet, nevertheless, he was the one who had roused the Silent Generation from its acquiescent torpor. He was the one who had created the climate in which youth was encouraged to challenge the status quo. And he was the one who had glorified the passing of the torch to a new generation. All that was heady stimulus for the youth of Amer-ica. With torch in hand, they took it from there, to wage a full-scale assault on the values of age and authority—the values that Nixon, as Ike's designated successor, had sworn to uphold in the 1960 cam-paign.

Thus Nixon could view his comeback victory eight years later as vindication, as though the country had said to him: "Yes, if we had listened to you in '60, none of these terrible things would have happened. So now, this time, we turn to you to guide us back, to lead us out of this awful mess." Still, it was one thing to sense this mood in the faint and incoherent murmurings of the electorate, quite another to see it take on clarity and eloquence in the well-crafted prose of Pat Moynihan. For here was one of Kennedy's own telling him that the bright liberal promise of the JFK years had led to such a breakdown in the social and political order that his paramount mission as the new President must be to remedy it.

There was a key difference in Nixon's and Moynihan's thinking, of course, one that Nixon perhaps failed to notice, or at least ignored: in Moynihan's view, the upheavals of the middle and late sixties were a *post*-Kennedy phenomenon, in many ways triggered by the assassination itself; for him, the dark forces were set in motion by Kennedy's death, not his election. "I was and am a Kennedy Democrat," Moynihan insisted on more than one occasion after going to work for Nixon; as such, he hardly was interested in contributing to a revival of the Ike Age. What was this refugee from Camelot, this Harvard liberal, this Hell's Kitchen Irishman doing in Richard Nixon's White House? He was there because he perceived that the Kennedy obsession that had been twisting around inside Nixon over the past eight years was, in truth, a knife that cut both ways.

While much of Nixon's obsession with the Kennedy legend was negative and mean-spirited, deeply rooted in personal jealousy, there was more to it than that. A determination to learn from experience—especially adverse experience—has always been one of Nixon's stronger traits. And, although he never really understood the Kennedy legend that flourished in the sixties, he made an effort to try to understand it in hopes of being able to use it to his own advantage. Moynihan's presence in the Nixon White House was a significant part of that effort, which was something that Moynihan himself recognized.

To appreciate the depth of Nixon's Kennedy obsession, we should examine its origins. Having lived through so many years of their triumphs and tragedies, most of us have become a little jaded about the Kennedys; indeed, some of us (to be impolite about it) have had our fill of them. So perhaps we need to stretch our memories a bit to recall the sense of novelty and excitement John F. Kennedy engendered in 1960 when he set out to conquer America. There were his wealth, his social position, his Harvard background, and a record of heroism in World War II. There were the wit and charm that formed the base of his attractive personality. And there were the lean, athletic body, the movie star's face, and the stylish, jet-set wife who not only wore the latest Paris fashions but also conversed in French. Of course none of this had anything to do with issues or qualifications for the Presidency, but still, nothing quite like Kennedy had ever happened before in a national political campaign. To many Americans, he seemed almost unreal, like something out of a romantic novel. Our tradition had prepared us for Horatio Alger running for President, but not Jack Armstrong. This was what Norman Mailer was getting at when, in assessing the Kennedy impact on the country in 1960, he called it: "Superman Comes to the Super Market."

As it turned out, all these factors played to Kennedy's advantage, but it didn't necessarily have to be that way. A different kind of politician running in Nixon's place that year might easily have taken Kennedy's glamour and style and social status—and shoved them down his throat. Just imagine, for example, how much Harry Truman would have relished running against Harvard and Joe Kennedy's millions and all that snooty, jet-set swank. ("The little lady speaks French, does she? Well, plain, old-fashioned American is good enough for me and my Bess.") Oh, yes: a Common Man Harry, making the most of his modest background and "just folks" style, would have done everything he could to fit Kennedy into the striped morning trousers he used to trip up that other elitist—the fancy little man on the wedding cake, Tom Dewey.

But Nixon, cut from a much different cloth (no populist, common-man impulses stirring in those veins), went through the '60 campaign wearing all his insecurities on his sleeve. Though he ran hard against JFK on the issues (where there wasn't much difference between them), his problem was that he truly liked and admired Kennedy, and seemed more than a little awed by his opponent's various attributes. The poor boy from California who had to "settle" for Whittier and Duke may have resented Kennedy's Harvard education, and the social cachet that went with it, but it was a resentment born of envy;

he would have dearly loved to have had the same opportunity. The cautious introvert and poor mixer, who campaigned with a mortician's solemnity, was himself charmed by Kennedy's easy banter and jaunty style. The man who had been cruelly mocked for his ski-slope nose and Herblock beard had an uneasy appreciation of Kennedy's good looks, and the effect they might have on impressionable voters in the media age. The ardent sports fan and former benchwarmer, so painfully aware of his own awkward mannerisms, gazed with approval on a man who, despite chronic back problems, moved with the grace of a natural athlete.

Even Kennedy's valor in the war threw Nixon off balance, since it deprived him of what once had been a campaign plus. When he first ran for office, just after the war, he made much of the fact that he was a veteran (the late 1940s being the golden age of veterans), and of course he had every right to be proud of his record as a supply officer in the Pacific. Still, it wasn't quite the same as having a PT boat blown up in his face, so in 1960 he refrained from passing around his World War II snapshots, showing him in uniform, lest people draw the wrong comparison. And, finally, there was his wife: the loyal, hard-working Pat. She too had been an asset in past campaigns, but now, tossed up against Jackie's glitter, the "good Republican cloth coat"—that proud symbol of an earlier triumph—suddenly began to look a little threadbare.

In 1960, Nixon found himself back-pedaling at every turn, while all the time making it clear—perfectly clear—that he himself was bedazzled by the finesse and footwork that put him on the defensive. The millions of Americans who were taken in by the Kennedy magic in 1960 included the one man who could least afford to succumb to it. When Mailer's Superman arrived at the Super Market, he found his opponent among those gathered at the checkout counter, filling the air with his own "oohs" and "ahs." Though cast in the role of adversary, Nixon allowed himself to be caught up in the Kennedy mystique, and it greatly helped to bring about his defeat.

And, once caught up, he found he couldn't break loose. It was during his years of political exile that the Kennedy legend grew to full flower, taking on epic proportions in the aftermath of Dallas. Nixon soon discovered that in an odd sort of way he himself was associated with it. When he took his first tentative steps down the comeback trail in 1966 and '67, he learned that in the minds of many college students and other young people he was remembered chiefly as "the man who appeared on television with President Kennedy." Yet another demeaning identity. All during the Vice Presidential years, he had been viewed as a lackey. At last that image had begun to fade somewhat, only to be replaced by one just as humiliating, if not more so. It wasn't just the conventional "loser's" image we heard so much about in those days. Nixon was seen as a very special loser: the heavy, who had tried to prevent the "good guys" from settling the New Frontier; the patsy, over whose body the Kennedys trampled in their cavalry rush to power. But, if Nixon regarded this as a bitter pill, he was a smart enough politician to know that it was to his advantage to swallow it. Given the scope and intensity of the legend, better to be seen as Mordred than to have no role at all in Camelot.

So, as he ran for the Presidency the second time, Nixon often went out of his way to play up his Kennedy associations—to emphasize his *own* love for the sea, and to point out his *own* Irish background and that of his wife, "the former Patricia Ryan." No one can say exactly why he chose to do it or whether any of this helped him or not, but the point is the tendency was there. Out of one side of his mouth he might contend that the Kennedy call to youth was indirectly to blame for setting off the disorders of the sixties, and that the American people longed for a return to the tranquil climate of the Eisenhower years, with its inherent respect for age and authority. But another part of him was fully aware that many Americans believed, with Moynihan, that it was Kennedy's death that had brought on the darkness, and that the nostalgic mood he sensed in the country was, for many, a yearning to revive a spirit of hope, boldness and excitement. Thus he might try to respond to that too, since in his own peculiar way he carried with him into the Presidency a legacy from both eras. Trained under Eisenhower, he had been tempered in battle with Kennedy, and both experiences had left their indelible marks. Inside that Ike jacket he clutched so tightly about him, there lurked a closet Kennedy struggling to express himself—with whatever "vigor" he could manage.

As Nixon began his Presidency, the ghost of John F. Kennedy hovered over the White House, and of all the men who gathered in and around the Oval Office none discerned its presence more clearly than Moynihan. Understandably. As one of Kennedy's men, he was especially sensitive to nuances of that sort. Moreover, it helped him comprehend exactly why he, of all people, had been summoned to the new President's inner circle—why Nixon, a man he had never met, would call him down from Harvard to play with the Republicans. Insofar as there was to be a visible link with Camelot, he was it.

Moynihan, of course, had to be discreet. He was on alien ground, surrounded by enemies, and therefore he could hardly set out to establish an overt connection with the New Frontier. That would have been gauche, though he did go so far as to pass out White House matchbooks depicting the Presidential seal and Presidential yacht, but inscribed with the words *Honey Fitz*. And when Republican recipients, recognizing this JFK label, raised their eyebrows, Moynihan would break into an elfin grin, and say: "That's how frugal we are on government expenses. We're even using leftover matches." But harmless pranks were one thing. On the adult level, he came up with a far more subtle ploy whereby Nixon's Kennedy hangup could be exploited to liberal advantage.

Once he ingratiated himself with all his tough talk about "restoring authority" (which had a nice, firm law-and-order ring to it), he proceeded to play his high cards—again appealing to Nixon's reverence for history. In their casual late-afternoon chats in the Oval Office, Moynihan told the President he had a grand opportunity to become a modern Disraeli. He pointed out that when Benjamin Disraeli was Britain's Prime Minister in the 1870s he utterly confounded Gladstone and other opponents by advocating a series of social reforms which they, as Liberals, were honor-bound to support. In this way, Disraeli broadened his political base, increased his power, and established the tradition of Tory Reform—the art of clothing liberal policies in conservative dress.

It was Moynihan's contention that as a Republican President with solid conservative credentials, Nixon could pull off a similar coup. He would want to pick and choose his spots carefully, of course, but the right kind of bold and unexpected move would leave his political enemies jabbering to themselves. By skillfully muscling in on their own territory, he could beat the Kennedys and their liberal friends at their own game. This was a most ingenious maneuver on Moynihan's part; having taken the measure of his new boss, he sensed that the way to bring out the least politically conservative tendencies in

Nixon was to pander to his desire to "get back" at the Kennedys for all they had done to him. In growing up on the tenement streets of Hell's Kitchen, he obviously learned at an early age how to play the con artist.

Nixon, at least as much as Kennedy and Johnson, came to the Presidency determined to do something great. In foreign affairs he had some definite ideas about what he wanted to try. But in domestic affairs he had no deep-seated notion of what the "something great" might be or even a personal philosophic basis for determining what might or might not be great. At his core he wasn't certain that he was a dedicated conservative but he knew he didn't want to appear, much less be, a dedicated liberal. Nevertheless, he was determined to do "something great," or as he once put it to a Moynihan aide he wanted "to make a difference." Moynihan skillfully played upon this longing in Nixon.

Nevertheless, he took a hell of a chance in citing Disraeli as Nixon's historical model. For one thing, Disraeli was primarily known not for his domestic reforms, but for the aggressive, gunboat imperialism of his foreign policy. He was an unabashed jingoist who rejoiced in flaunting Britain's imperial power before the world; during his premiership, Britannia ruled the waves more arrogantly than ever before or since. Was it Moynihan's intent to draw a parallel here as well? Was he slyly taking note of Nixon's own pre-Presidential reputation as a knee-jerk anti-Communist who loved to wave the flag of American imperialism? If so, such an association was not especially helpful to the "new Nixon" who had just recently proclaimed the "era of negotiation."

As for Disraeli's social reforms, both his contemporaries and later historians recognized that they stemmed from motives of the utmost cynicism. As an aristocrat who deeply believed in the class system, he didn't care a whit about improving the lot of the lower orders. His support of reform legislation was not that of a man moved by conscience (he had nothing but contempt for Gladstone's moral fervor), but that of a rank opportunist—a "Tricky Ben" willing to go along with anything that might enhance his own power. Was this also meant to be part of the analogy? Was Moynihan suggesting that Nixon align himself with Disraeli's unprincipled motives, and thus give emphasis to his own lingering image as a man ever ready to play any tune the voters wanted to hear? To dispel that image had to be one of Nixon's chief aims on becoming President, but to become identified with Disraeli was hardly the way to go about it.

Yet, if Moynihan was indulging in a bit of covert mischief here, he got away with it. For such was the seductive power of his central argument that the darker aspects of Disraeli's reputation, with their embarrassing implications for Nixon, were blithely overlooked. Already intrigued by Moynihan's personality, the President became intrigued by Moynihan's vision of him as a Tory Reformer. By the spring of 1969, he was eager to trot out his new identity, to pit his Disraeli against Teddy Kennedy's Gladstone. All he needed was an issue large enough and dramatic enough to get the message across. So Moynihan, having guided matters along so smoothly up to this point, now played his ace: welfare reform.

The welfare bill that came out of the White House that summer was downright revolutionary in its basic proposal: to provide every American family with a guaranteed annual income. This went far beyond anything offered by Nixon's two Democratic predecessors and, needless to say, Moynihan's fingerprints were all over the measure. Having induced the President to don the Disraeli robes of Tory Reform, he then persuaded him to sponsor the most radical social legislation since the New Deal. So there was no question about it: the Kennedy liberal, the Harvard outsider, was running circles around the Nixon White House.

Eight

THE "welfare mess" had been one of Nixon's favorite targets in the '68 campaign. "The time has come to get people off the welfare rolls and onto payrolls" was the line he liked to deliver before well-dressed crowds at suburban shopping centers. And, once inside the White House, he was determined to do something about it. But what? As was the case with other domestic issues, he did not come into office with a concrete plan or coherent policy. All he knew for certain was what he did *not* want, and on this he was adamant: a guaranteed-income scheme was out of the question. He was not going to be the kind of President who took taxpayers' money and, with no questions asked, just gave it away to people who did not work.

This was the hard-line Nixon stand Moynihan encountered when the welfare question first came up in the early weeks of 1969. As for his own views, welfare—and the poverty problem in general—had long been a major concern. For years Moynihan had been arguing in favor of some kind of income maintenance for the poor, either in the form of a guaranteed income or through a program of support payments for families with children, with so much allotted for each child. (The latter policy, as he often noted, had been successfully put into practice in Canada and Western Europe.) But he was well aware that Nixon would never buy the conventional liberal argument for income maintenance, and that if he tried to sell it on that basis he would only paint himself as a bleeding-heart type eager to help those who refuse to help themselves. Hence, he knew from the first that he would have to go about it another way—and he did. With his unerring instinct for getting to Nixon where he lived, Moynihan came up with another brilliant ploy.

The trouble with our present welfare system, he told the President during their philosophical chats in the Oval Office, is not that we give all this money to the poor, but that so much of it goes to the government services that have become part of the system: the social workers, the paper pushers, and all the rest of the bureaucratic tangle. The advantage of direct cash payments under a plan of guaranteed income is that ultimately we could eliminate the services. That way, the poor would still get the money they need, but the social engineers and other do-gooders with their graduate degrees in sociology would have to find other ways to make a living. We may not be able to put an end to welfare, said Moynihan, but we can certainly break up the welfare bureaucracy. Moreover, he went on, direct cash payments with a minimum of government interference adhered more to the Republican philosophy. Let those who are mired in poverty have the money, but let them lead their own lives without having to answer to the social planners. Such a policy, Moynihan concluded, was both humane *and* conservative—and thus in the best tradition of Tory Reform.

So once again the maverick liberal hit all the right nerves. As

Moynihan presented it, guaranteed income was still a radical concept, but radical in the right direction—i.e., *away* from the custodial, government-as-nursemaid approach that had been in effect since Roosevelt's time. The government would continue to put up the dough (or dole), but that's all. The recipient, the individual—a favorite conservative word—would be allowed to take it from there, without a lot of bureaucratic meddling.

This was heady, intoxicating stuff, and strong enough to bring Nixon around to the point where he was at least receptive to Moynihan's argument. But, for all its novelty and shrewd, unorthodox appeal, it still failed to resolve the central dilemma. Everything about Nixon's Horatio Alger background, from childhood days through the long, hard years of struggle to get to where he finally got, rebelled against the idea of giving people money for doing nothing. And, as long as that dilemma remained unresolved, there was no way that he could play Tory Reformer on the issue of welfare—Disraeli or no Disraeli.

The eventual solution to this problem did not come from Moynihan (the man, after all, had only so many cards up his sleeve), but from a thoroughly unexpected source: Labor Secretary George Shultz. It was at a high-level meeting on welfare that Shultz suddenly spoke up and said that what Moynihan's plan needed was something for the *working* poor. Although still a minor and relatively obscure member of the Cabinet, Shultz had impressed Nixon, even before this, with his calm intelligence and unassuming manner, particularly in the way it contrasted with the evangelistic bombast of some of his other domestic Cabinet officers, especially Romney and Hickel. And now at this meeting, having mentioned the sacred word "working" Shultz was asked by Nixon to weave into the welfare scheme some ideas that would make the program more attractive; which is to say, more than just a form of government handout.

Shultz delivered on two counts. First, he emphasized work *incentives*. The welfare rolls would be expanded to include the rock-bottom working poor. Those who work but who earn less than $60 a month (or $720 a year) would continue to receive full welfare payments. The idea was to discourage dependency as a way of life; that is, to put an end to the prevalent practice whereby the head of a family would turn down certain menial jobs because he (or more often, she) could make more living off welfare. Furthermore, under

Shultz's plan, a man who starts earning more than $720 a year would still be entitled to *some* of his welfare allotment; for every dollar earned, he would only give up 50 cents in welfare until the combined income reached a certain level ($3,290 for a family of four). Then he would be on his own. Shultz's major contribution was to shore up the provision for work *requirements*. Except for the disabled or mothers of preschool children, all welfare recipients would be required to accept work that was available, or take part in vocational training that might lead to jobs.

As it turned out, his work on the welfare package proved to be a boon to George Shultz's own career. From this point on, his views were sought on a wide range of issues, and his rise was swift. He left the post of Labor Secretary, with its narrow jurisdiction, and took up a position inside the White House, where he promptly became the President's top economic adviser, that role, in turn, eventually leading to his appointment as Treasury Secretary. In a broad overview of Nixon's Presidency, Shultz must be ranked among the top six or seven men who have had decisive influence on policy, and it was his contributions to welfare reform that carried him to the threshold of power.

Their more immediate effect, however, was to give Moynihan's program the element of "cover" Nixon thought it needed. The President now felt he could run the risk of a guaranteed-income policy so long as it honored the sanctity of the Puritan work ethic. In other words, he could have his cake of Tory Reform and eat it too. Thus it was that in the late spring of 1969 Nixon moved to embrace a principle that just a few months earlier he had declared anathema. But, before committing himself completely, he gave the opposition within his administration a chance to have its say—and that opposition was considerable.

Since he was surrounded by Republicans who had not been exposed to the full force of his ingenious arguments, Moynihan had few allies in his fight for a guaranteed income. The only Cabinet officers who gave him their full support were Shultz and HEW Secretary Bob Finch. (Even before Moynihan launched his own campaign, Finch and his HEW deputies had reached the conclusion, based on their own studies, that some kind of income maintenance was the only way out of the "welfare mess.") But most other members of Nixon's official family were either opposed to the plan or extremely wary of it.

When Burns, for example, first heard that Moynihan was pushing for a guaranteed income (which would entail a program so costly that, in Burns's view, it would wreck any hope of curbing inflation), it merely confirmed his worst suspicions, that Moynihan was a Kennedy wolf in sheep's clothing, who was determined to spread havoc in a Republican administration. Still, he was confident that, knowing Nixon as he did (or thought he did), the crazy scheme wouldn't get anywhere, and he was appalled when he later found out that Moynihan was making real headway. Moving to intervene, Burns set down before Nixon all the familiar Republican arguments against lavish spending programs for the poor.

For a time, Burns was effective in his criticisms of the highly technical aspects of Moynihan's proposals. Moynihan, with backing from Finch, had become more strident in his advocacy but was having an increasingly difficult time countering the technical criticisms. It was in this area that Shultz was of such immense value. It was, in part, to mollify Burns's objections that he proposed adding stiffer work requirements ("eyewash," a White House aide later called it) and articulated ways to integrate the plan with income-tax laws. That saved it. Burns had nothing in his repertoire to match the combination of Shultz's practical skills as a mediator and Moynihan's visions of Disraeli Reincarnate.

Nor did anyone else. Although Vice President Agnew and a number of Cabinet officers joined Burns in trying to dissuade the President, their efforts were in vain. By midsummer, Moynihan knew he had the thing nailed down. As he remarked to one of his aides, "I have the pleasure of holding a poker hand nobody can beat."

The final decision came early in August. Nixon chose to unveil the new program in a nation-wide television address, and on the day of the speech he sat down with Moynihan to work in some last-minute refinements. Moynihan already was in an exultant mood, and his spirits brightened even further when, at one point, the President suddenly turned to him and said: "Of course you know perfectly well that it has always been Tory men with liberal principles who have enlarged democracy." So, on top of everything else, the young professor was accorded the ultimate tribute: his prize pupil had become an echo, tossing back at him lines from his own lectures, almost word for word.

Moynihan had every right to be pleased with himself. To have persuaded Richard Nixon—a man known for his deeply-ingrained sense of caution—to endorse so radical a measure was, by any criterion, a remarkable achievement. With his success, Moynihan became the man of the hour in Nixon's White House, and there seemed every reason to believe that this was just the beginning; that he would move to extend his power over the full range of domestic policy, and that guaranteed income would soon be followed by other bold initiatives, all in the name of Tory Reform. But, unfortunately for Moynihan, the fight for welfare reform did not end with Nixon's acceptance of it. From the White House, the struggle moved into a larger arena, and the setbacks encountered there helped to bring about Moynihan's own downfall. Having won the battle, he went on to lose the war.

At first, everything went according to plan: Nixon's television address was an enormous success. Although he managed to get the point across that the main feature of his welfare bill was to guarantee every American family an annual income (a minimum of $1,600 for a family of four), he carefully adhered to the Tory tradition of couching liberal policies in conservative language. The official name was itself a master stroke of blandness. It was designated the Family Assistance Plan (or FAP), thus steering clear of the inflammatory phrase "guaranteed income." And in his speech Nixon went out of his way to stress the work-ethic aspects that Shultz had contributed to give the bill respectability. (What the country needs, he sternly declared, "is not more welfare but more *work*fare.")

The immediate reaction was not only favorable but overwhelmingly so. Conservatives rushed to applaud the move to prod "welfare chiselers" into doing a little work for their handouts. And, at the other end of the spectrum, Nixon's political opponents got the message intended for them. Fully aware of the progressive concept that lay at the heart of the proposal, liberals had no choice but to offer their compliments and voice their support. But naturally they were stunned. Some of them even lapsed into vague mutterings on the mystical power of the Presidency to uplift and ennoble any man who assumes its burdens, and make him into something new and wonderful. But the widespread euphoria of this initial response was fleeting; for within no time at all, doubts began to set in like ice on a pond.

Predictably, it did not take long for conservatives to sober up.

Once they recovered from their gleeful vision of chain gangs being formed to make the shiftless earn their keep, they began to take note of how much the damn thing was going to cost. Ironically, it was the other Moynihan-Shultz clause—the one calling for work incentives —that many conservatives found most disturbing. Since the plan to expand welfare to include the working poor would add about thirteen million people to the rolls and raise the cost at least four billion dollars more a year, they clearly wanted no part of that. (Both Shultz and Moynihan argued that the extra cost would be only a comparatively short-range problem; that over the long haul, as incentives worked to reduce dependency, less and less would have to be spent on welfare. But conservatives had heard that song and others like it many times before, and they remained disbelieving.)

Beyond this specific concern, many Republicans simply thought the whole idea of a guaranteed income was nuts, and that it ran counter to the party's best interests. A vigorous spokesman for this view was Ronald Reagan. Visiting with Nixon in the late summer of 1969, he reportedly reminded the President that he owed nothing to the welfare blacks, and the poor in general. What's more, he told Nixon, the people who elected him, his natural constituency—the hard-working middle class—resented this scheme to dole out more money to people. And finally Reagan confessed that he personally was puzzled as to why the President had allowed himself to become identified with such a boondoggle. In response, Nixon informed the California Governor that he had his reasons, though there is no evidence that he bothered to enlighten him on the subtleties of Tory Reform. So much for the opposition that formed within the President's own party. The disaffection on the left was a more complex matter.

Since leaving Nixon's White House, Moynihan has written his own account of the fight over welfare reform. In it, he acknowledges that conservative resistance helped to defeat the plan, but for the most part he minimizes that and excuses it on the grounds that it was only natural for Republicans to be against the bill's key proposal: guaranteed income. (Moynihan was one person who had no illusions about the work-ethic ploy; he knew from experience that conservatives judge a book by its cost, not by its cover.) His central point, however, is that the measure failed in Congress because (a) some liberals chose to oppose it, and (b) many others gave it only lukewarm support when their full and enthusiastic commitment was needed to get it passed. And he attributes to these liberals unworthy political motives, contending that they could not bear the idea of such land-mark social legislation emanating from a Republican President, espe-cially one named Richard Nixon. Like a Parisian discovering a great French restaurant in Germany, the shock of seeing their own spe-cialty done well by the enemy was so great that they could not resist the impulse to find fault; to make petty complaints about the service or the dessert. In this way, Moynihan asserts, liberals who should have been the bill's most ardent defenders actually helped to destroy it with their carping criticisms that it didn't go far enough in allotting funds for the poor—when, in fact, it went farther than anything proposed by Nixon's Democratic predecessors.

There is much to be said for Moynihan's argument—as far as *it* goes. The welfare debate on Capitol Hill *was* marked by a narrow, partisan bickering that did little to honor the spirit of Solon; and there's no denying that most liberal Democrats who did support the bill would have done so much more aggressively if it had come down to them from a Kennedy or Johnson White House. But the trouble with Moynihan's thesis is that it doesn't go nearly far enough; and its overall effect is grossly self-serving, in terms of both his own role in the struggle and that of his employer.

In the first place, conservatives weren't the only ones concerned about the cost. Many liberals who endorsed the principle of a guaran-teed income seriously wondered if the economic and political cli-mate was right for passing such a radical measure. Noting that the inflation and the war which created it were still going strong (and with no sign that the end to either was in sight), they had to ask: Is this really the time to hit the hard-pressed taxpayers with another big spending program for the poor? Nor was this the only economic drawback. At the time Nixon submitted his welfare proposal, unem-ployment figures already were rising sharply, and some critics (lib-eral and conservative) pointed out that if this trend continued the increase in cost and number of recipients would be even greater than initial estimates indicated—and those estimates were alarming enough. And the trend did continue. By the following spring, as the welfare bill moved toward a point of decision in the Senate, the miracle of "Nixonomics"—deepening recession in the midst of infla-tion—had taken hold of the country. So there were some liberals who held back on the welfare bill because they sincerely felt it wasn't consistent with the President's fiscal policy—his much-heralded "game plan." As they saw it, Nixon the Tory Reformer was being undermined by Nixon the economic bungler.

Other liberals, however, went beyond that, and questioned the President's own sincerity. Some of this, as Moynihan contends, no doubt reflected the years of anti-Nixon bias in the liberal community, a chronic inability to believe anything good about the man. But that was only part of it. In presenting his welfare program to the country, Nixon classified it as his "top domestic priority," yet in the weeks and months that followed he behaved as if it were anything but that. During this time, he almost never brought the subject up himself, and when others did, his general attitude seemed to be one of pious indifference; he acted as though he couldn't care less. More than a few Democrats were baffled by this. Accustomed as they were to the arm-twisting techniques of their own recent Presidents (they had a vivid recollection of the kind of muscle LBJ applied to *his* domestic priorities), they soon began to ask themselves: Why isn't Nixon out in front on this thing? Why isn't he using the power of his office to *push* for welfare reform? Moreover, this lack of pressure from the White House encouraged those Republicans who didn't like the bill, anyway, to think they could line up against it without incurring much in the way of Presidential displeasure.

And, on those rare occasions when Nixon did address himself to the issue, he usually chose to emphasize its hard-line feature—the demand for work requirements. Although this was in keeping with the Tory strategy of using conservative rhetoric as a cloak to hide the dagger of guaranteed handouts, in many ways it achieved the reverse effect. Conservatives, once they caught sight of the dagger, were no longer distracted by the cloak. And among liberals there arose the suspicion that Nixon actually was playing the opposite game: putting forth the income proposal as a smoke screen to lull Congress into giving him the regressive, *anti*liberal clause he really wanted. Before long, harsh terms like "forced labor" and "involuntary servitude" began to infect the debate over welfare reform. Confronted with a White House atmosphere of, at best, apathy and inertia, punctuated only by occasional tough talk about the need for "workfare" to get "welfare idlers" off their butts, many liberals became convinced that (a) Nixon didn't really care what happened to his "top domestic priority," or (b) if he did like it, it was for all the wrong reasons.

And what of Moynihan's role in the affair? Since he was Richard Nixon's showcase Democrat, as well as the man who personally sweet-talked the President into going along with welfare reform, it was widely assumed that Moynihan would serve as the bridge between the White House and the liberals in Congress. The word went out that Nixon himself shared this assumption: Let Pat be the one to bring the liberals in line. They're *his* people. Well, they were and they weren't—and there was the rub.

As we noted earlier, the Pat Moynihan who went to work for Nixon was known as an unorthodox liberal, who had built up his reputation by engaging in open and spirited squabbles with other liberals. Some prominent black leaders, in particular, viewed him with suspicion, and that alone was enough to put him in a tight spot as the chief spokesman for welfare reform. Since the welfare issue is unfortunately viewed by many as a race issue (under Nixon's Family Assistance Plan, 43 percent of the recipients would have been black), solid support from the Negro community was deemed vital if the bill was to have any chance of success. And Moynihan simply was not the man to inspire widespread trust among blacks.

His difficulties in that area go back to 1965, when he was still Assistant Secretary of Labor. (He was one of the many New Frontiersmen Johnson chose to keep on the job after the assassination.) These were the salad days of the civil-rights movement. In the midst of it, Moynihan stirred up a howling controversy with a report he put together on the breakdown of the Negro family. The report argued, among other things, that the crumbling family structure in urban ghettos, with their high rate of illegitimacy and fatherless homes, put lower-class blacks at a severe disadvantage in a society dominated by a white middle class. The report had good intentions written all over it, but it was marred by flashes of rhetorical excess. (At one point, Moynihan described the Negro family condition as "a tangle of pathology.")

Black spokesmen immediately denounced the report as "patronizing," and accused Moynihan of being "an apologist for the white power structure" and a "subtle racist." Since the last person Johnson needed around him at that moment was a Kennedy intellectual who antagonized civil-rights leaders, no one was surprised when, a few months later, Moynihan left the administration. (LBJ once said he thought of Moynihan in much the same way he thought of Arthur Schlesinger—"Harvard, all right, but the kind of Harvard smarty who couldn't find his ass with both hands.")

Undaunted by this jarring experience, Moynihan proceeded, during his post-Washington years at Harvard, to cultivate a reputation as a liberal critic of liberal policies and attitudes. He found fault with many of the Great Society programs, especially the "war on poverty" (which he had had a hand in creating), charging that it raised absurdly high expectations that could not possibly be met, and that it was critically hampered by poor administration. And in 1967 he became the complete heretic when he told a group of liberals (at a meeting of the Americans for Democratic Action, no less) that they had much to learn from conservatives, especially from their skeptical view of the idea that the federal government has the answer to all of society's problems. It was this particular speech that inspired Nixon to praise Moynihan as a "thoughtful liberal." That was his opinion. Liberals saw this attitude as betrayal, and a year later, when Moynihan joined the Nixon administration, they smelled sellout.

This was the cross Moynihan had to carry into the battle for welfare reform. Indeed, running through the proposal itself were several Moynihan touches that stood out as echoes from past disputes. The major thrust of Moynihan's arguments for the bill focused attention on the problems of poor black families, and while some Negro leaders praised the measure as a step in the right direction, others related it to Moynihan's previous effort on their behalf—and the memory of that still rankled. In their view, a white liberal professor who saw black family life as a "tangle of pathology" was someone whose motives were still suspect. Moynihan and the President could have aided the bill by embarking on a campaign to emphasize that many whites on the lowest end of the economic scale—down-and-outers in the cities and victims of rural poverty, such as those in Appalachia—also would be helped. But they didn't. Then, too, one of the bill's basic aims—to eliminate social services and the cumbersome welfare bureaucracy by shifting to a policy of direct cash payments—only reminded some Johnson Democrats (who, after all, had voted to establish many of these services) of Moynihan's earlier attacks on the Great Society.

Still, these past resentments might have remained nothing more than minor irritations, festering beneath the surface, had it not been for subsequent actions taken by Moynihan—and others. During the weeks immediately following the President's announcement of his new welfare plan, when the first wave of favorable reaction pointed toward swift and easy approval, Moynihan couldn't resist the temptation to crow a little. He went around Washington chortling over how the President had really socked it to the liberals—or "libs" as he called them. "You know, the libs will never forgive Richard Nixon for this," he said in one of many interviews typical of this period. "And you know why? Because he's done what they wouldn't do, what they didn't *dare* do. And they can't stand that." Comments such as this one no doubt gave Moynihan a great deal of psychological satisfaction, but they did little to enhance his position as the White House link to the "libs" on Capitol Hill. And the worst was yet to come.

In April, 1970, the House passed the welfare-reform bill, virtually intact, and sent it on to the Senate. The critical moment was approaching. If the bill could be steered through the labyrinth of the Senate Finance Committee and go to the floor for a vote, nothing but a last-minute disaster could prevent the most ambitious social legislation since the New Deal from being passed into law. But a disaster of sorts already had taken place. At the time when the full force of liberal support was most urgently needed to push welfare reform through, the White House liberal most closely identified with the measure once again was embroiled in a bitter controversy. Pat Moynihan had become the victim of White House leaks.

Just a few weeks earlier, in March, some of Moynihan's private memos to the President found their way into the hands of the *New York Times* and other newspapers, which gave them a big splash. The memos were newsworthy, no doubt about that. Liberals and blacks in particular read them with more than routine interest.

The published memos included the pre-inaugural missive already referred to, in which Moynihan stressed the need to restore authority and observed that LBJ had been "toppled" from office by a "mob of college professors, millionaires, flower children and Radcliffe girls." Some of his former Harvard colleagues who had participated in the antiwar movement of the Johnson years loved that. Somehow they had been under the impression that their protest activities had taken place entirely within the democratic process, especially since their efforts eventually found expression in the insurgent candidacies of

Eugene McCarthy and Bobby Kennedy. Some of them remembered seeing Moynihan himself flitting around the edges of Bobby's '68 campaign.

Other former colleagues in the liberal community were less dis-turbed by the content than by the obsequious, courtier-to-His-Wor-ship tone they detected in this and other memos made public at the time. Now, this admittedly was a subjective judgment (one man's gush of flattery is another man's show of proper respect), yet, never-theless, more than a few old friends were distressed. Poor Pat, they murmured, not only has he sold out, but he's proud of it. Being seen in this way did not exactly deepen liberal trust in Moynihan, or in the welfare-reform bill he was promoting.

Far more damaging, however, was the furor caused by another leaked memo. Written to the President just a few weeks earlier (January, 1970), it dealt with the question of race relations, and the Moynihan sentence that produced all the headlines was this one: "The time may have come when the issue of race could benefit from a period of 'benign neglect.' " With those two words, "benign ne-glect," another ten-strike in racial misunderstanding was scored. Again, as in his report on the Negro family five years earlier, Moyni-han was motivated by all the right intentions. The purpose of the memo (as an irritated Moynihan later tried to explain) was to bring some perspective to the black revolution, and the white reaction to it. What prompted him to write it was the heavy attention being given at the time to the Black Panthers and similar extremist groups. Too many white Americans, he argued, were overreacting to the inflammatory rhetoric and menacing image of the Panthers, and thus losing sight of the fact that the vast majority of Negroes were not in sympathy with these radicals, and did not resemble them in any way.

One of the memo's more subtle aims was to needle John Mitchell. Then at the height of his power as Nixon's Attorney General, Mitch-ell lately had begun to talk about the Black Panthers as though they were a potent revolutionary force, getting set to destroy white American suburbs. Moynihan's point was that the overall cause of Negro progress might best be served if an effort was made to tone down the stridency of racial rhetoric among both blacks and whites. In other words, a little "benign neglect."

But that is not how the phrase was interpreted by black leaders and their white liberal allies. Already alarmed by the direction of the

Nixon administration's racial policies, especially at the steps taken by Mitchell and others to slow down the pace of school desegregation, they saw it as a disgusting attempt on Moynihan's part to pander to Nixon's cherished Southern Strategy: Stop talking about all those Negro issues, and the George Wallace voters will be sure to reward you at the polls. This clearly was not Moynihan's intent, but he had only himself to blame for the confusion. As in the earlier flap over the Negro family, he was done in by his zest for literary flair. Like other facile writers who become enamored of their own style, his affection for an arresting phrase tended to exceed his critical judgment. Had he been equipped with what Hemingway once called a "built-in shit detector," he surely would have taken the red pencil to "tangle of pathology" and "benign neglect."

This controversy left Moynihan in a completely untenable position as a lobbyist for welfare reform. Liberals on Capitol Hill, already sensitive to criticisms of the bill from black militant groups, now had to cope with charges that the plan's principal author and advocate was privately advising the President to adopt a policy of "neglect" toward blacks and their problems. (The "benign" touch was perceived as a genteel redundancy; neglect was neglect.) What's more, the storm broke at a time when conservatives, increasingly encouraged by Nixon's personal aloofness on the issue, became bolder and more vocal in their opposition. Thus a proposal originally conceived as a daring attempt to forge a new political alliance between liberal and conservative became trapped in a relentless left-right crossfire, with each side trying to outdo the other in gunning it down.

By the late spring of 1970, it was obvious that welfare reform was in deep trouble. And over the summer and fall, as the battle was fought in the trenches of the Senate Finance Committee, its prospects steadily dwindled until finally in November—in a lame-duck session following the midterm elections—the bill was killed in committee, without ever reaching the Senate floor.

The suspicion lingers that Nixon knew all along it would turn out like this. Or, to put it another way, the Democratic Senators who contended that the President didn't really care that much about his "top domestic priority" had reasons for believing they were on the right track.

Consider: Moynihan has stated that for a Republican President to have endorsed the concept of a guaranteed annual income—income as a basic right—represented nothing less than a "quantum leap" in U.S. social policy. Nixon, of course, recognized this, but he also may have sensed that it was an idea whose time had not yet come; that neither the country nor Congress was ready for such a radical step. (Two years later, George McGovern would come to grief in his clumsy effort to sell the idea of a guaranteed income.)

But, right from the start, Nixon could see the political value in having his name and his Presidency linked to such a bold proposal. During those tête-à-têtes in the Oval Office, as Moynihan unveiled his exotic arguments for Tory Reform and all the rest of it, it is not unreasonable to suspect that Nixon's mind already was racing ahead, putting together his own scenario. Yes, he would go along with the guaranteed-income scheme, up to a point. He would take welfare reform to the water's edge, but that's all: he would not get his feet wet. That way, if it met with vigorous opposition—as surely it must —he would be protected. Let Moynihan and others who were truly committed to the idea do what they could to get it passed. If they succeeded, fine: he would then make an honest effort to make the thing work. But if they failed, if the opposition proved too strong— well, even better: for then he could have the best of both worlds. He could claim credit among his contemporaries and before the bar of history for having introduced a landmark piece of social legislation, then turn around and pin the blame on Congress for depriving him of the opportunity to resolve the "welfare mess."

If, indeed, that was Nixon's secret strategy (in the judgment of many, Nixon friend as well as foe, it is the only conclusion that satisfactorily explains his own apathetic behavior), then this was modern Disraeli with a vengeance: you steal the other fellow's clothes, but you don't necessarily wear them. And while this theory doesn't exactly enhance Nixon's reputation as a straight shooter, it says wonders for his political acumen. Ben Disraeli, the patron saint of the enterprise, would have stood up and cheered.

One final note: when the next Congress convened in January, 1971, Nixon resubmitted the welfare-reform bill, once again calling it his number-one domestic priority. Over the next twenty months, the earlier drama repeated itself, with only a few slight variations. This time, leadership and support from the White House was even more tepid, one reason for that being the fact that Moynihan was no longer around. (Having read the writing on the wall in the first defeat, he left the White House staff at the end of 1970 to resume his academic career at Harvard.) Once again, the bill was passed by the House (in June, 1971), and once again, when it moved on to the Senate Finance Committee, it got caught in the pincers of a left-right squeeze. This time, however, there was much less suspense and much less fanfare. Like a terminal cancer patient, welfare reform was allowed to linger on, without hope or purpose, until finally, in September, 1972, it was put to sleep, once and for all.

By then, it was difficult to think of guaranteed income as a Richard Nixon proposal, and all but impossible to recall the White House atmosphere in which it had been approved three years earlier. For by then radical social legislation ran counter to every other course of action the administration was pursuing in its domestic policy. By the fall of 1972, the Tory Reformer had long since been placed alongside the other skeletons in the cluttered graveyard of Old Nixons.

Nine

So Pat Moynihan did not become the domestic counterpart to Henry Kissinger in Richard Nixon's White House, and that is a point of no small significance. For there is no question that if he had been able to establish himself in that role the domestic policy of the first term would have been drastically different, both in tone and substance, from the one that did evolve under the aegis of Haldeman and Ehrlichman. And, while the difficulties Moynihan encountered during the long and futile fight for welfare reform certainly helped to hasten his downfall, they were not the whole story. Indeed, even before that project began to go sour, he had ceased to be a voice of major influence inside the White House. As early as the fall of 1969, when his public reputation was at its height and he was being hailed as the "genius" behind the President's welfare initiative, he had already lost whatever chance he once had had of becoming Nixon's domestic czar.

Moynihan's strengths were ideas and personality. As we've seen, it was the novelty of his ideas (the "thoughtful liberal") that first captured Nixon's attention, and once he arrived on the scene, it was his engaging and flamboyant manner that quickly made him a Presidential favorite. Where he was weak, however, was in organization. In the world of Richard Nixon's Presidency, where efficiency ranked second only to loyalty as the supreme virtue, Moynihan's unstructured approach proved to be a serious handicap. Even his staff meetings became notorious for their disorder and bull-session casualness. One former White House aide who often sat in on them recalls that a typical Moynihan staff meeting was "like a scene from an Andy Warhol movie."

The free-and-easy style also was evident in the various reports and studies that were put together and sent on to the President. As a result, it did not take Nixon long to become aware of Moynihan's tendency to "wing it," to make do with generalities, when hard, specific facts were needed to back up a point. His early draft on welfare reform was shot through with technical deficiencies, an example which Arthur Burns, for one, took delight in pointing out to the President. (Aside from their political and philosophical differences, Burns regarded Moynihan as a careless scholar who relied a lot on bluff and blarney to gloss over his slipshod research. Burns himself was just the opposite: he generally was thorough and meticulous to a fault. He had built a whole school of economic forecasting on detailed charting and analysis of minute detail. Once Burns completed a project, the facts and details would be in perfect order, but he would have taken seemingly forever to assemble them.)

So, even in the early going, Moynihan came to be viewed as someone who talked a good game, but who had trouble delivering on the nitty-gritty. While his mind was an anthill of fertile and useful ideas, he seemed to lack the organizational skill to carry them forward into action and policy. Superb in the field of overall strategy, he was judged a poor tactician, who had no firm grasp of operational details. In one sense, it could be said that he and Burns did have something in common: both professors brought too much of the classroom with them into Nixon's White House. Too often, when confronted with a problem or issue, they would succumb to the pedagogue's vice, and give a lecture. Moynihan's lectures, unlike Burns's, were stimulating and fun and frequently charged with clever insights. But even the most brilliant and colorful talk is still only talk, and what was needed was more in the way of follow-through. As for his famous memos, they were more of the same—"written" lectures, dealing too much with broad, overview themes and general problems, rather than with specific solutions.

The importance of the failure of first Burns and then Moynihan to put together a domestic apparatus similar to Kissinger's operation for international affairs cannot be overemphasized. One of the reasons for this failure is the fact that domestic policy is in many ways tougher to handle than foreign affairs. The forces and interests in this area are close at hand; the conflicts in objectives are often on the cutting edge, for they concern questions which intrude on the daily lives of voters. Also involved was the President's own lack of interest in domestic as opposed to foreign policy. His failure to devote much time to domestic problems, as well as to think out in advance exactly who should be delegated what authority, contributed to the general confusion. And, as we shall see, still another factor in the downfall of Burns and Moynihan was Haldeman's low opinion of them both, an opinion fueled, in part, by his ambitious desire to promote Ehrlichman and himself into positions of expanding power. Yet Burns and Moynihan themselves deserve a large part of the blame. In the end, each in his own way, they created a vacuum in the area of domestic affairs, into which Haldeman and Ehrlichman eventually moved.

No one can say with certainty, but things might have been different—and clearly it would have helped—if Burns and Moynihan had assembled different staffs around them. But the men they chose as their staff assistants reflected to an extreme degree their own strengths and weaknesses. Moynihan's staff was very young, fascinated by Moynihan himself, quite brilliant. Most of them were facile writers who could put words together in a way that glittered. But Moynihan's men—Richard Blumenthal, Checker Finn, and others—were not seasoned problem solvers. They were weak on researching technical details and they were sadly short on follow-through.

Burns's staff was more scholarly, more experienced than Moynihan's, but his men (Charles Clapp, for example) still were not at bottom experienced at solving problems. They tended toward slow deliberation and reflection rather than action. Their writing and their arguments were often dull and confusing. Also, Burns tried to muddle through with a staff that was much too small in size to handle the complexities of the job. Things also might have been different if Burns or Moynihan—perhaps especially Burns—had challenged, head-on and early, Haldeman's arrogant ways.

Nor did it help to have Kissinger around as a constant point of comparison. Kissinger, like Moynihan, knew how to impress the boss with intellectual chatter, but this was a skill he chose to use sparingly, and therefore to maximum effect. Besides, he was strong where the other two professors were weak. Unlike Burns, he knew how to attack a problem with speed and concision. And, unlike Moynihan, he had the kind of orderly mind that could easily translate strategy into tactics, ideas into action. Kissinger was, in short, both an intellectual *and* a model of efficiency.

Nixon soon discovered that when he gave Kissinger a problem he got results—*fast* results. On leaving the Oval Office, Kissinger would immediately repair to his mini-empire in the White House basement, and apply the Prussian lash to his overworked staff. (If Moynihan's staff was an Andy Warhol movie, Kissinger's more closely resembled scenes from *Mutiny on the Bounty*—which is one reason why he lost a number of good people in the early months.) Kissinger demanded a miserable pace, even when there was no apparent need and even when a slightly more deliberate one seemed needed. He drove himself and he drove those under him, often with caustic verbal whippings. Those assigned to work with Kissinger on a problem would wearily pick up the phone to inform their wives that, once again, they would not be home for dinner. The burning of midnight oil in Kissinger's sweat shop was such a frequent occurrence that some staffers found themselves yearning for an occasional power failure. Not that it would have done them any good; Henry simply would have sent out for a box of candles.

The next morning, up bright and early, Kissinger would be back in the Oval Office, laying it all out on the table. The problem would be reviewed, then crisply he would turn to the possible solutions, the options: bang, bang, bang, bang; A, B, C, D. And when asked, he would come right back with his own recommendation, a suggestion that perhaps C would best serve the national interest, in terms of immediate objectives as well as long-range goals. And the reasons for that would be rattled off in precise order, with subtlety shading subtlety, nuance piled on nuance. Out of this would flow the delicate process of decision: to invade Cambodia . . . to side with Pakistan in the Bangladesh war . . . to modify the U.S. position at the SALT talks.

This, then, was Kissinger: a virtuoso at dealing with the here and now, the immediate problem, the day-to-day crisis. His consummate skill in this area only emphasized the shortcomings of both Burns and Moynihan. Thus, by the summer of 1969, around the time Burns was perceived as a Super Bore who preferred ponderous lectures to vigorous action, it became equally evident that Moynihan lacked the organizational talent to seize firm command of overall domestic policy. Neither man, it turned out, was especially suited for the role of a domestic Kissinger.

But while this wrapped it up for Burns, putting him on a downhill course that would continue until the end of 1969, when he was granted safe passage to the Federal Reserve Board, this was not the case with Moynihan. At first, the fact that he was no super-organizer, no empire builder, seemed to have little or no effect on his privileged status as a policy adviser. His big triumph, after all, was achieved that summer, and however annoying his inefficiency may have been, it clearly didn't prevent him from getting his way during the in-house debate on the welfare question. He won that fight by making the most of his strengths: his penchant for bold and large ideas, envisioned across a broad sweep of history, and the force of personality he brought to his arguments. As long as Nixon was responding favorably on that level, Moynihan could count on being near the center of power. But, as time went on, even these, his best attributes, began to work against him; and once that happened, his Andy Warhol working habits merely helped to grease the skids for his departure.

The trouble, finally, was also that Moynihan cut *too* conspicuous a figure in the Nixon White House; he stood out *too* much from the rest of the crowd. Even his physical height was a factor here. At six feet five inches, he towered over the Cabinet officers and other colleagues. Thus, in any stand-up conversation, in a West Wing corridor or outside a meeting room, he inevitably gave the impression of talking *down* to Burns or Ehrlichman or Mitchell, or even the President himself. And this impression was enhanced by the breezy arrogance that was so much a part of his personality. In point of fact, he usually *was* talking down, in the figurative sense as well. (At Harvard, he often shared the giraffe role with John Kenneth Galbraith, another six-and-a-half-foot giant, whose arrogant charm appears to be an extension of his natural height advantage.)

Moynihan's facial features, on the other hand, were deceptive— and that too could be disconcerting. At first glance, his heavy eyelids, his apple cheeks, and his sagging jowls put one in mind of a slouching and sluggish basset hound. Yet Moynihan in action was the antithesis of that; more like a Yorkshire terrier, frisky as hell and endlessly yapping. With his florid, theatrical personality, he was always "on," like an actor ever-conscious of how he enters a room. (One former colleague who knows him well has shrewdly observed that "Pat was always a better performer than thinker.") This sense of drama helped to shore up the image of a commanding presence, a man accustomed to dominating any setting he finds himself in.

Moynihan also was adept at using his verbal gifts to draw atten- tion to himself and throw others off balance. One of his favorite weapons was the pithy non-sequitur. At an early White House meet- ing on the welfare question, he tried out the stratagem of treating the idea of a guaranteed income as though it were nothing more than a routine alternative to the existing welfare program. It worked, too, as far as most of those present were concerned, but one of Arthur Burns's deputies (Burns himself was not there) was sharp enough to see through it, and in an effort to alert his fellow Republicans to the radical menace he suddenly blurted out: "Now, wait a minute, let's call a spade a spade."

To which Moynihan replied: "Anybody who wants to call a spade a spade should be made to use one." Though it seemed utterly irrele- vant to the discussion at hand, the remark was not entirely without point. As a young man fresh off the streets of New York, Moynihan worked on the docks as a longshoreman, and he was confident that in a room filled with white-collar Republicans, he was the only one who had had that kind of experience. In essence, then, he was saying: "Look, I've been a manual laborer. I've used a spade. And maybe if you tried it, you'd have a better idea what it means when we talk about putting these people to work."

On other occasions, his putdowns were less subtle. Once at a background briefing for newsmen, with Press Secretary Ron Ziegler standing at his side and looking very much like a frightened puppy in need of its mother ("mother" being Bob Haldeman), Moynihan gave this reply to a question: "I don't know the answer to that, and if I did Mr. Ziegler wouldn't let me answer. I live in constant terror of his disapproval." Ziegler somehow managed a wan smile, but the quip was later deleted from the transcript. And there was the time Moynihan presented a book to Haldeman's more important protégé with the inscription: "For John Ehrlichman—*achtung!*"

Moynihan was not only different from the Nixon men around him, but defiantly so. Whereas the other Harvard outsider, Kissinger, made a prudent effort to blend in with the group (only later, after he was absolutely sure of his own status, would Henry allow *his* irreverent wit to surface with any regularity), Moynihan went out of his way to dramatize the fact that he was, in Hugh Sidey's fine phrase, "a volcano in a cornfield."

But that didn't mean the cornfield had to like it. As time passed, more than a few of the staid bankers and businessmen, the straight-arrow lawyers and admen, grew to resent Moynihan's flippant remarks and arrogant manner, which so often took the form of intellectual snobbery. His passion for lecturing and fancy, historical name dropping was not confined to private communications with the President; when it manifested itself at White House meetings with Cabinet officers and the like, some members of the team who did not have Moynihan's academic background experienced pangs of discomfort. "As you know, Mr. Secretary," Professor Pat might begin in his flaunting way, "it actually was Lord Durham who first proposed . . ." And Mr. Secretary would nod in agreement, though somewhat warily since in all likelihood he had never even heard of Lord Durham, much less of what he had or had not proposed; and often, on such occasions, those present were left with the suspicion that Moynihan was purposely trying to show the other fellow up. Yet, as long as he continued to rack up brownie points with his one-on-one performances in the Oval Office, the good, gray Republicans around him had no choice but to grin and bear it. They could only hope that in time he would wear out his welcome there as well—and that is precisely what happened.

Moynihan was at his most endearing during the first, heady months of the administration when Nixon himself was caught up in the spirit of a bold new adventure. As long as that mood prevailed, there was an honored place in the "cornfield" for an active "volcano," ever erupting with fresh ideas. Yet, as time went on and the new regime settled into the flow of day-to-day routine, Nixon grew weary of Moynihan's combustive style. The Kennedy Democrat simply overdid it. The flurry of memos and the incessant lectures, with their snappy, relevant quotes and intriguing historical parallels—all this was finally carried to excess. What started out as stimulating eventually became a strain for Nixon, and a distracting one at that. Like Shakespeare's surfeit of honey, Moynihan became "by much too much."

Although the analogy is a bit racy, the situation was not at all unlike that of a middle-aged man who, after years of strict adherence to marital fidelity, suddenly finds himself enmeshed in an affair with a high-powered femme fatale who knows from experience how to get the most out of a relationship. At first, the fellow rejoices in the dalliance and in his new role as swinger; he feels rejuvenated, all bright-eyed and bushy-tailed, and eager to try just about anything. But he can't keep it up. Before long, he reaches the point where the intensity of it all becomes too much for him. So, after a few weeks or months, he decides, with a sigh of relief as well as regret, to go back home, to return to the undemanding wife he knows he can handle with ease and equilibrium.

Something like that happened to the Nixon-Moynihan relationship. If Burns proved to be a bore who put the President to sleep, the younger professor went too far in the other direction. By the end of 1969, with the Berlin Wall firmly in place, Moynihan discovered that his visa no longer guaranteed him automatic passage through "Checkpoint Haldeman." So he began to press, to extend his reach beyond his grasp. The man who had gloated the previous summer that he had "a poker hand nobody can beat" now experienced the frustration that comes from trying to fill too many inside straights. In this respect, the famous memo on race relations he wrote early in 1970 may be viewed as a desperate attempt to regain advantage, to rekindle the spark, to get the old juices flowing again.

But it was too late. The old magic just didn't work any more. Having had his fling with the volcano, Nixon now preferred to nestle in among the cornstalks he had always been more comfortable with. Not that there was an open rift between them. No "Dear Pat" letter or anything like that. Like his pet project, the welfare-reform bill, Moynihan was allowed to linger on, in a position of steadily diminishing importance, until his departure from the scene at the end of

1970. But, in an exquisite irony that must have registered on Professor Pat himself, he became the victim of his own recommendation. During those last few months on the job, he was the one who was treated with "benign neglect."

Symbolic of his irreverent chiding of the clean-cut organization men to the very end, and of the gadfly as opposed to manager he saw himself to be, was a note Moynihan left Ronald Ziegler on his last day at the White House. It read: "Well, you won't have Pat Moynihan to kick around anymore."

The start of Moynihan's decline in the waning weeks of 1969 was part of a major shift in the whole course of Nixon's Presidency. To appreciate its significance, we must freeze our focus for a moment on the state of affairs that existed at the end of his first six months in office—around the time he presented the welfare-reform plan to the country. Viewed from that vantage point, even some of his harshest critics had to admit that the new President was off to a promising start. And, in terms of his own loosely-defined goals, he had every right to be pleased with the way things were going.

First of all, the "Eisenhower Revisited" theme was working out nicely. The new administration, though clearly Republican in character, was pursuing a moderate, centrist course designed to encourage bipartisan support. In dealing with his most critical foreign-policy problem, Vietnam, Nixon's decision to begin withdrawing American troops (first announced in June, 1969) was seen as neither the screech of a hawk nor the coo of a dove, but rather as an in-between, compromise move. And, while there was some grumbling from the left because it wasn't fast enough or unequivocal enough, it generally was welcomed as a first step down the road toward disengagement, which, once taken, could not be reversed. At the time, however, few people, perhaps not even the President, realized how long the road would stretch before the light-at-the-end-of-the-tunnel would finally be reached. On the domestic front, there was a general slowdown in the pace and volume of new legislation, but just as Ike chose to leave intact New Deal and Fair Deal measures that were on the books when he assumed office, so Nixon shied away from a sweeping effort to dismantle the New Frontier and Great Society programs he inherited.

Beyond that, with his other eye cocked on the more subtle

Kennedy legacy he also brought into the Presidency, Nixon spiced things up that first summer with a couple of bold initiatives that caught everyone by surprise. One of these was the welfare reform already discussed, and the other was a diplomatic breakthrough. Just a few days before the welfare program was unveiled, Nixon made a triumphant visit to Rumania, thus becoming the first American President to set foot in a Communist country since visits by FDR and Truman to Yalta and Potsdam in the closing days of World War II—when the "bad guys" were still allies. (The full significance of the Rumanian visit as an augury of more ambitious journeys to come would not become known until much later.) With both ventures, Nixon served notice that he intended his Presidency to be more than a cautious "holding action." Taking a cue from the more activist Democrats, he demonstrated that he too could be innovative and strike out in new directions. Both moves met with widespread approval on Capitol Hill, in the press, and among the general public, and therefore helped to prolong the traditional post-inaugural "honeymoon."

Even more impressive, perhaps, was the way Nixon seemed to be making good on the conciliatory "bring us together" pledge of his inaugural theme. He was exerting leadership, but in a quiet, unobtrusive way that fit in well with his avowed desire to dispense balm to a troubled nation. By the summer of 1969, the voices of protest *had* lowered, and the riots and demonstrations of previous "long, hot summers" had tapered off considerably. There had been a number of campus disorders the preceding winter and spring, following a trend that began in the Johnson years, but they too showed signs of abating.

It should also be said that this effort to invoke a spirit of national togetherness was given an enormous boost by the big historic event of that summer: man's first visit to the surface of the moon. For a country embittered by years of war and domestic strife, the great space achievement was a welcome tonic. And, although it was essentially a cosmic thrust into the future, it was also an old-fashioned triumph, reminiscent of the World War II era when Americans felt a common bond and could rejoice in unison. As such, it was tailor-made for Nixon's recurrent appeal to his countrymen to take pride in "what's right with America." The fact that the moon landing was the culmination of programs launched by previous Presidents

(Kennedy and Johnson) was really beside the point. It was entirely within Nixon's prerogative to exploit the feat to the fullest, which he did. In recalling the harmonious, upbeat mood in Washington that summer, as the moon landing, the trip to Rumania, and the welfare announcement occurred in rapid succession (all within a span of twenty days, from late July through the first week in August), Moynihan would later write that "these were rather splendid hours for the new administration."

And so they were. But they were soon to end.

By mid-autumn, the euphoria had given way to a mood of stress and turmoil as the White House became involved in a series of troubles and hostile acts. The President and his men themselves caused no small number of these troubles. Many of the difficulties and hostilities did not come from the outside. There was, for instance, the dispute with the Senate over Nixon's nomination of Clement Haynsworth to the Supreme Court, which, after Haynsworth's rejection, led to the far more venomous fight the following spring over the subsequent nomination (and rejection) of G. Harrold Carswell. The Haynsworth-Carswell controversy did much more than end the "honeymoon" with Congress. It created the atmosphere of distrust and enmity which, from that time forward, would define the administration's relations with Capitol Hill.

Even more abrasive was the unleashing that fall of Spiro Agnew. His attack on the television networks (and sundry other groups that might, in any way, qualify as "effete snobs" or "nattering nabobs of negativism") was the opening round in the administration's holy war against the press, which, two years later, would be carried to the Supreme Court in the Pentagon Papers case, and would continue on afterward with ever-deepening hostility. The President himself added to the turmoil. It was in a television speech that fall, given in an effort to blunt the resurgence of the antiwar movement (marking the end of another honeymoon), that Nixon first made his famous appeal to the "silent majority," thus driving a wedge that much deeper between Americans who sympathized with Vietnam protesters and those who regarded them as traitors.

All this commotion was a far cry from the low-key, centrist approach, reminiscent of Ike. No longer was there any pretense that the Nixon White House might serve as a forum of conciliation, a temple of togetherness. By the fall of 1969 it had become an embattled fortress, complete with invisible moat and drawbridge. Within its walls, hidden from public view, there festered a poisonous climate of fear and suspicion, of brooding rancor—the "us-versus-them" mentality that would affect so many future decisions, up to and including those that led to Watergate and related crimes. As it took shape that first autumn, it reflected the new power structure that had formed like a shield in and around the Oval Office.

Of the original troika of Ivy League professors brought in to direct and coordinate policy matters, only one—Kissinger—had by fall, 1969, succeeded in nailing down a position of enduring influence. Arthur Burns was about to move on to the comparative serenity of the Federal Reserve Board, while Pat Moynihan was beginning to fade into the limbo of benign neglect. In their stead stepped two men who, given the parochialism of their West Coast backgrounds, were the very antithesis of Ivy League academe, which Burns and Moynihan represented.

All through 1969, Haldeman and Ehrlichman had been steadily expanding their spheres of influence, and by the end of that first year they had joined Kissinger at the top of the White House hierarchy. This fact was not fully appreciated at the time, and even in the months and years that followed most of the country would remain unaware of their vast importance. Indeed, for many Americans the names Haldeman and Ehrlichman would mean little or nothing until the spring of 1973, when the Watergate exposures brought them into the glare of public scorn. But those who were engaged in what John Osborne so aptly calls "the Nixon Watch," and observed them taking over that first year, began to ask by the end of 1969: Just who are these guys? How did they manage to acquire such power? In the answers to those questions lies the key to understanding much of what already had happened, and much more of what would later unfold in the course of Richard Nixon's Presidency. And, to look for the answers, we must start by going back to the early years of Nixon's own career.

PART III

The Knights of
the Woeful Countenance

Ten

He was just a freshman in Congress when, in 1948, he latched on to the Hiss case and propelled himself to national prominence. Yet, even before that, Nixon had done his best to exploit the emerging issue of Communist subversion. In the '46 campaign that sent him to Congress, he accused his opponent, New Deal Democrat Jerry Voorhis, of accepting support from a Communist-front group in the labor movement. And just a few months before the Hiss case broke he co-sponsored an antisubversion bill to place Communists in this country under tight control. But it was his dogged pursuit of Alger Hiss and the perjury conviction that ultimately followed that gave both the Congressman and his cause the impetus they needed. More than anyone else, it was Richard Nixon who got the anti-Communist movement of the postwar years off the ground and helped to make it a national obsession. (Senator McCarthy, whose name has since defined the era, was actually something of a Joseph-come-lately: he didn't swing into action against Communism until 1950, though it is true enough that, once he got going, he more than made up for his slow start.)

So his role in the Hiss affair gave Nixon a leg up, a head start, on the issue that was to dominate American politics all through the late forties and early fifties. And, as a young Congressman very much on the make, he was determined to maintain the edge. He couldn't expect to come up with an Alger Hiss very often; for all the furor of those times, there simply weren't that many public figures around who could realistically be accused of having a Communist past or

present. Nixon had an answer for that. Although still a relative new-
comer to politics, he already had discovered the value of what would
soon come to be recognized as vintage McCarthyism: if you can't find
a Communist, then attack a *non*-Communist. The main thing was to
keep the issue alive.

This was the strategy he carried into his 1950 Senate race against
Helen Gahagan Douglas, whom he accused of being "soft on Communism"—or as one of his campaign circulars dubbed her "The Pink
Lady." (During one whistle stop, at a particularly low point in the
unedifying contest, Nixon charged that "Helen Gahagan Douglas is
pink right down to her underwear.") Then, with his elevation to the
Senate, it was just a short hop, two years later, to the Vice Presidential nomination and his first national campaign. What had been sauce
for Mrs. Douglas was now sauce for the Democratic Presidential
candidate, and Nixon went around the country in 1952 denouncing
Stevenson as "Adlai the appeaser . . . who got a Ph.D. from Dean
Acheson's College of Cowardly Containment." (This flair for allitera-
tion would reappear two decades later in the harangues of Nixon's
own Veep.) Other Democratic leaders that year, including the outgo-
ing President Truman, were vilified by Nixon as "traitors to their
party."

There exist today millions of Americans who are simply too young
to have witnessed all this. Like late arrivals at the theater who miss
the first few scenes, they grew to political awareness after Nixon's
long career was well under way, after he had begun to hone down
the rough edges and refine his image—a process of dilution which has
given us, over the years, a multitude of "new Nixons." But those who
were, in Acheson's phrase, "present at the creation" have never
forgotten the young Nixon of the Congressional and Senate years.
They remember him well as Nixon the Fierce, Nixon the Zealous,
Nixon the Ungloved—the one and original "Old Nixon." And those
who were victims of his early tactics, or who identified with his
victims, plus many who were simply repelled, have never seen fit to
forgive him.

Thus, at the Democratic convention in 1960, Sam Rayburn urged
his protégé Lyndon Johnson to run for Vice President with John
Kennedy (after first advising him to decline the offer) because he felt
everything must be done to prevent the White House from falling
into Nixon's hands. As Speaker Rayburn put it, "that other fellow

called me a traitor, and I don't want a man who calls me a traitor to
be President of the United States." And from theater gossips we have
been hearing for years that actor Melvyn Douglas, Helen Gahagan's
husband, would get up and leave a room whenever Richard Nixon's
name was mentioned in his presence.

Nixon's enemies, however, aren't the only ones who remember
those early years with untempered passion. While the methods he
practiced then aroused contempt and revulsion in some, they stirred
in others admiration, even devotion. For all the liberals and middle-
of-the-roaders in both parties who were turned off by the "Old
Nixon," there were plenty of conservatives and middle-of-the-road-
ers, Republican and Democrat, who were turned on. Especially in
the early Nixon political years, conservatives particularly were ecstatic about him. Among those most deeply smitten was an impressionable crew-cut collegian on the campus of UCLA named Harry
Robbins Haldeman—known to his friends then, as in the years ahead,
by the nickname "Bob."

Given his background, it is hardly surprising that young Bob
Haldeman became a Nixon disciple. Although a third-generation
Californian, his deepest roots, like those of Nixon himself, reached
into the Middle West, his grandparents on both sides having mi-
grated from Indiana. This was part of a massive trend that has run
all through the twentieth century. For better or for worse, modern
California (i.e., *southern* California, a land and culture that must be
distinguished from the older frontier tradition of San Francisco's
gold-rush days) has been largely the creation of transplanted Mid-
westerners, restless ones who pushed themselves to the far edge of
America in search of a better life out there in the sunshine. Babbitry
came with some. But, whether they brought that or not, many came
with strong beliefs in self-reliance, Protestantism, and national isola-
tionism. It has often been observed that southern California is not a
replica of the Midwest so much as an exaggerated version of it, or as
one critic has put it, "the Midwest gone berserk." It is almost as if the
values and attitudes of the heartland developed a kind of elephantia-
sis once they were given a chance to sprout in that rich California
soil. Yet, when the great modern migration began in the first years
of the century, no one could have predicted that the road from Main
Street would lead to the network of swimming pools and gleaming

shopping centers that begin somewhere around Santa Barbara and stretch, almost as a continuum, all the way down to Tijuana; or that the modest pleasures of an old-fashioned county fair would someday evolve into the garish wonders of Disneyland. Those early immigrants from the Midwest, a group that included Nixon's parents as well as Haldeman's grandparents, had no way of knowing they were the forefathers of our brave new world.

Both of Haldeman's grandfathers were small businessmen. One made his money as an automobile dealer and the other established a pipe and building-supply company. The two men also brought with them to California the conservative politics of "Main Street" they had known back home in Indiana: business-oriented, isolationist, and solidly Republican in every way. In their era, they belonged to that class of citizenry which kept sending native sons of Ohio to the White House—McKinley, Taft, and finally Warren G. Harding. Haldeman's paternal grandfather (the pipe-supply man) in particular had a strong conservative bent. He was, in fact, one of the nation's first anti-Communists. In the aftermath of World War I, when the Bolshevik threat first reached our shores (they called it the "Red Scare" in those days), he helped found the Better America Foundation, a kind of forerunner of the John Birch Society. And the fervor of his cause was dutifully passed on to both son and grandson.

Haldeman's father took over the pipe-supply company, but the small business foundered in the Depression. In 1933 he started a new venture, selling heating and air-conditioning units. Old friends of the family remember the senior Haldeman as "an energetic, look-ahead guy" who had a shrewd gift for anticipating market trends—a trait his son would later manifest in his advertising career. The country's mania for "keeping cool," via air conditioning, must have been one trend Papa Haldeman saw coming even in the Depression years when most Americans could ill afford such a luxury. Incidentally, he also was named Harry, yet like his son, preferred to be known socially by a nickname, in his case "Bud."

Haldeman's new business prospered, and "Bob" grew up in that model of modern suburbia, Beverly Hills. From all accounts, he passed through what is usually described as "a normal childhood" in that sheltered, upper-middle-class setting, experiencing none of the poor-boy traumas and resentments that scarred Nixon's youth. When he was twelve, the family swapped homes with actor Dick Powell and his wife, Joan Blondell, and moved out to the San Fernando Valley—no slum, either. Though later much would be made of his high IQ (said to be in the "genius" range), he was, in his early school years, a poor student who brought home report cards depressingly cluttered with Ds. The problem, which would greatly amuse those who came to know him later, was a lack of discipline, and his parents solved it by enrolling him in a no-nonsense private school. He thrived in that atmosphere of strictly-enforced rules and protocol—all those reiterative "yes sirs" and "no sirs"—and in this respect the child was very much father of the man. A zest for regimen and rigid command structure would become a Haldeman trademark in later years. So would his belief in the sanctity of orders; once given, they should be carried out with no questions asked.

Haldeman was just young enough to miss the war. Graduating from high school in 1944, he took part in the Navy's V–12 program, first at Redlands University, then later at Southern California, before settling in, for his final two years, at UCLA. There he became absorbed in campus politics, and in the larger, more volatile issue of Communist subversion.

Those early postwar years were lively and gratifying times for a serious young man who had been brought up to believe in the righteousness of his grandfather's fight against Communism; and UCLA was just the place to be. In years to come, southern California would be identified with anti-Communism in much the same way that Sicily is associated with the Mafia or Vienna with Freud. Indeed, the issue came alive there with such intensity that, long after McCarthy was dead and the hysteria he helped to foment had simmered down in most parts of the country, southern California was still offering such picturesque diversions as steely-eyed minutemen standing guard over their fallout shelters and "little old ladies in tennis shoes" assuring us all that we'd be better off dead than Red. And it was there, back in the mid-forties, that the storm first broke with telling force.

In the early months of 1947, when the House Un-American Activities Committee (the platform from which Congressman Nixon launched his pursuit of Hiss) began in earnest to look into Communist subversion, most of its early focus was on southern California—especially that part of Los Angeles known as Hollywood. For it was those hearings that brought on the great purge in the motion-picture industry to root out Communists and their fellow travelers, and to make sure that all those who refused to repent were nailed to the cross of the Hollywood blacklist. The convulsions that rocked the film colony in those days sent reverberations through southern California and, in time, across the rest of the country as well. But, since the UCLA campus was on the doorstep of Hollywood, it caught the first wave. And there, riding its crest, was Harry II—Bud's son, Bob.

Haldeman was a big wheel on UCLA's Interfraternity Council, which was where most of the student action was in that era of saddle shoes and cashmere pullovers, and there were times during his two years there when he seemed determined to put out his own blacklist. (Years later, he would get in on this sort of thing again, on a much grander scale; by then it would be called the White House Enemies List.) At one point, convinced that the staff of the student newspaper had been infiltrated by Communists and their sympathizers, he organized a campaign calling for the campus-wide election of editors. The prevailing practice then was for the staff to pick its own editors, but Haldeman feared that if it was allowed to continue the subversives would gain control. (Even then, he was keeping a sharp and wary eye on the press.) That particular purge attempt did not succeed, but what makes the story worth noting is that one of the editors of the *Daily Bruin* at the time was Frank Mankiewicz, who later on would also surface in national politics, as Bobby Kennedy's press secretary and, after that, as a top man in the McGovern campaign. Mankiewicz remembers the Haldeman of UCLA days with a kind of chilling awe. "You know," he once said during the period when Haldeman was riding high in Nixon's White House, "I don't think I ever saw him laugh." Then, with a chuckle of his own, Mankiewicz added: "And . . . he hasn't changed a bit. Even his crew cut's the same."

For the sake of perspective, let it be emphasized that a case can be reasonably argued that fears of possible Communist penetration of campus organizations in the 1930s, '40s and even early '50s were not, in every instance, necessarily far-fetched. Taking that into account, it is still fair to say that Haldeman, even in the context of his campus days, was much more fearful than most other students, and far more zealous in pursuing Communist influences, real or imagined.

Despite Haldeman's most zealous efforts, student organizations

Attorney General John N. Mitchell, Secretary of the Treasury David
M. Kennedy, and Secretary of State William P. Rogers

Secretary of Defense
Melvin R. Laird

Postmaster General Winton M. Blount

Secretary of the Interior Walter Hickel

Secretary of Agriculture
Clifford M. Hardin

Maurice Stans, Secretary of Commerce

George P. Shultz, Secretary of Labor

Robert H. Finch, Secretary of Health,
Education and Welfare

George Romney, Secretary of Housing
and Urban Development

John A. Volpe,
Secretary of Transportation

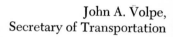

Elliot L. Richardson

Arthur Burns

Daniel Patrick Moynihan

Henry Kissinger

Charles Colson

John Ehrlichman

H. R. "Bob" Haldeman

suspected of being Communist-front groups (such as the American Youth for Democracy, or AYD) continued to exercise their First Amendment rights on the UCLA campus. In his senior year, they became especially worked up over the antisubversion bill Nixon had co-sponsored and was then trying to push through Congress. Years later, Haldeman would recall: "I was fascinated by their opposition to it. It wasn't so much the substance of the bill, but the reaction by the Communist-front AYD. They came out in demonstration against the bill, and in those days that was unique. It intrigued me." On another occasion, speaking of "those days" in a similar context, he remarked that "to a degree, you can judge a man by his enemies as well as his friends." So it was then that Haldeman fastened his gaze on the young Congressman from Whittier, who was arousing the bile of all the right enemies. The more he saw, the more he liked, and he began to feel the first stirrings of hero worship.

Like young love, political attachments formed at college age are often impassioned. A politician who is able to engage the idealism and romanticism of youth automatically becomes a candidate with a following of true believers. We have seen examples of this on a mass scale time and time again over the years, and at both ends of the political spectrum. In 1964, the Young Americans for Freedom would have cut off—well, even their right arms, if by doing so they could have elected Barry Goldwater President. And four years later there were the "Keep Clean for Gene" kids who trudged through the snows of New Hampshire for McCarthy.

Nixon has never been much of a campus hero. Over the years, it is true, he has had his share of students who campaigned and voted for him, but more often than not they did so quietly, in a lukewarm manner, without the kind of pep-rally enthusiasm other politicians have been able to inspire. But Haldeman was a real exception. The commitment he made to Nixon during those days of anti-Communist turmoil was not only deep but enduring. It would become his guiding light, his northern star, through all the years ahead. As the Jesuits, who know a thing or two about true believers, are so fond of saying: "Give us the child, and the man is ours for life."

Eleven

Nixon was just beginning to hit his stride when Haldeman graduated from UCLA in 1948. The Hiss business started up in the late summer of that year, and within a few months the three principals in the affair—Nixon, Hiss, and Whittaker Chambers—had acquired the status of household names. (For the benefit of those who came in late on Nixon's career, it was Chambers, the repentant ex-Communist, who persuaded Nixon that Hiss, a recent big shot in the State Department, had been a fellow Red back in the 1930s. Hiss denied the charge, and at the time almost everyone believed he was telling the truth and that Chambers was lying, instead of the other way around, but Nixon remained steadfast to Chambers, and between them they eventually got their man on a perjury conviction.)

As one who already was a Nixon enthusiast, Haldeman followed the Hiss case with the kind of absorption that, a quarter century later, would characterize those Americans who sat with glazed eyeballs in front of their television sets for hours on end while the Watergate hearings droned on and on. For back in 1948 and '49 it was Congressman Nixon who, in the eyes of his admirers, was cast in the Sam Ervin role: the righteous guardian of freedom determined to dig out the truth, regardless of the obstacles placed in his path. (President Truman called the Hiss probe a "red herring." That was his version of "wallowing in Watergate.") So, as the Hiss headlines grew bigger and, to Haldeman's lights, ever more satisfying, the young man's ardor for the bloodhound Congressman waxed strong. And in 1950, when Nixon bet all the chips he had won in the Hiss case on a shot at a seat in the Senate, Haldeman naturally was among those cheering him on in his bare-knuckle campaign against Helen Gahagan Douglas.

Yet all this time he was still just a spectator, a fan applauding Nixon from his seat in the bleachers. On leaving UCLA, Haldeman made no effort to get involved in politics in a professional way.

Having majored in business administration, he first gave some thought to hotel management, then opted, instead, for a career in advertising. He started out as a market researcher for Foote, Cone and Belding, but quickly moved on to J. Walter Thompson. His early years with JWT included brief stints in San Francisco and New York (the latter being a city and part of the country he has always loathed), but by 1952 he was back home working in the agency's Los Angeles office, where he remained, off and on, over the next sixteen years. The off periods were election years, when he would take a leave of absence from J. Walter Thompson to work for Richard M. Nixon.

It was on a visit to Washington in 1951 that Haldeman had his first face-to-face meeting with The Man, who by then had become Senator Nixon. A girl he had known at UCLA was working in Nixon's office at the time, and she arranged the audience. It was not a terribly auspicious encounter; no immediate vibes of rapport or intuitive meeting of minds, or anything like that. Haldeman himself remembers it as just "the customary courtesy handshake." Still, there was no slackening of interest on his part, and the following year he volunteered to help in Nixon's first Vice Presidential campaign. But, as he later recalled, "I was unable to work out any role at that time, so I faded away and came back in 1956." He was taken on then as one of the Vice President's advance men, and while that didn't exactly put him at the heart of "Campaign Central," it did give him entrée, and a chance to show his stuff.

An advance man's job is to do pretty much what the term implies. He and his cohorts descend on a campaign site ahead of time to set things up, to make sure, for example, that there are plenty of adoring faces on hand when the candidate puts in his appearance. Some advance men become truly inspired in their work and devise clever little refinements to improve the act. For example, Jerry Bruno, who advanced some of the campaign stops for both John and Robert Kennedy, had a special fondness for soft, collapsible barricades which he hoped would induce gullible reporters to write: "So enthusiastic were the crowds that they broke through barricades to get to the candidate." Such tactics were frivolous, innocent versions of what later would be known as "campaign tricks," and in the years ahead Haldeman would spend a lot of time trying to think up ways to deceive the press and the voters in a political campaign. Some of the Watergate disasters were the ultimate fruit of such efforts. But back in 1956 advance men generally played it straight, and he was no exception. What Haldeman brought to his campaign labors were the same managerial skills that were making him a success in advertising: crisp organization, precise attention to detail, and a strong sense of image, or media; and beyond that, of course, a fervid personal commitment to Richard Nixon. By the time the '56 campaign was over, he had begun to impress all the right people, and four years later, when the Nixon team saddled up for the big run against Kennedy, he was called on to serve as chief advance man.

Through the years leading up to 1960, the men who had been most closely associated with Nixon's career were three other Californians: Murray Chotiner, Herb Klein, and Robert Finch. Chotiner had been Nixon's first political mentor. An aggressive lawyer who had managed the victorious campaigns of other California Republicans, he took the young Navy veteran on as his pupil in 1946 and schooled him in the cut-and-slash techniques that proved so successful in that first campaign for Congress and in the others that followed. ("The Pink Lady" circular was a Chotiner inspiration. So was the famous 1952 "Checkers Speech," when Nixon turned what was supposed to be a defense of himself into a sharp attack on the Democrats and/or Communists who were trying to discredit him.)

Klein also hooked up with Nixon in 1946, when, as he once said many years later, "neither of us amounted to much." It would be difficult to argue with this assessment, since at the time Klein was a reporter for a small California paper, something called the *Alhambra Post-Advocate*. As for Finch, he was working in Washington in 1947 for another California Congressman when he struck up an acquaintance with the freshman from Whittier, whose office was just down the hall; there soon developed between them the close friendship that has endured through all the years since.

By 1960, Chotiner was no longer a key man on Nixon's campaign staff. He had become something of an embarrassment, a skeleton best left buried in the closet. For in 1960 all the emphasis was on the "new Nixon"—the experienced statesman, the dignified candidate of Presidential mien—and strenuous efforts were made to expunge from the voters' memories the scowling hatchet man of earlier campaign brawls. Hence, that year Chotiner was, publicly at least, kept away from his pupil. One of Chotiner's—and Nixon's—problems was the fact that in 1956 Chotiner had been brought before a Senate investigating committee to answer for alleged influence peddling.

But Klein and Finch were not so closely identified with the more abrasive aspects of Nixon's past, and they both were very much in the picture in 1960. Klein was Nixon's press secretary, and Finch was the Vice President's campaign manager. Moreover, they were the ones most responsible for bringing Haldeman along; it was, in fact, Finch's decision to put the eager young adman in charge of the overall advance operation.

Haldeman, for his part, was properly appreciative of the helping hands extended to him by Finch and Klein, but he didn't let his gratitude blur his judgment of their own performances in 1960. Long before the campaign was over, he found himself disapproving of the way the two senior aides were running things. He blamed Finch for not keeping a tighter rein on Nixon's schedule, and for letting the candidate involve himself in the most trivial details of the campaign. The result was that Nixon wore himself down to a frazzle. The most painful moment came the night of the first debate, and Haldeman did a slow burn as he watched his wan and exhausted hero fritter away the large advantage he had enjoyed going into the campaign. In Haldeman's view, that dismal scene and others like it could have been prevented if Finch had taken firmer steps to husband Nixon's strength. And Klein, he felt, only aggravated the situation by making the Vice President too accessible to the press, thus further cutting into his time and draining his energies. At the time, of course, Haldeman was still too much of a new boy in camp to make his objections an issue, and he was careful not to say anything that might sour his personal relations with Finch and Klein. As a matter of fact, he remained on friendly terms with both men then and through the years that followed. But in the course of that '60 campaign he had quietly taken their measure, and much later, when the levers of power in Nixon's White House were his to control, he would deal with them accordingly.

Nixon's narrow defeat by Kennedy brought an end to the long winning streak Nixon had been riding since his first election to Congress. More than that, there seemed every reason to believe that never again would he come this close to the Presidency. Up to that time, after all, no losing candidate in this century had ever gone on to win a Presidential race; and the few who had been given a second chance (Bryan, Dewey, Stevenson) succeeded only in diminishing their stature that much more. Richard Nixon was destined to be the one to shatter that tradition, but in the immediate aftermath of 1960 there weren't many people around who were willing to bet on that happening.

So, as the campaign operation broke up that year, most of the bright young Republicans who had tied their own ambitions to Nixon's career in the belief that he was headed straight for the White House took stock of the situation, and decided the time had come to look around for another meal ticket. Nixon himself was enough of a realist to understand this and he could only assume that among those moving on in search of greener pastures would be his chief advance man. As he saw it, there was no reason to suppose that Haldeman would do otherwise. He had gotten to know Haldeman by this time, but only in the casual, superficial way a national candidate becomes acquainted with his middle-echelon people in the heat of a campaign. There was no special bond between them, no strong alliance reaching back over a number of years. Therefore, he was surprised, as well as pleased, when Haldeman volunteered to stay around after the '60 campaign and help research the book that he, Nixon, was planning to write—that stirring apologia that was to become *Six Crises*. This was the first real indication Nixon had that Haldeman was different from the others; that he was a man without political ambitions of his own whose primary allegiance was neither to cause nor to party, but a personal one to him—Richard Nixon. And it was during these months following the '60 election that Bob Haldeman became a Nixon intimate.

This was a period of intense soul searching for Nixon. Indeed, the writing of *Six Crises* was in itself an exercise in therapy. His confidence had been shaken by the loss to Kennedy, and now, out of office for the first time in fourteen years, he was faced with an uncertain future. He was, of course, all too familiar with the dismal record of previous losing Presidential candidates. In *Six Crises* he sought to justify—to himself as well as to others—the key decisions that had brought his career to this point; and in the process to regain the stature he once had had, but which he now knew was slipping away. Although the book dealt with the past, the battles already behind him, its real purpose was to build himself up for the struggles that lay ahead. Thus it wasn't a memoir so much as a rehabilitation project.

What Haldeman did, during this period, was to serve as a combination sounding board and cheerleader. That made him an ideal helpmate. In Nixon's presence, he was able, to an extraordinary degree, to subjugate his own ego and personality and sit for long stretches in attentive silence as Nixon rambled on about the major events of his political career, the designated crises. Yet he was more than just a good, self-effacing listener. On those occasions when his hero seemed to falter, to doubt and second-guess his past decisions, Haldeman would be quick to give him a boost, to offer reassurance that he had been absolutely right in all he had done; that in such endeavors as chasing down Hiss or standing up to Khrushchev in the Moscow kitchen Nixon had brought honor to himself, his party, and his country.

In the years to come, Haldeman would bring many qualities to his service to Nixon: zeal, efficiency, unflagging loyalty, and his adman's gift for media exploitation. But, on a purely personal level, it was his ability to listen, to comfort, to bolster, to reassure that made him a Nixon favorite. And these attributes first came to Nixon's attention in 1961 when, in his new and uneasy role as private citizen, he was struggling to pull the shattered pieces together, and was therefore most receptive to someone who still believed in him as fervently as Haldeman did. By the time *Six Crises* was finished, Haldeman had become one of the few men ever to penetrate the veil of privacy Nixon has always kept tightly around him. He had joined Robert Finch in a very exclusive club: men who had won Richard Nixon's personal trust.

Both Haldeman and Finch advised Nixon not to run for Governor of California in 1962. But the impatient warhorse, smarting from defeat and determined to dispel as quickly as possible the loser's image that now hung over him, persuaded himself that Pat Brown, the incumbent Governor, would be easy pickings (no Kennedy charisma there to work against him), and that a fresh victory on his native turf would give him rail position for another run at the Presidency. Sensing the disaster to come, Finch chose to steer clear of any direct involvement in the '62 race. (In contrast to Haldeman, he *did* have political ambitions of his own, and four years later he ran for Lieutenant Governor on the Reagan ticket that finally ousted Brown from office.) Finch's decision to step aside opened the way that much more for Haldeman, who, despite his misgivings, was eager to play the good soldier, the super loyalist. So he became campaign manager in '62 and helped to engineer the humiliating defeat that convinced just about everyone, friend as well as foe, that Richard Nixon's political career had come to a decisive end.

Haldeman's major contribution to that '62 adventure came in the murky area of "dirty tricks." Midway through the campaign, registered Democrats in California began receiving circulars from a group that called itself the "Committee for the Preservation of the Democratic Party." The circulars warned that Governor Brown had become the captive of left-wing extremists who were out to destroy the party. The apparent purpose of the mail campaign was to trigger an anti-Brown movement among Democrats that, in long-range terms, would ostensibly benefit the party; in short-range terms, of course, the chief beneficiary would be Brown's opponent. As California's *official* Democratic leaders soon discovered, the committee was a phony, the creation of a public-relations firm hired by Haldeman. He, in fact, was the guiding force behind the ruse, though as it later came out he had acted with Nixon's explicit approval. Since the bogus committee was in clear violation of California's election laws, the Democrats took the matter to court and easily won their case.

Haldeman's reaction, once the fraud was exposed, was notable for its lack of remorse. "He was absolutely shameless," recalls Roger Kent, who was California's Democratic chairman at the time. "He didn't seem to think that there was anything wrong with it at all." Haldeman and Nixon always denied any intent to do anything illegal. Haldeman's real regret, apparently, was that the operation was handled in such a clumsy manner. In particular, he could hardly have been pleased with his failure to conceal the role that he and his boss had played. But, in fairness to him, it should be pointed out that he was still new at this sort of thing, and that he proceeded to learn from his mistakes. For in later years, as campaign "dirty tricks" on Nixon's behalf became more elaborate and extensive, Haldeman developed a special finesse for keeping a phalanx of "hit men" between himself and the field of action. That way, if anything went wrong, the intermediaries would have to fend for themselves, as so many of his later cohorts, like Dwight Chapin and Donald Segretti, John Dean and Jeb Magruder, would find out to their sorrow.

Although both Nixon and Haldeman were mentioned by name in the California court complaint, the Democrats stopped short of citing them as defendants and pressing for a full trial. That decision was prompted, in part, by a shortage of funds; but even more so it was influenced by the result of the '62 election, and all that it implied. Like everyone else, the California Democrats had seen the "last press conference," and taking Nixon at his word, they could only assume that they too would not have Nixon "to kick around anymore."

What was not generally known about that bizarre valedictory was that its chief instigator was Haldeman. He was among the handful of aides gathered around Nixon in his Los Angeles hotel suite in the early-morning hours as the moment came to throw in the towel. To detached observers, actually, that moment was long overdue, for the election was in no way a cliffhanger; Brown had led all through the night and would end up winning by a comfortable margin of 200,000 votes. Yet, even though the outcome had been evident for several hours, Nixon held back on his concession and the customary wire of congratulations to the winner. In one sense, of course, his reluctance was understandable. For, as the verdict became clear, he grasped, better than anyone else, the full enormity of its message. He knew that, barring a miracle (and there were no miracles in sight that dark and desolate morning), this defeat in his home state, coming on the heels of his loss to Kennedy, meant that it was all over for him as an active, office-seeking politician. And, while it is one thing to concede an election, it is quite another to rush headlong into one's political grave. So he held back.

Yet, as the morning dragged on, the reporters assembled downstairs in the hotel began clamoring for Nixon to face up to his cup of hemlock so they could wrap up their stories and get some sleep. Their impatience was duly noted by Press Secretary Herb Klein, who returned to Nixon's suite and gently suggested that perhaps the time had come for the candidate to put in an appearance. According to an eyewitness account, Nixon's response to this was "Screw them." He must have liked the sound of that, for he promptly repeated it two or three times. Then to Klein he issued the order: "You do it. You make the statement." For all his ill temper, this was not a bad idea. There is, after all, nothing in the rules that obligates a defeated candidate to put on his stiff upper lip and present himself in public as the gallant loser. (In fact, much of the time it makes for a rather ghoulish spectacle.) So, even though he was physically exhausted and emotionally distraught, Nixon still was responding to his best instincts, which told him that, given his mood, his black despair, it would be a mistake for him to appear before the press and the public. Most of his aides who were with him that morning were quite relieved by the decision. They could plainly see that his nerves were at the breaking point, and that it wouldn't take much to unhinge him. Thus it was left to Klein to handle the concession formalities; with his crinkly eyes, his Cheshire-cat grin and his bland, impenetrable manner, he could be counted on to glide through the ordeal without flinching or losing his cool.

As Klein headed downstairs to carry out the assignment, Nixon and the others who stayed behind huddled around the television set. What they wanted to see was not so much Klein's routine statement but the reaction to it. They were certain the assembled reporters would seize the occasion to ask hard questions, and they were right about that. That, of course, is what reporters are paid to do, but Nixon and the people around him have always had some difficulty understanding that. The tone that morning in Los Angeles was set by the first question hurled at Klein after he finished reading the telegram to Governor Brown.

"Where's Nixon?"

To the men watching upstairs, the very bluntness of the query had a metallic and insolent ring to it. Although their candidate, the private citizen, no longer had an official title, this didn't give some pushy reporter the right to show such blatant disrespect. For Nixon himself, it was especially grating since it brought back unpleasant memories of his Vice Presidential years when Eisenhower, with his brusque, military view of subordinates, referred to him that way. "Get me Nixon," Ike usually barked to Sherman Adams or one of his other aides. Almost never was it "Get me the Vice President." (When he became President, Nixon did the same thing to his Veep. To his top aides, it was always "Where's Agnew?" or "Get me Agnew.")

"The boss won't be down," said Klein, hiding behind his Buddha's mask, the broad and placid grin that turns his eyes into wrinkled slits. "He plans to go home and be with his family."

This was greeted by a snicker or two. The men upstairs were certain of that. They distinctly heard snickers. Then the derisive and demeaning questions came on in a rush, a flurry. ("Herb, now that he's . . ." "Herb, just where does he go from here. . . ." "Herb, does he still think he can . . .")

Upstairs, in Nixon's suite, Haldeman flew into a rage. All through the night and into the morning, the anguish and bitterness had been building up inside him as well. For him, after all, this had hardly been an impressive debut as a campaign manager. In that role, he had made several serious mistakes, not the least of which was his decision to set up the phony committee of Democrats. On the issues level, he had helped to persuade his candidate to campaign as the "Old Nixon," the militant anti-Communist. Between them, they had done their best to revive the old crusade, as though it were 1950 and Helen Gahagan Douglas all over again. But that strategy, not very sound in the first place, soon backfired. For in the fall of 1962, while Nixon was raising the cry about the Democrats being "soft on Communism," his great nemesis, the Democratic President, was busy staring down Khrushchev and his missiles in Cuba. As Dean Rusk so vividly phrased it at the time, "We were eyeball-to-eyeball, and the other guy blinked." In the face of all that, it wasn't easy to make a case for softness.

But Haldeman was in no mood that morning to admit that the Nixon forces had brought defeat on themselves. Glaring at the television set, he saw who the real villains were and launched into a tirade. It was, he told Nixon, the hostile liberal press that had tipped the balance to Kennedy in 1960. Now the same crowd had done him in again. And here they were, on television, jumping at the chance to rub salt in his wounds. They were mocking him down there, having themselves a high old time, and they shouldn't be allowed to get away with it. They should be told just where the hell to get off.

Haldeman's diatribe aroused all of Nixon's combative fervor. Whereas before he had been more depressed than angry, now he was out for blood. It suddenly occurred to him that by staying up in his suite he was playing into the hands of the reporters, leading them to think he was afraid to confront them. Well, he wasn't afraid, and he would prove it. His career might be over, but at least he would go down fighting. The press had been having fun at his expense for a long time, and now it was his turn. He would have the last word.

So, a few moments later, Nixon was down there himself, facing the reporters, putting together his famous performance—the rambling, semicoherent gripe about how the press had given him "the shaft," and all the rest of it, getting around eventually to his big line, the celebrated parting shot, so laden with bitter sarcasm: "I leave you gentlemen now, and you will now write it. . . . But as I leave you, I want you to know, just think how much you're going to be missing: You won't have Nixon to kick around anymore because, gentlemen, this is my last press conference. . . ." With that performance, he hit rock bottom. It was as though, faced with a defeat that he himself interpreted as his political death, he decided to riddle the corpse with bullets, just to make sure it would never stir again. Only later, when the time came for him to play Lazarus, would he look back on that morning with regret. ("A great mistake," he called it in 1967 when he was edging toward another run for the Presidency.)

So came the down years—the move to New York and a new life, away from politics. But Nixon was not that easily forgotten; his two defeats had left too strong an imprint on the national consciousness. He had become an object of ridicule. He was viewed, during this period, as a political counterpart to the Edsel, another product that received a big buildup but failed to deliver on performance. Indeed, his very name became a synonym for "loser." Even many Republicans who had supported him with enthusiasm in the past now succumbed to the fashion and found themselves laughing at all the shrill jokes about "Tricky Dick," the man you wouldn't buy a used car from. But this was never true of Haldeman. Nixon was still his hero, and all through the dark years of derision he staunchly kept the faith. "I didn't have any supernatural premonitions," he later recalled at the White House, "but I honestly felt that, despite the events of the early sixties, he was not through." Yet, as we shall see, Haldeman was not particularly eager to back up his faith with good works. When the time finally came to go into battle again, he would hold back, for the longest time, before committing himself to another campaign. Others may have believed in Nixon less intensely, but they at least were with him when he started out on the long road back. Haldeman was not.

For Haldeman, during Nixon's years out of public affairs, it was onward and upward in the world of advertising. By the early 1960s he had become a vice president at J. Walter Thompson, and as manager of the agency's Los Angeles office he directed the handling of several lucrative accounts. Among them were Disneyland, 7-Up, and a whole slew of household products manufactured by the Boyle-Midway Company: Aerowax, Aero Shave, Saniflush, Griffin Shoe Polish, Easy-Off oven cleaner, Black Flag bug spray, and a host of other

modern miracles that no American home would be complete without. (As a Christian Scientist, Haldeman declined to take on cigarette
or liquor clients, but he did agree to sell beer.) Of all his triumphs at
J. Walter Thompson, the most memorable, perhaps, was the advertising campaign he put together for a product called "Snarol." Snarol,
it was promised, would do to snails what Black Flag was reputed to
do to roaches and such. Now, up to this time, it is true, hardly anyone
realized that snails, of all things, were worthy of such attention; they
were not exactly perceived as your everyday sort of pest. But, since
the whole point of advertising is to alert us to perils we might otherwise fail to heed (bad breath, antisocial armpits, and the like), Haldeman's campaign made it clear that snails were prolific in warm
climates, like California's, and that they could be quite a nuisance,
especially for people with gardens. This was a melancholy moment
in the long and tranquil history of *l'escargot*, for soon Snarol took its
place on scores of shopping lists, right up there with the other essen-
tials.

Knowing how to get the message across was one of Haldeman's
strengths at J. Walter Thompson. He had made a careful study of
television, and he learned how to exploit it to maximum advantage.
Yet, for the most part, his value to the agency was not in the creative
sphere. Hugh Sutherland, a close friend since childhood who later
worked for Haldeman at JWT, makes the point that "Bob was not a
great writer or a great artist, but he was a good critic of advertising."
In other words, once the product was packaged, he had a gift for
recognizing whether or not it would sell, and, if so, exactly what
advertising and publicity techniques would be most effective. But
Sutherland and everyone else who knew him agree that Haldeman's
most impressive skills were managerial and administrative. He was
adept at finding the kind of people he wanted and, once they were
under his wing, he knew how to mold them into a tightly-organized
staff.

Through the early and middle sixties, he recruited a corps of
earnest young junior-executive types, most of whom were just out of
college. To a man, these up-and-comers were the antithesis of the
college "kids" we generally associate with the sixties, the beards and
longhairs who brought on the hippie movement and all the other
social upheavals that marked the era. In attitude and appearance,
Haldeman's protégés seemed to come from the fifties, young men

who still adhered to the conventional and acquiescent values of the "silent generation." This being the case, it is hardly surprising that they shared his enthusiasm for Richard Nixon; a few of them, in fact, had worked as volunteers on the '60 and '62 campaigns while they were still in college. And in time no fewer than five of these well-scrubbed straight arrows—Ronald Ziegler, Dwight Chapin, Larry Higby, Ken Cole, and Bruce Kehrli—would move on, with Haldeman, to Washington and the Nixon White House.

By 1967, the notion that Nixon might become the next President of the United States was no longer dismissed as a Harold Stassen fantasy. Because of what the Goldwater debacle had done to the Republican party in 1964, and what the Vietnam war was then doing to Lyndon Johnson's Presidency, Nixon suddenly was back among the living. His political resurrection had begun the previous fall when, in the course of an extensive campaign tour on behalf of Republicans running in the midterm election, he discovered he still had widespread support among the party faithful. Moreover, those '66 election results indicated the country was starting to turn against LBJ. So all of a sudden 1968 held out the promise of being a Republican year, and Nixon, having tested the waters and sized up the competition, was convinced he had an excellent chance of becoming the Republican nominee. Thus, in the early months of 1967, he quietly moved into the preliminary stages of another run for the Presidency.

In the fall of '67, while still immersed full time at J. Walter Thompson, Haldeman sent Nixon a lengthy memo, suggesting guidelines for the campaign ahead. His central thesis was that because of television the traditional, barnstorming approach to a national campaign was now obsolete. He pointed out that a Presidential candidate could now reach more people in a thirty-second TV spot than he could in ten months of shouting himself hoarse on the hustings. Therefore, he went on, what Nixon should do this next time was structure his campaign around a high-powered television blitz and keep his public appearances to a minimum, thereby conserving his energy and reducing the risk of unpleasant confrontations. (If all this sounds overly familiar, it is only because we have become so accustomed to Haldeman-style campaigns. At the time, it was quite a novel idea, for until then no one had ever attempted a TV-oriented campaign on anything approaching the scale Haldeman had in mind.)

Haldeman knew, when he wrote this memo, just how wary Nixon was of television; he knew that his man still bore deep scars from the debates with Kennedy in 1960. So he stressed the point that this sort of television campaign was not at all the sort of thing he was proposing. There would be no debates, no unstructured skirmishing with the opposition or the press, or any of that. Everything would be controlled, rigidly controlled, right down to the last cue card. The whole idea was to present the candidate in his most favorable light, to show him at his attractive best; in other words, to *package* him, just as one would a new shaving cream—or the latest in snail killers.

Several months would pass before Haldeman would break away from J. Walter Thompson to give his full attention (and commitment) to Nixon's second bid for the Presidency. But the guidelines he set down in that 1967 memo formed the basis of the strategy Nixon would eventually take into his '68 campaign. And in pushing for a campaign that relied heavily on television, Haldeman was also, rather shrewdly, looking out for Number One. For, once Nixon made the decision to go that route, Haldeman would be assured of a prominent role. He, after all, was the adman, the professional image maker, the one who knew all about "media." His talents, therefore, would surely be needed.

In the meantime, as 1967 drew to a close, he was content to sit back and wait, to remain in California while all the action was "back East," in New York. There, Nixon's recently-assembled campaign team, composed of many new faces (in accordance with the unveiling of still another New Nixon), was busy gearing up for the first phase—the early primaries. But, although Haldeman chose to stay away from direct, personal, on-scene involvement in all that, he did make a point, throughout this period, of keeping in touch—not only with Nixon, but with another man as well, one he had known since college days and who now had a thriving law practice in Seattle. This other man also was a veteran of past Nixon campaigns, having been lured into that world by Haldeman himself. And now, in the waning weeks of 1967, Haldeman wanted to make sure that when the right moment came—if it came—his close friend, John Ehrlichman, would be ready, once more, to march for Richard Nixon.

Twelve

UCLA was where they met, and where their friendship began. Like Haldeman and many of the others, Ehrlichman came to that campus as a hometown boy of sorts. That is, he did most of his growing up in the LA area, in the city of Santa Monica, a community that is best described as a kind of peninsula-in-reverse. While one side of it looks out on the Pacific, it was doomed, early on, to be surrounded on the other three sides by the urban sprawl of Los Angeles itself. But unlike his good friend Ehrlichman is not a native of California. He was born in Tacoma, Washington, and his family roots are planted there, and in Seattle.

Ehrlichman's paternal grandfather immigrated to Seattle from Austria in the late nineteenth century, at a time when the Pacific Northwest was still regarded as a frontier outpost, the end of the line on the old Oregon Trail. One of Seattle's pioneer merchants, he also was a founder of the city's first Orthodox Jewish congregation, the Bikur Cholim synagogue. Ehrlichman's grandfather remained steadfast in the Jewish faith even after his wife discovered Mary Baker Eddy and became a Christian Scientist. But, although their four children started out attending synagogue services, they later followed their mother into Christian Science; subsequently, all four of them married within that faith. So, by the time John was born, in 1925, Christian Science was firmly established as the family religion.

Ehrlichman tended to be somewhat sensitive about his family's earlier heritage. In the summer of 1973, when he was giving his testimony at the Watergate hearings, a Seattle newspaper ran a story quoting a local rabbi as saying that both his father and uncle had been, at one time, "synagogue-going Jews." When a Washington, D.C., reporter, assigned to do a background story on Ehrlichman, questioned him about the Seattle report, he denied it, then warned that, if such a story were published, "I'll sue." A few moments later, however, having been stricken by an attack of second thoughts, he broke into a grin and told the reporter: "I hope you realize that last remark was off the record. I just realized how it would sound [sic] in print." In any event, it is certainly true that Ehrlichman has never, in any way, identified himself with the faith of his fathers. When he was at UCLA, he belonged to Kappa Sigma, a fraternity which at the time did not accept Jews.

The family star of his father's generation was John's uncle, Ben Ehrlichman. An investor who gambled for high stakes in land development, he amassed a fortune in real estate and insurance; in the process, he became something of a legend in Seattle business circles. To this day, Ben Ehrlichman's portrait is on display on the mezzanine of the Olympic Hotel in Seattle, a hallowed gallery reserved for the city's all-time great citizens. In 1972, when he was at the height of his power in the White House, Ben Ehrlichman's nephew, John, was named Seattle's "First Citizen of the Year" by the city's board of realtors, and soon his portrait took its place in the Olympic's pantheon.

Ehrlichman's father, Rudolph, was also an investor, and although he did all right for himself, he never had the instinct for the big killings that made his brother a millionaire. A restless spirit, he left Seattle as a young man, motivated in part (old friends suggest) by a desire to get out from under brother Ben's shadow. He first moved to Tacoma, where John was born, then later decided to try his luck in New York. So the family moved east, to New Jersey, just across the river from Manhattan, where John started grade school. After a brief stay there, they packed up again and returned to the West Coast, this time to Santa Monica. There they finally settled down.

Ehrlichman's great passion during the Santa Monica years was the Boy Scouts. He devoted almost all his spare time and energy to scout activities; he was especially fond of hiking and weekend camping trips in the mountains, and the day he became an Eagle Scout was the crowning moment of his adolescence. Even in later years, after he had fought in the war and gone on to become, first, a highly successful lawyer and, after that, a man of great power in Richard Nixon's Washington, Ehrlichman would still look back on getting his Eagle as one of his proudest achievements. He would insist, for example, on having it listed, along with his adult citations, in *Who's Who*.

With the onset of World War II, Rudolph Ehrlichman became restless again. More than restless, really, for as his son recalled many years later: "He was very concerned about the world at that time, and he wanted to do his part." At first, Ehrlichman senior tried to enlist in the U.S. Army, but he was rejected as too old. He promptly went up to Canada, and joined the Royal Canadian Air Force. Not long after, he was killed in a plane crash. In the meantime, his son, having graduated from Santa Monica High School in 1942, started in at UCLA that fall. But after his freshman year, and not long after the death of his father, he left college to join the U.S. Air Force. He became a B–24 navigator and, during the next three years, he flew twenty-six bombing missions over Europe. After the war, he returned to UCLA as a sophomore, this time on the GI bill.

It was in his junior year that he became acquainted with Bob Haldeman. What brought the two classmates together was their mutual interest in campus politics. Although they did not belong to the same fraternity, they were both big shots on the Interfraternity Council, and generally found themselves in agreement on the burning issues. As an example, Ehrlichman supported Haldeman's campaign to purge the *Daily Bruin* of "subversives." Another bond between them, obviously, was the fact that they were both Christian Scientists. As their friendship grew, they even began to do their courting together. Both Haldeman's future wife, Joanne Horton, and Ehrlichman's, Jeannie Fisher, were UCLA students at the time, and soon all four of them became extremely close, in the traditional double-dating manner. In fact, when Jeannie Fisher decided to run for vice president of the student body, she called on her boy friend's best buddy to manage her campaign. But Haldeman blew it: she lost.

Yet, for all the rapport between them, there were some significant differences. For one thing, even then Ehrlichman was inclined to be more of an "out-front" guy than Haldeman—more open, more gregarious, more relaxed in the presence of others. He was, in fact, often at his best in public situations, which helped to make him an outstanding member of UCLA's debate team. On one occasion, in a debate with nearby Occidental College, his opponent was none other than Robert Finch. In contrast, Haldeman was reserved, intense, and, for the most part, wary of strangers. While Ehrlichman enjoyed debating in open forums, Haldeman already revealed a strong preference for staying in the background, for pulling strings from behind the scenes—for managing Jeannie Fisher's campaign, rather than running for office himself.

Ehrlichman also was far less ideological in his view of the world beyond UCLA. The Communist thing was not an obsession with him the way it became with Haldeman. He considered himself a Republican, but his leanings were moderate rather than conservative. As a political-science major, he took a natural delight in discussing and arguing politics, yet he seldom was so strongly committed to a position that he could not be receptive to an opposing view. This quality helped him as a debater, since it made it easy for him to argue either side of a question with force and conviction. Ehrlichman also was not caught up in Haldeman's passion for a new California Congressman named Richard Nixon. As a Republican, he was inclined to view Nixon in a favorable light, but he did not become absorbed in his career, or his crusade, the way Haldeman did. In short, John Ehrlichman was in those days a far cry from being a true believer. That would come later.

From UCLA, Ehrlichman went on to Stanford Law School, where one of his closest friends was a future enemy of the Nixon White House named Pete McCloskey. A fellow Republican, this was the same Pete McCloskey who, in 1967, would get himself elected to Congress by beating Shirley Temple; once having sunk the "good ship Lollipop," he would go on to become a vigorous opponent of Nixon's Vietnam policy, even to the point of running against the President in the 1972 New Hampshire primary. For that act of disloyalty, he would lose his friendship with Ehrlichman, by then no longer receptive to opposing views. But, even after the rupture between them, McCloskey still remembered the Ehrlichman of their Stanford years with warmth and affection. And for good reason. In 1950, when McCloskey went off to fight in Korea and become a much-decorated hero (a fact that gave a certain bite to his later antiwar stand), John and Jeannie Ehrlichman took in Pete's pregnant wife, and helped her through those first difficult weeks.

Ehrlichman received his law degree from Stanford in 1951 and promptly nailed down an offer from a firm in Los Angeles. But, before starting in there, he took his wife on a short vacation to the "old country"—to Seattle, where his family still had ties. Years later, he recalled that trip with an almost boyish exuberance: "I had been telling her about the water and the trees and the fishing. And when we got there, the sun was shining and the strawberries were big and fat. We stayed awhile, then packed our things and went to Los Angeles. The smog was terrible, the traffic was terrible, and one of the few pretty places to live was Malibu, which a young lawyer can't afford. So we came back to Seattle."

In Seattle, his Uncle Ben, the city's living legend, set him up as an attorney for one of his many enterprises, the United Pacific Insurance Company. After a brief apprenticeship there, Ehrlichman opened up his own practice, in partnership with a friend of his uncle's named Jack Hullin. Years later, Hullin's son, Tod, once a star quarterback for the University of Washington Huskies, would go to work for Ehrlichman in the White House, where Ehrlichman saw to it that young Tod stayed out of trouble. Another protégé, Egil ("Bud") Krogh, would not be so lucky. Krogh also started out with Ehrlichman in the Seattle law firm, and went on with him to the Nixon White House. But Krogh's later service there led, in time, to the Plumbers' Unit, the Ellsberg burglary, and finally to prison.

From the beginning, Ehrlichman dabbled a lot in real estate (Uncle Ben's connections opened all the right doors), soon becoming a specialist in land use and zoning laws. Fairly dull stuff perhaps, to some people, but not in that neck of the woods, where land developers and environmentalists long have regarded each other with a hostile and suspicious eye. Conservation was a major concern in the Pacific Northwest years before it was rechristened Ecology. In any event, this rather narrow branch of the law became Ehrlichman's life, his consuming interest, his sole occupation, with a few exceptions, through the years right up until 1968.

He was good at it. By the 1960s, Ehrlichman was recognized as the best in his field—Seattle's foremost zoning lawyer. "He had a passion for detail and was indefatigable," recalls another Seattle attorney who knew him then. "And that's what made him good. Land use tends to be boring, but he could just outwait you. He never let up. He was going flat-out all the time." In the recurring battles between property owners trying to preserve natural values, and commercial interests pushing for development, Ehrlichman was just as apt to be on one side as on the other. In the words of another former adversary, "he knew how to beat City Hall or win for City Hall, depending on whose corner he happened to be in." He was, in short, the super advocate, who would pull out all the stops for a client once he agreed to take his case. In later years he served Richard

Nixon that way, regarding him as his client, his one-and-only client.

Ehrlichman prospered there, on the banks of Puget Sound, and found himself the good life. Once he built up his reputation, he began knocking down $50,000 to $60,000 a year, and the area he lived in featured homes in the $100,000 range. Moreover, he rejoiced in all the opportunities available around Seattle for outdoor recreation. As in his youth, he went in for hiking, though by now, having developed a paunch, he was inclined to be a "huffer-and-puffer." And there were camping trips in the nearby mountains, during which he took special delight in impressing others with his Eagle Scout lore—cleaning fish, exploring old trails, identifying strange animal sounds in the night. All in all, the good life.

But no politics—none at all in Seattle during these years. He made no effort to become involved in local Republican affairs. Part of this, no doubt, was calculated, in deference to his law practice. Since a zoning lawyer must deal constantly with city and state officials of *both* parties, it was to his advantage to be thought of as apolitical. But it probably went deeper than that. He simply wasn't all that interested in party politics, for he was still very much the non-ideologue. In fact, his political profile was so low that later, when he suddenly surfaced with so much muscle in Nixon's White House, all the top Republican politicos in his home state could do was shake their heads in bewilderment. And when reporters and other interested parties, seeking to get a clearer picture of Ehrlichman's background, came to them with their questions, they simply threw up their hands and said, in effect: "Hell, we don't know a thing about him. He was just a zoning lawyer here, that's all. He never had anything to do with us."

Actually, what these local party leaders did not know was that Ehrlichman had indeed been playing around in politics during these years, but always far away from Seattle. Like a furtive alcoholic who does all his drinking in bars on the other side of town, he was careful never to be seen "under the influence" in his own neighborhood.

Ehrlichman's connection with politics was through his friend Bob Haldeman. Although they had taken separate paths since leaving UCLA, Haldeman and Ehrlichman, along with their families, kept their friendship alive through the years after college. Thus, in 1959, when Haldeman was given the job of chief advance man for Nixon's

'60 campaign, and the go-ahead to line up some of his own people, one of the first he called was his old buddy from the Interfraternity Council. "I wanted him to find out what this kind of thing was all about," Haldeman once said years later. It would be fascinating to know exactly what he meant by "this kind of thing," since Ehrlichman's first major assignment as a Nixon operative was to engage in a little casual spying.

In 1960, Governor Nelson Rockefeller of New York, then a brand-new face on the national scene, was going around the country trying in vain to drum up Republican support for his own Presidential hopes. Ehrlichman's mission was to shadow the Rockefeller forces, infiltrate their ranks if possible, and find out as much about them as he could. He took on the job with all the zest of an Ian Fleming addict, and his favorite moment came in North Dakota when, in his secret agent's role, he drove a car in Rockefeller's motorcade. Some years later, he still bragged about this with great relish: "Oh, it was wonderful. The Rockefeller people thought I was from North Dakota, and the North Dakota people thought I was with Rockefeller." So much for his introduction, through Haldeman, into the world of Richard Nixon.

It should be said, not only in Ehrlichman's defense but also to clarify, that, while he didn't see anything wrong in the Rockefeller assignment, he also didn't think it was terribly serious or important. He regarded it as something of a lark, a harmless escapade. And he had a point: as an isolated incident, seen in the context of that time, his gumshoe mission *was* innocuous, about as frivolous a deceit as Jerry Bruno's collapsible barricades. There wasn't much, after all, that Ehrlichman, prowling around the edges of the Rockefeller camp, could hope to find out that wasn't readily available to a good reporter, and therefore the public. Only from a later perspective does this "campaign trick" take on a certain significance; for only in hindsight does it come into focus as an early marker on the long road to Watergate.

We must be careful here, for the John Ehrlichman of 1960 was not the same man who in 1973 at the Watergate hearings would defend burglary and other crimes on grounds of national security. If, in 1959 and '60, he was only too eager to play the games Haldeman asked him to play (and after trailing Rockefeller he would be sent to the Democratic convention to snoop around there), it was largely because he thought of them in precisely those terms—as games. For Haldeman, of course, this 1960 race was deadly serious—in his view, nothing less than the survival of the Free World was at stake—and, in time, some of that conviction would rub off on Ehrlichman too. For in the course of the 1960 Presidential campaign, he became truly committed to Nixon, though more in a personal than an ideological sense. At the end, when Kennedy won, he was as wounded and crestfallen as the other loyalists.

But at first he thoroughly enjoyed himself. It was his first taste of the big time, and he soon became caught up in all the hoopla of a national campaign. He discovered that politics on this level was fun, a stimulating change from the parochial concerns of Seattle and the narrow world of legal disputes over land use. Even after he cast off his James Bond role and settled into the more routine chores of helping Haldeman advance the campaign, Ehrlichman went about his tasks with verve and exuberance.

He had such a good time, in fact, that in 1962, when the California Governor's race came up, he jumped at the chance to do it again. This time, however, it wasn't so much fun. Gone was the glamour and heady excitement of a national campaign, and as the battle against Pat Brown became increasingly ugly and acrimonious, Ehrlichman's own attitude hardened into bitterness. In that contest, he encountered the full fury of the hatred Nixon inspired, most of it from those who still remembered and could not forgive the Old Nixon of earlier campaigns. Like Haldeman, Ehrlichman started hating back. The lesson he took away from the '62 disaster was that, ultimately, politics wasn't fun; the game itself didn't mean a thing. All that really mattered was winning.

Having failed to win, they were through. He was convinced of that. Haldeman, during the bleak years which followed, may have clung to the belief that Nixon still had a political future, but Ehrlichman was more in tune with the conventional wisdom that the "last press conference" had been exactly that. So he returned to Seattle and his good life: the prosperous law career in a pleasant environment of clean air and natural beauty. Having had his two flings as a Nixon campaigner, he now was back home and there he intended to stay.

But those mysterious forces which were determined to make Richard Nixon President had a different fate in store for Ehrlichman.

In 1966, Nixon asked Haldeman to come to New York to help train some new advance men he had lined up for his midterm campaign travels, the essential first step in Operation Comeback. But Haldeman politely begged off and suggested Ehrlichman instead. Ehrlichman took on the assignment, and during his brief stay in New York he became persuaded that Nixon might really have a chance in 1968. That feeling grew stronger in the aftermath of Nixon's success in the '66 campaign, and within himself, by this time, the old competitive fires had begun to stir. So in 1967, when the calls began coming in from Haldeman, his answer was: Yes, he certainly would be available for another run on the big track. But not full time, no full commitment, not right away. He agreed with Haldeman that they should hold back for a while, to see what developed.

Haldeman did help with strategy-planning meetings in late '67. With Ehrlichman as his field-man-in-charge, he directed most of Nixon's travel and some of his advertising in the primaries of early 1968, including the demolishing of Romney in New Hampshire. But the Haldeman-Ehrlichman combination did not work full time, as permanent staff, traveling and working every day, every week with the candidate the way, say, Patrick Buchanan did. They continued to hold back, at least a little, for the longest time.

Some people who were close to Nixon then and later had the impression Haldeman was holding back partly because he was reluctant to make another full commitment, out of his remembrance of agonies past, partly because he was not convinced Nixon could again get the nomination, and, near the end, partly because Haldeman wanted Nixon to plead for his return. The latter would insure him an inside top position, a job running things, rather than playing second fiddle to any New Yorkers. It is one thing to volunteer for a campaign, but it is quite another to be asked. Ehrlichman, following Haldeman's lead, naturally wasn't going to gamble on risking all unless and until Haldeman did.

It was not until June of 1968 that Haldeman and Ehrlichman joined the Nixon campaign team on a full-time, permanent basis. When they finally did sign up completely, it was just a few days after the May 28 Oregon primary (the last one Nixon entered that year), which has induced some of their critics to contend that the two super loyalists purposely waited until after that final hurdle had been cleared. Only then, it is argued, were they convinced their man would go on to win the Republican nomination. The trouble with this argument is that it places undue importance on the Oregon primary. By the time of the Oregon primary, Nixon's nomination was a foregone conclusion, and had been for many weeks, ever since late March when Nelson Rockefeller decided not to challenge him there. So in reality Oregon was as meaningless as the other primaries in which Nixon had faced only dormant opposition. But, if the critics focused on the wrong event, their conclusion was right on target. The majority opinion among those in positions to know at the time is that in choosing to hold back Haldeman and Ehrlichman mostly had been waiting for some proof or sign that Nixon was moving on a triumphant course. And finally it had come. But the Oregon primary may have been the least of it. Comments and hints they dropped later, stories from friends, and circumstantial evidence all indicate that the prime factor in their decision may not have been the Oregon primary, but may well have been something that happened one week later, several hundred miles to the south, in Los Angeles—Robert Kennedy's assassination.

All through 1967 and into the early weeks of '68, Nixon had been psyching himself up to run against Lyndon Johnson, who he knew had become a deeply unpopular President. Then in March came the first cataclysmic events of that incredible year: Eugene McCarthy's strong showing in New Hampshire, the sudden entry of Kennedy into the race, and, at month's end, LBJ's abdication. Johnson's decision in particular threw Nixon off balance, for it meant that now the Democratic nominee would be either Hubert Humphrey or Bobby Kennedy. There was a lot of brave talk in the Nixon camp about how they really hoped it would be Kennedy, for then their man could avenge 1960 and vindicate himself.

But among themselves, in private, they were singing a much different tune. A Kennedy nomination, they knew, could only mean trouble for Nixon. For one thing, it would surely make Vietnam the central issue of the fall campaign, and Bobby, having changed his mind about the war, and having emerged as an impassioned peace candidate, would savage Nixon on that. Nixon himself, by this time, had begun to edge away from his earlier hard-line stand on Vietnam, but he had been on record for too long as a militant hawk (his earlier criticisms of Johnson had been that he wasn't prosecuting the war vigorously enough), and Kennedy would be sure to pound away at that record, without mercy or letup. All this would come at a time when antiwar sentiment was rising in full force across the country, and even if Nixon made an about-face and tried to align himself with the doves, there was no way he could outmaneuver Kennedy on the peace issue. And beyond that Bobby would have all the Kennedy nostalgia going for him: the romantic afterview of the New Frontier, the slain prince, and now his devoted brother vowing to revive it all. The combination of Camelot and the peace issue would make Robert Kennedy a formidable opponent for any Republican in 1968, but especially for one named Richard Nixon.

Just the mere prospect of a Kennedy nomination was enough to send tremors of dismay through many Republicans. For, if they did nothing else in 1968, they were determined this time not to repeat the mistakes of the past. They were tired of being ridiculed for their suicidal follies, for having sent Barry Goldwater out as cannon fodder in 1964. Many of them felt that to give their blessing to another Nixon-Kennedy race would only bring on the 1960 nightmare all over again. A lot of these nervous Republicans were convention delegates who were willing to accept Nixon under normal circumstances—against Johnson, say, or Humphrey—but who regarded a Kennedy threat as something clearly abnormal. So this was the mood that was taking hold within Republican ranks during the weeks of April and May, following Johnson's withdrawal. If by convention time it looked as though the Democrats were going for Kennedy (and the Republicans would not know for certain since their convention was first), then to hell with Nixon and having to go through all that again. Instead, they would turn to another candidate; perhaps to Rockefeller, whose position on the war was more equivocal and who could challenge Bobby on liberal domestic issues; or if not him, then Reagan, who could counter the Kennedy charisma with his own cosmetic appeal.

Haldeman and Ehrlichman were aware of this sentiment. They knew well that a strong Kennedy threat greatly diminished Nixon's chances of being nominated. They also had to ask themselves: If Nixon did get the nomination and then Kennedy became the Democratic candidate, did they really care to be a part of that? Did they really want to slave and suffer through a campaign that could lead to another Kennedy victory at Nixon's expense? The answer was no. Neither of them had the stomach to endure the pain of another 1960.

So they bided their time, delaying decision—until that night in Los Angeles when Sirhan Sirhan settled all the immediate political questions, sewing up the Democratic nomination for Humphrey and making Nixon a shoo-in at the GOP convention. With Kennedy dead, the Republicans could relax. Humphrey promised to be the weakest possible opponent, a man who would have to run on Johnson's war record without having the power of the Presidency to use as leverage in the campaign. Hence, the Republicans felt secure enough to go with Nixon, despite his past performance chart. Under these circumstances, 1968 was shaping up as the kind of campaign Haldeman and Ehrlichman would enjoy working on, so they promptly hopped aboard. Because there is room for doubt, perhaps fairness dictates saying that it is possible the pair—Haldeman, at least—might have risked their all for Nixon in the summer of 1968 anyway. Some of their friends and co-workers are convinced of that; one even says Haldeman and Ehrlichman had fully committed their time and future long before it publicly appeared that way. Whether they or we are correct, Haldeman and Ehrlichman did not appear to most inside and outside observers to have decided irrevocably to commit themselves until mid-June of 1968.

Haldeman was appointed campaign chief of staff, a title created for him. He immediately started making changes. Through the primary campaigns that spring, there had been occasional signs that this time there might be something more to the New Nixon business than the usual propaganda. The New York years seemed to have mellowed Nixon a bit; long-time Nixon observers found him less strident, less uptight. He even made a conscious effort to improve relations with his old bête noire, the press. On his forays into the primary states, he went out of his way, now and then, to mingle with reporters. On occasion, there were even attempts at a little Kennedyesque banter—with mixed results, to be sure, but he was given high marks for trying.

One of Haldeman's first moves was to apply the ice to all that. Henceforth, on the campaign jet, the curtains were tightly drawn between Nixon's forward cabin and the press section. Haldeman, remembering Nixon's fatigue in the 1960 campaign, set up a protective cocoon around the candidate to spare him the ordeal of having to cope with open and unstructured situations. (Haldeman once said that "the key to an effective Richard Nixon is to keep him relaxed."

Nixon himself would seldom admit it, but he tired easily, physically and mentally. So Haldeman decided that if Nixon was to remain relaxed over the forced march of a long national campaign, as opposed to a few quick forays into primary states, he had to stay rested.) Soon Nixon became remote, inaccessible, not only to the press but to local politicians and the less-privileged members of his own campaign team.

Deciding just who was privileged and who was not also became a Haldeman responsibility. Right from the start, he elbowed aside all those who incurred his displeasure. He was especially suspicious of the new faces, the people who had hooked up with Nixon in recent years, since the move to New York (lawyer John Sears and writer Richard Whalen, to name just two). For the most part, they were Easterners—New York and Washington types—and therefore not to be trusted, unless they could prove themselves worthy. Staffers who went in for drinking or socializing with the press were certain to be put on short rations, if not dropped altogether from the entourage. And, as a general rule, anyone who tried to make personal contact with Nixon on his own initiative was crisply told by Haldeman to state his business in writing; the candidate was busy or resting, and was not to be disturbed. Thus, even at this early stage, construction had begun on the Berlin Wall.

All this met with the full approval not only of Nixon, but also of the official campaign manager, John Mitchell. Absorbed in the big picture, the overall campaign—essentially, the Southern Strategy, the quest to nail down as many Wallace voters as could be pried away from the feisty Alabaman—Mitchell was more than content to let Haldeman take charge of field operations, the day-to-day details, and to act as Nixon's personal guardian and nursemaid. What's more, he was in total agreement with the sequestering of the candidate. In Mitchell's view as well, the more Nixon stayed out of public view and the less he said on controversial issues, the better his chances of winning. So, even though they were just getting acquainted, Haldeman and Mitchell soon discovered they saw eye to eye on how to elect Richard Nixon President. By campaign's end, in fact, the two men had formed a fragile alliance that would continue through the early White House years. They were never exactly comfortable with each other. Haldeman, especially, was suspicious. But in general there was mutual respect. Only toward the end of Nixon's first term would they turn on each other in a struggle for power that would carry both of them to their Watergate ruin.

Ehrlichman's assignment during the early summer weeks of 1968 was to set up Nixon's convention headquarters in Miami Beach, and to ride herd on the various plans for convention week. Among other things this gave him a direct hand in the great aesthetic triumph of that '68 Republican convention—the Festival of Balloons. It was his job to make sure that on acceptance-speech night hundreds of Nixon balloons were synchronized for release at the precise moment the nominee's arms shot upward into a V. After the convention, Ehrlichman was put in charge of logistics for the fall campaign. To carry out these mundane tasks—overseeing hotel reservations and other travel arrangements—he was given the imperious title of Tour Director.

As it turned out, however, there wasn't that much touring to direct. With the cocoon around Nixon firmly secured, Haldeman began, after the convention, to bring to fruition the television strategy he had planned months before. Working along with other media experts who had been hired for the purpose, he helped package the candidate for display to the voters. This included not only the routine commercial spots, but more elaborate TV "specials," such as question-and-answer sessions that featured Nixon testing his wits and cool against panels of civic-minded citizens, all carefully screened beforehand. Nixon spent as little time as possible out on the campaign trail, "pressing the flesh" as LBJ used to call it. It was ironic that Nixon, who felt he had been sabotaged by television in 1960, would choose to make most of his second run for the Presidency from within various TV studios. It was also a major innovation in our national politics, and it worked—though barely, just barely.

So at last in November, 1968, the dream came true, and Haldeman and Ehrlichman were on hand to savor the long-awaited moment. What now lay in store for them? In all their labors for Nixon over the years, they had learned a few things about politics and campaigning, but that was behind them. Having finally won, Richard Nixon now must govern. And neither Bob Haldeman nor John Ehrlichman had taken the time, up to this point, to give much thought to what governing might entail. The world ahead, the world of Washington, the White House, the vast empire of the federal government, was utterly foreign to them. What they might be able to do in that world was unclear; would there even be a place for them, and if so, what would it be?

Thirteen

Ehrlichman, in particular, viewed the future with uncertainty. In the first place, he wasn't sure he wanted to go to Washington. He had a realistic appreciation of his total lack of experience in government work. He was a good zoning lawyer, and he knew how to bring efficiency and order to the chaos of a campaign. But he was fully aware that these talents did not qualify him for a top job in the federal government. And he certainly wasn't interested in going to Washington to get lost in the shuffle, to be swallowed up by the giant bureaucracy. One of the reasons he had stayed in Seattle all these years was because he preferred being a big fish in a small pond—especially when the pond happened to be situated in such an attractive setting. For that too entered into Ehrlichman's indecision. During the inevitable post-election letdown, after having been on the road for several months, he could feel the old, familiar lure taking hold of him; visions of those big, fat strawberries once again danced through his head. So, although he was thrilled to have been part of the victory, and deeply relieved that the future course of America was in Richard Nixon's hands, his first impulse was to chuck it all at this point, and return to Seattle.

He had several talks with Nixon during this period, and there was at least one firm job offer that he turned down. He has steadfastly refused to reveal what it was except to say he would have been "a round peg in a square hole." Then eventually, through Haldeman's intercession, he was offered a job as White House counsel, a rather modest post that eventually he would pass on to John Dean.

He was attracted to the position of counsel in large part because of its narrow jurisdiction. The job would be legal work, for which he clearly had the credentials, yet at the same time he would not be thrust into the heavy, controversial issues (such as school desegregation) that the lawyers at Justice and other departments would have to confront. More than anything else, he would be Nixon's personal attorney, in charge of handling routine matters generally having nothing to do with the big Presidential policy decisions. In addition, he learned from Haldeman he would be called on from time to time to help out on certain political chores, such as keeping the lines of communication open to party officials and others who had worked in the recent campaign. That also appealed to him. Another thing which appealed to him was that the job would place him directly in the White House, under Haldeman, instead of off in some department or agency where he would have to work with strangers.

Through the early weeks of the new regime, Ehrlichman devoted almost all his time to two projects: drawing up a conflict-of-interest code for members of the White House staff and other Nixon appointees, and managing the President's personal finances. Among other things, he played an instrumental role in the purchases of the two Nixon homes at Key Biscayne and San Clemente. (At the time, this task seemed innocuous enough, though four years later, during the Watergate avalanche, it came out that these transactions involved certain irregularities—including the use of taxpayers' money to improve the President's own property.) Even after he settled in at the White House, it was still Ehrlichman's intention to stay just a few weeks—three or four months at most—and then go back to Seattle. However, he would soon be given ample reason to change his mind about that.

In Haldeman's case, there was never any doubt, in his mind or in Nixon's, about where he was going or what his official position would be. Unlike Ehrlichman, he did not feel any lure drawing him back to his former life. In fact, by this time he had become just a little bored with advertising; it was no longer the challenge it once had been. He felt ready to move on into a larger, more demanding sphere. Even when he was at J. Walter Thompson, he once told Hugh Sutherland, his boyhood chum and agency colleague, that what he'd really like to be, more than anything else, is "the executive secretary of a major corporation."

This was the kind of job Haldeman now envisioned for himself: he would hover on the doorstep of power, but his own position would not be endowed with any great authority. His duties in the White House, he knew, would be similar to those he had undertaken in the past. He would continue to serve as the overseer of Nixon's image, his top media man. For it was understood that the selling of the President did not end with the election; the carefully-packaged product was a delicate plant that would need to be watered regularly throughout the years ahead. And in addition he would be applying his managerial talents to the White House staff operation, seeing to it that all the internal administrative machinery hummed along at peak efficiency. That much Haldeman knew, for these assignments had been spelled out in his pre-inaugural conversations with Nixon. Beyond that, it was all rather vague; they would just have to wait and see.

Haldeman certainly did *not* expect to be given the kind of heavy-handed authority over Nixon's schedule and privacy that he had exercised during the recent campaign. The Presidential campaign had been a special situation, something he had had experience with —and he had been determined that Nixon not wear himself out, fussing over trivial details, the way he had in the past. His authority, buttressed by Mitchell's approval, had been total. It was also true that the people he had muscled out had only been speechwriters, grabby local politicians, and other nonentities; it had been very much in the candidate's interest to keep all those hangers-on at bay. So Haldeman had acted with confidence. At the White House, however, it would be different. There the people asking to see Nixon would be men of stature: foreign dignitaries, Cabinet officers, Congressional leaders, distinguished policy advisers. And, since Haldeman knew next to nothing about Washington and how the federal government worked (and was, therefore, just a bit intimidated by the strange world he was entering), he had no intention, at this point, of standing in the way of the ex-Governors and highbrow professors who were to be entrusted with forming policy for the new administration. It was essential, he believed then, that these men get in to see the President as often as possible. So, even though he might have control over access to the Oval Office (and he had been given to understand this would be one of his duties), Haldeman had reason to believe it would not be the same as it had been during the campaign. Then he had been a stern sentinel, jealously guarding Nixon's privacy. Now his role would be that of a smiling, deferential gatekeeper, ever ready to usher in the men of importance whose wise counsel the President would need in order to govern the country.

Yet, if at first Haldeman viewed his post as White House Chief of

Staff in fairly modest terms, he was not entirely a shrinking violet. Right at the beginning he moved to assert his authority over some key areas, and one in particular. Given his attitude toward the press, he was determined to make sure that *it* was taken care of. This meant that something would have to be done about Herb Klein, campaign press secretary. He liked Herb all right, and respected the fact that his fellow Californian had been one of the earliest soldiers in Nixon's army. But Klein still was prone to making the mistakes Haldeman first took notice of back in 1960. He still was too accommodating with the press, much too willing to concede that reporters covering Nixon had certain prerogatives. For a long time Haldeman had suspected that part of the problem was Klein's background. Herb himself was a former newspaperman, and still felt a certain camaraderie with those people. He enjoyed fraternizing with reporters over drinks and such. Well, this was not the sort of atmosphere Haldeman wanted to encourage at the Nixon White House. Press relations were to be strictly official, formally correct—and that's all.

So in the period just after the election, when all the various jobs were being filled, he persuaded Nixon to approve a new arrangement. Klein, the senior man with the broad experience, was anxious to avoid the grind of day-to-day press briefings. So he agreed to take on a newly-created post called Director of Communications, in which he thought he would be responsible for the press relations of the entire executive branch, with special focus on the Cabinet. Meanwhile, the routine, daily briefings at the White House would be handled by young Ron Ziegler, whose title would be simply "Press Assistant"—thereby downgrading, in one neat stroke, both his role and that of the reporters he'd be briefing. There would be no Press Secretary in the traditional sense. (Not long thereafter, Haldeman relented and gave Ziegler the official title.)

At first, every effort was made to convey the impression that Klein was taking on a position of real importance, but in reality he was being "kicked upstairs," away from the center of power. This would soon become a familiar Haldeman tactic. Pat Moynihan and Robert Finch, as well as others, were to receive similar "promotions," which turned out to be one-way tickets to limbo. In any event, it didn't take an old pro like Klein long to realize he had been had. He never complained though; in public he was always as bland and conciliatory about his own defeat as, in the past, he had been about Nixon's. Klein had it in him to be a communications adviser to the President in the mold of Eisenhower's Jim Hagerty, had he really been given a chance. But he wasn't. Or perhaps it was, as Haldeman and others later claimed, a case of Klein having the opportunity and not making the most of it.

Ziegler, naturally, was a Haldeman protégé. In fact, Ron had been his prize pupil at J. Walter Thompson, the junior staff man to whom he had entrusted the much-coveted Disneyland account. There was a wonderful, symbolic fitness to this. For in earlier years, while a student at the University of Southern California, Ziegler spent his summers working at the Mickey Mouse wonder spa as something called a "Jungle Boat Tour Guide." Later, at the White House, in his awkward attempts to be one of the boys, he would give reporters a rendition of his old Disneyland spiel: "Hi. This is Ron, your tour guide. Take a good look at the land, folks, because it may be your last look." Then, after the jungle boat had penetrated a bit into the Disney bush, Ron would point out to the folks: "On the left are natives on the bank. . . . The natives have only one aim in life and that is to get a-head."

In 1962, just one year out of college, Ziegler worked as a press drudge in Nixon's gubernatorial campaign, passing out handouts and that sort of thing. But his enthusiasm and dedication to Nixon impressed Campaign Manager Haldeman, and soon thereafter Ziegler started in at J. Walter Thompson. In the '68 campaign, he again worked as a press aide, though on a slightly higher level; sometimes he filled in as a "spokesman" and issued statements. Klein, of course, was still the head man, Nixon's official press secretary, and he remained in that customary role until after the election, when Haldeman came up with his sleight-of-hand maneuver.

Therefore, as the Nixon Presidency began, reporters assigned to the White House were greeted every day by a twenty-nine-year-old adman who, unlike the wayward Klein, had never been tainted with a working background in journalism. Blessed with what Mary McGrory has described as the face of a "sinful cherub," Ziegler would venture into press briefings, during those early weeks, with a cockiness that was not matched by performance. At times, his first response to a question would be to lapse into a catatonic gaze—what Army psychiatrists, accustomed to dealing with the fear of combat, call the "thousand yard stare." Nor were his verbal replies much better. His fractured syntax and cryptic, ad-world jargon were such that his answers became known as "ziegles" or "zigzags," and after a typical briefing reporters would compare notes, not so much to double-check accuracy, but in an effort to break the code. An example or two of typical ziegles will suffice: Question "Is General Hershey's replacement under consideration by the White House?" Answer: "There is no information that I have that would lead me to respond to that question in the affirmative." Question: "Was the decision also made prior to Friday's meeting to resume the B–52 bombings?" Answer: "I think I made it clear that when we were discussing the B–52 matter—the decision to delay flights of the B–52s for a period of 36 hours—that it related to the fact that the decision, when it was made, related to a period of 36 hours, and there was not a decision point after the decision to delay the flights for 36 hours to again order the resumption." To veterans on the beat who had dealt with the professionalism of his predecessors, from Jim Hagerty to George Christian, Ron would remain an object of mirth and wonder. Ziegler's nice-guy personality and dedication to hard work were appreciated by the press, but his lack of knowledge about the news business and his placing of loyalty to Haldeman above the public's right to know were not.

But Ziegler had no need of friends and supporters in the press corps; he had more than enough buddies around him inside the White House. He was only the most visible member of the young flock (all under thirty) which Haldeman had brought with him to Washington. There was Tim Elbourne, another ex–Disneyland man, who went on the payroll as an assistant to Ziegler in the press office. Dwight Chapin was named Nixon's appointments secretary. And Larry Higby, John Brown, and Ken Cole were appointed to Haldeman's personal staff. Chapin and Higby were especially close to Haldeman, and had carried out important assignments for him during the period leading up to the '68 election. Although Haldeman declined in 1966 to be personally on hand for the launching of Operation Comeback, he had sent Higby out from LA to join the small Nixon entourage put together for that midterm campaign. And in 1968, during the early run through the primaries, Chapin accompanied Nixon on every trip, serving as his personal aide. Both young men, of course, were also serving Haldeman, acting as his eyes and ears at a time when he, personally, was not marching at Nixon's side.

They reported back frequently, keeping Haldeman well informed.

The J. Walter Thompson Agency was not the only old school tie. Just as Haldeman and Ehrlichman first formed their alliance as classmates at UCLA, so was there a similar link binding the younger group of Californians—only more so. Ziegler and Elbourne were classmates at USC (1961) and belonged to the same fraternity, Sigma Chi. Chapin graduated from USC two years later. One of his classmates was Gordon Strachan, who also went to work for Haldeman in the White House, operating from there as his liaison with the Committee to Re-elect the President in 1972. Strachan finally appeared on TV screens as one of the more disillusioned witnesses at the Watergate hearings, and was later indicted in the Watergate coverup. Still another buddy from that USC class of '63 was Donald Segretti, whom Chapin later hired to do some political espionage in the 1972 Democratic primaries—a series of "campaign tricks" that later led to the criminal convictions of both Chapin and Segretti.

This then was the core of what was to become Haldeman's empire. In time there would be others, all of them cut from the same earnest, young-man-in-a-hurry mold. Jeb Magruder and John Dean are two more names that spring immediately to mind. But they came a bit later; this original band of California admen and fraternity brothers formed the nucleus.

Because of the heel-clicking, busy way they scurried about the White House, the first group soon became known as the "Beaver Patrol" (Haldeman, like Ehrlichman, has an Eagle Scout background), and they were as indistinguishable as crabs crawling over each other in a bucket. They all had the same short, spartan haircuts, though never quite as severe as Haldeman's Marine Corps brush. They all wore the same expressions of waxen solemnity, meant to convey their high purpose and noble calling. They all affected the same crisp, junior-executive manner to stress the point that they were busy, important people who had no time for amenities. They all kept their conservative-colored and -cut suit coats on, their collars buttoned and their ties firmly knotted in place. This last was a Haldeman preference: no working in shirtsleeves and no ties askew. And, because Haldeman disapproved of "mod" innovations and usually wore white shirts himself, white shirts became, for them, a required part of the uniform-of-the-day. Once in a while Ziegler, yielding to a reckless impulse of self-assertion, would show up in something as raffish as a "television blue" shirt, but that was definitely the outer limit. The members of the "Beaver Patrol" were, in short, physical and temperamental extensions of the man who brought them there.

This point became increasingly important as Watergate unfolded. Haldeman attracted, yea *demanded*, people who executed his orders. He did not welcome questioning. Important posts in the administration, just below the top, and later posts in the 1972 Nixon campaign were filled with Haldeman choices (Magruder, Strachan, Chapin). The Haldeman men were conditioned to translate ideas—even dumb ones—into action. They were not accustomed or encouraged to say, "Wait a minute, have you thought about this?"

When some of them became entangled in the barbed wire of Watergate, William V. Shannon of the *New York Times* would write: "They are Richard Nixon's children, these sad young men who come day after day before the Senate committee." This was true, but for most of them Nixon was an austere, aloof parent, one who certainly inspired awe and devotion, but always from a distance. As a father, he was not in the habit of visiting the prep school to see how the lads were doing. Through their years of service, their guardian and headmaster was Haldeman. He was the one who made sure they minded their manners and were always neat in appearance. And he was the one to whom they were truly beholden, to whom they gave their most intimate loyalty. They belonged to him.

This dependency, loyalty and personal devotion came out, almost poignantly, in the spring of 1973 when the scandal broke and Haldeman the Fierce suddenly became Haldeman the Fallen. On the day his forced resignation was announced, an ashen-faced Ron Ziegler confessed to a White House reporter, in his halting and sheepish way: "I guess—well, I'd have to say that I—I really love Bob Haldeman." It was the first and only time the reporter ever heard the word "love" used at the Nixon White House.

As the new administration opened for business, however, Haldeman was just one of several men Richard Nixon trusted enough to take into his confidence. Cabinet officers like Bob Finch, Bill Rogers, and John Mitchell also were Nixon intimates; in fact, these three friends were probably closer to the President, in a personal sense, than Haldeman was at first. Arthur Burns too had been, in his formal and academic way, an old Nixon friend. And although the other two professor advisers, Henry Kissinger and Pat Moynihan, had come into the White House as comparative strangers, there were signs that they too were establishing cordial personal relations with the new President.

Yet from the beginning Haldeman was in a unique position, and it gave him a decisive edge on the other insiders. Given the nature of their jobs, the Cabinet members and the advisers were concerned, first and foremost, with policy questions. When they visited the Oval Office, the emphasis was on the impersonal business at hand: charting goals, discussing options, planning and initiating programs for the new administration. Haldeman's situation was different. His role was essentially administrative. He was the man in charge of the President's daily schedule, the one who met with Nixon the first thing each morning to help set up the day's priorities and appointments. As such, he dealt directly with personnel matters, and so it was only natural that the President would choose to confide in him—not about policy so much, but about the policy makers themselves. Thus it was that in the course of these early weeks, through the winter and spring of 1969, Haldeman became privy to Nixon's innermost thoughts about the men he had hired to give shape and definition to his Presidency. Here was information no one else received in quite the same intimate way, and it proved invaluable.

From Nixon's own lips he learned that the President was generally pleased with his foreign-policy people. He approved of Mel Laird's orderly plan for withdrawing American troops from Vietnam; and he liked the way Laird was bringing the Pentagon generals and Congress into line behind the new war policy. Over at State, his friend Bill Rogers was concentrating on the Middle East; the major goal there was to work out an agreement with the Russians on settling the Mideast problems that could open the door to détente, and a new era in U.S.-Soviet relations. The President was confident that Rogers was making the right start on all that. But the man who came in for the most glowing praise was Kissinger. The President considered Henry a real find. From reading the professor's books and articles he had assumed that they would get along philosophically. What he had not known beforehand was that Kissinger's working style would blend in so well. Henry was always very thorough and well organized. No matter what the problem was, he always made sure that all the options were put on the table for consideration. And he was not one to blow his own horn. He waited to be asked before

offering his own recommendation. All in all, the President was enthusiastic about his foreign-policy team.

But the domestic operation was something else again; there the
reviews were mixed. Among Cabinet officers, John Mitchell was singled out for high marks. The President fully approved of the steps
his Attorney General was taking to put some law-and-order muscle
into the new administration. That was one campaign pledge he was
determined to keep, and John was doing his best to see to it. Another
bright spot in the domestic Cabinet was the quiet fellow he had put
in over at Labor, George Shultz. The President had known nothing
about this man previously, but he found himself responding favorably to Shultz's keen mind and efficient, unassuming manner. Yes,
Shultz was someone he would want to keep his eye on.

With some of the others, however, he was not so happy. The three
former Governors, in particular, were a source of irritation to him.
George Romney at HUD, for example. He could do without Romney's self-righteous, evangelistic style, his insistent tendency to turn
every meeting into a platform for sermons. What especially rankled
the President was the way Romney had badgered him into continu-
ing the Model Cities program. He had not wanted to keep that
program going (he considered Model Cities one of the worst boon-
doggles left over from Johnson's Great Society), but Romney had
blustered so hard for it that the President went against his better
judgment and gave in. He knew it was a mistake, however, one that
he'd later have to rectify.

John Volpe, his Transportation man, was another fast talker—
smoother than Romney, but the general effect was the same. Volpe
had coaxed the President into approving the SST project, and he was
afraid that was another decision he'd regret, especially if Congress
refused to go along with it. (Congress did refuse, and Nixon did regret
it.)

As for Wally Hickel at Interior, Nixon considered him to be just
another fist pounder, another blowhard who kept shooting his mouth
off at Cabinet meetings about matters he didn't know the first thing
about. In short, the President was sorry he had named the three
Governors to his Cabinet. To a large extent, of course, they had been
political appointees—payoffs of one kind or another—but nevertheless, if he had had it to do over again, he would have bypassed all
three of them.

On a more personal level, the President was dismayed by the way

Bob Finch was performing over at HEW. His long-time friend was proving to be indecisive and wishy-washy. Instead of taking over HEW the way Mitchell had taken over Justice or Laird the Pentagon, Finch seemed to have become the captive of the liberals and social engineers who were so deeply entrenched in that massive bureaucracy. Some of his major appointments to key sub-Cabinet posts were so flagrantly liberal that they had provoked cries of outrage in Republican circles. Most disturbing of all, from the President's point of view, was the fact that his two close friends Finch and Mitchell were heading on a collision course over school desegregation, and other sensitive issues including voting rights for blacks and aid to education.

The point Nixon kept coming back to time and time again in his private talks with Haldeman was that he didn't want to get bogged down in all this. He wanted to be left alone so he could devote the bulk of his time and attention to foreign policy. The gears were meshing there, and plans were moving forward in an orderly manner. These were his priorities: first deal with Vietnam, and after he had succeeded in turning that around, then on to the larger quest for a new order of world stability—what he would later define as the "generation of peace." With all that to concentrate on, the last thing he needed was George Romney and John Volpe barging into the Oval Office to pressure him into approving their pet projects. And under no circumstances did he want to be put in the position where he, personally, would have to act as mediator in the ugly disputes that were starting to flare up between his two friends Bob Finch and John Mitchell.

What he needed, he kept insisting, was someone inside the White House to take charge of this domestic mess and bring some order and cohesion to it. What he needed was someone to organize domestic affairs the way that Kissinger, with his calm, impartial judgment and efficient working habits, was organizing foreign policy. His original choice for that role had been Arthur Burns. That had been the whole point in naming him Counsellor and giving him Cabinet rank. He was the one who was supposed to coordinate the entire domestic program; it had all been spelled out at the time of his appointment. But that was another appointment the President was having second thoughts about. Arthur was a good man, and absolutely brilliant in his field—no one better when it came to forecasting business cycles.

But he was, alas, no generalist; he had no feel for issues and problems beyond economics. And, to be blunt, he lacked drive and spark. No, Arthur was not working out the way the President had hoped he would.

Nor was Moynihan the right man for the job he had in mind. The President was very high on Pat, very high indeed. Like Kissinger, he was considered a real find. As we've noted, there was no one the President would rather summon to the Oval Office for long chats than Moynihan. His flair for generating ideas and coming up with novel and innovative approaches to domestic policy was a constant delight. But Pat's value at the White House, while considerable, was also limited. He was poor at organization, which is largely what the job of domestic coordinator called for. Perhaps most important, he was too much of a liberal and Democrat. It was one thing to give him a free rein on an isolated project, like welfare reform, but if he were put in charge of organizing the entire domestic program, Burns and Mitchell, as well as others, would be sure to howl. So Pat also had to be ruled out. But if not Burns or Moynihan, then who? Who could the President call on to serve as his domestic Kissinger?

As we know from the White House transcripts, Haldeman became increasingly bolder in his personal relations with Nixon once his unchallenged power within the administration was secure. But in the course of these early confidential sessions he was still deferential even to the point of obsequiousness. So, as Nixon rambled on, Haldeman himself said little. Every now and then he might toss in a remark to buttress a point the President had made. He might disclose that he too found Arthur Burns rather tedious; or with great delicacy he might remind the President that there always had been a certain indecisive streak in their good friend Bob Finch. For the most part, however, he just sat back and listened; he was content to serve as Nixon's sounding board, just as he had been back in 1961 when their close relationship was formed during the gestation period that brought forth *Six Crises*. But finally, at one point, after Nixon had complained for the umpteenth time about his need for someone to coordinate domestic policy and take all that off his back, Haldeman suggested that perhaps John Ehrlichman could be of help. John didn't have that much to do as White House counsel and he would be only too glad to be of assistance.

The President welcomed the suggestion, but frankly he had his reservations. He had nothing but praise for Ehrlichman as a campaign man, for his ability to take charge of advance procedures and other logistical problems. Nor did he doubt for a moment that John had been a good lawyer out in Seattle, but his field of expertise was rather narrow, and he really didn't have the background in any of the major domestic issues he would have to deal with if he took on these other responsibilities.

That was true, Haldeman agreed. But, as he understood it, the President wasn't really looking for another policy expert; he already had all of those he needed, both in the Cabinet and at the White House. As he understood it, what the President needed most was precisely someone who did *not* have his own policy axe to grind, but who was good at organizing and pulling all the loose ends together. The President needed not an advocate but a broker who could bring together policy ideas for full, balanced consideration and decision by the President. That is, someone who would represent the President's interests alone, rather than always promoting his own favorite program or project. Well, these were John Ehrlichman's strong points: efficiency and personal loyalty. He had demonstrated that time and time again, most recently in the last campaign.

Now it was Nixon's turn to agree. Put in that light, Ehrlichman didn't seem like such a poor choice, after all. So he decided to give it a try. He authorized Haldeman to bring Ehrlichman into the domestic area on a sort of trial basis. There would be no upgrading of title or anything like that—at least not at first. John would remain White House counsel, but with the expanded responsibility of trying to iron out some of the wrinkles in the new administration's domestic policy.

At this moment, a certain Rubicon was crossed. Though reached quietly, almost secretly, in the period between spring and midsummer of 1969, this decision would prove as significant as any Nixon would make in all his Presidency. For one thing, it signaled the start of John Ehrlichman's rise to power. But, even more important, it brought the Haldeman-Ehrlichman axis directly into the sphere of policy formation, and for both men that was a quantum leap from the modest duties that had previously been their sole concern. Of course, none of this was perceived at the time. It would, in fact, be months before the effect of the decision would be felt in government circles, and years before its full impact would register on the country Nixon had been elected to govern.

It is altogether possible that John Ehrlichman would have succeeded as a domestic Kissinger even if he had been entirely on his
own. That, however, is something we'll never know. For from the
start his friend and patron was there at his side, guiding and advanc-
ing him along every step of the way. And, as Haldeman moved to
clear the decks for Ehrlichman, he steadily solidified and expanded
his own authority over the Nixon administration. One of Haldeman's
first targets was Arthur Burns.

One morning that first spring of 1969, as Burns emerged from a
meeting with the President, he suddenly remembered something he
had meant to tell Nixon but had momentarily forgotten. But as Burns
turned to go back into the Oval Office, there was Haldeman blocking
his path. "Your appointment is over," he said curtly. Burns protested
that it would only take a moment, but Haldeman stood firm. (In his
view it was just like this absent-minded professor not to have properly prepared himself for a meeting with the President.) He told
Burns to put whatever it was that had slipped his mind in writing and
he would be sure to include it in the President's reading folder.

Since at the time Burns was still very much the senior man on the
White House staff, it is interesting to speculate on what might have
happened if he had chosen to pull rank. But he didn't force the issue.
In fact, he really wasn't angry at Haldeman so much as contemptu-
ous. During his long career in academia, Burns had come across
many a dean's secretary who, because of his or her proximity to the
boss, had taken on ludicrous airs of self-importance. He put Haldeman in that category. Because Haldeman was always so servile and
obsequious in Nixon's presence, and because he sometimes performed menial tasks, such as bringing the President coffee (something Burns himself would never dream of doing), the professor
made the mistake of assuming that Haldeman was nothing more than
a glorified flunky, a mistake that others would also make. Like Burns,
they would live to regret it. Burns considered it unseemly for a man
of his position to get into a petty argument with this officious clerk
Nixon kept at his side. So, with an airy wave of his hand, he let the
matter drop and returned to his office. That incident taught Haldeman all he needed to know about Arthur Burns.

It was also during this period that Haldeman made his first, tentative moves to assert his control over the Cabinet. Men such as Kissinger, early, and Connally, later, understood power and the symbols

and gestures due it. Each of them, in their own way, made Haldeman grant them direct access to the President. But members of the original Nixon Cabinet either had no such understanding of power, its symbols, and the importance of maintaining its privileges, or failed to act on the understanding quickly enough. (Laird was an exception. He fought but lost, partly because among Cabinet men he was alone, and partly because Kissinger, as well as Haldeman, was boxing him out.) For members of the original Cabinet, however, telephone conversations with Haldeman began falling into the following pattern:

"I'll do my best, Mr. Secretary, but it doesn't look good. The President plans to be tied up all week on Vietnam. If you could possibly put it in writing and get it over here, I'll make sure he sees it first thing in the morning."

This would be greeted by a sigh on the other end of the line, though of course no loyal Cabinet officer could object to the President spending so much of his time on Vietnam. Then: "Okay, whatever you say, Bob. But I was hoping to talk to him in person about this. We need a final decision fairly soon."

"I'll convey your wishes on that point, Mr. Secretary. But, if you really want to speed things along, it might be a good idea to talk to John Ehrlichman."

"Ehrlichman? Why Ehrlichman? I thought Arthur Burns was—"

"Well, yes, of course, Dr. Burns should be kept up to date on what you're planning. But, as I understand it, he's also tied up at the moment on a special assignment. And the President has asked John Ehrlichman to lend a hand on some of these matters."

"Ehrlichman, huh? Okay, Bob, I'll give him a call. Thanks for the tip."

"Don't mention it, Mr. Secretary. Anything we can do to help. That's what we're here for."

Often, after concluding a conversation like this, a tight little smile must have crossed Haldeman's lips. Based on the testimony of his aides, who were acquainted with his mood and manner of operating, it was apparent that Haldeman was discovering that these big shots, these so-called men of stature, were as easy to push around as the hangers-on he had beaten off during the campaign. They might know a lot more than he did about Washington and the federal government, but they did not know Richard Nixon the way he did. As time went on, it became more and more apparent to him that the government and Richard Nixon were one and the same. Without the President, these other people could do nothing, and he, Bob Haldeman, was the person they had to deal with to get to the President. Having dallied with personal power on a modest scale in the past, he now was getting a taste of the real thing—and he liked it. He liked it enough to desire more. A lot more.

Fourteen

BY THE summer of 1969, Haldeman could feel the arteries of power in Richard Nixon's Washington flowing in his direction. In these first few months, he already had accomplished a great deal. Through the seemingly calculated and programmed daily ineptitude of Ron Ziegler, he exerted—with the President sometimes directly involved—total control over the White House press relations. With the other members of the "Beaver Patrol" carrying out his every command, he was in control of much of the administrative machinery inside the White House. And now, through the rising influence of John Ehrlichman, the whole apparatus of domestic policy was starting to fall into line within his orbit. Yet, for all of this, Haldeman's view of the world around him was not entirely serene. Even within the White House itself, there were still a few people who made him uncomfortable, and whom he viewed with suspicion. For example, there was almost no way he could adjust to the flamboyant presence of Daniel Patrick Moynihan.

Glancing around the table at a meeting of the White House senior staff, Haldeman's eyes would sometimes come to rest on Pat Moynihan. Whenever that happened, he found himself looking at everything that he was not. He was the supreme Nixon loyalist looking at a man who had served and loved the Kennedys. He was a conservative Republican looking at a liberal Democrat. He was a Los Angeles adman looking at a Harvard professor. He was Beverly Hills looking at Hell's Kitchen. He was a country-club WASP looking at the son of an Irish barmaid. He was a teetotaling Christian Scientist looking at a self-indulgent papist. It wasn't so much that he personally disliked Moynihan; indeed, there were times when he too could be charmed by the man's wit and flashy brilliance. It was just that deep down, in his viscera, Haldeman could not come to grips with the astounding fact that this Kennedy-Harvard-Irish-Catholic-Democrat was actually *there*, working with *them*, in Richard Nixon's White House. It was like coming across a revised edition of *The Iliad* and finding Odysseus on the side of the Trojans; or going to a Civil War movie and seeing Stonewall Jackson riding alongside Sherman, through Georgia. It was surreal.

But the professional in him, the polished adman who knew just how to woo a client, could not help but admire the suave selling job Moynihan had done on his boss. In many ways, he had done much the same thing; back in the early 1960s, when he had moved to ingratiate himself with Nixon, flattery and an eagerness to please also had been his chief weapons. But the great difference, in Haldeman's view, was that he had meant it: he had been a *sincere* sycophant who truly did worship Nixon, his hero. Whereas Moynihan, he suspected, was simply a con man playing games, trifling with Nixon's affection so that he might influence Presidential power to achieve his own sinister, Kennedyesque goals. Moreover, Haldeman was personally frustrated because his favorite tactic, the one that had worked so well to keep others at arm's length, only backfired when he tried it on Moynihan. Insisting that Moynihan state his business in writing only inspired him to dash off one of his fancy memos, and that, invariably, enabled him to sink his hooks even deeper into Nixon.

Still, Moynihan did have his vulnerable points, portions of soft underbelly here and there, which Haldeman did his best to work over. For example, his slipshod working habits and those of his staff. The President was aware of all that, and surely he could not have approved. Then, too, there was his brashness, his flippant putdowns; his general attitude of disdain toward other members of the White House staff. In particular, Moynihan's condescending treatment of Ron Ziegler ("Ronald, you really should read a book now and again") and the rest of the "Beaver Patrol" did not endear him to Haldeman.

Best of all, for Haldeman's purposes, were the reports of his drinking, the stories—true or not—that kept filtering back to the White House of Moynihan in his cups, staggering out of Georgetown bars late at night and hollering, rather coarsely, for his government limousine. To make sure no one gets the wrong idea, there was never the slightest suggestion that Moynihan did any sipping on the job, or that he was afflicted with what is sometimes described as a "drinking problem." To clarify further, there's a line from a play written by another American Irishman, Eugene O'Neill, in which a character, taking issue with the charge that Shakespeare was a lush, retorts: "I don't doubt he liked his glass—it's a good man's failing—but he knew *how* to drink." So, like Shakespeare, Pat Moynihan may have "liked his glass," but that never, in any way, interfered with his work. (Friends claim he got better by the glass.)

However, to the strictly abstemious Haldeman and Ehrlichman, liking one's glass (even in moderation) was not "a good man's failing," but simply a failing, period, a sign of moral weakness. So it was that the two of them fell into the habit of referring to Moynihan, in the presence of visitors, as "our Oscar Wilde." It was all very jolly and innocent on the surface, a playful tribute to his Irish wit and epigrammatic prose style. But implicit in it was the less-flattering side of Wilde: the dandy, the dilettante. And, lurking beneath that, the darker side: the decadence, the self-indulgence.

Still, they had to be careful. It was all right to drop hints here and there about Moynihan's general behavior and life style, but it would not have been wise for Haldeman and Ehrlichman to make their objections more strenuous than that. This was especially true during the spring and early summer weeks of 1969, when they had just begun to edge their way into the domestic policy area and were, therefore, not entirely sure of their ground. For this was precisely the period when Moynihan's own influence was at its height. These were the days when he was busy cajoling the President into approving his bold scheme for welfare reform. Both Haldeman and Ehrlichman had come to realize by now what lay at the heart of Moynihan's strength. It wasn't so much his charm or his Harvard background or his "thoughtful" liberalism, as the President called it. They were all assets, no doubt, but the real secret of his success with Nixon was his close identification with the Kennedys. Begrudgingly, Haldeman and Ehrlichman had learned to appreciate the value of this connection—though they did not agree with his appointment to Nixon's staff —as a gesture on Nixon's part toward balance, or as an attempt to establish a link with Camelot. To Haldeman and Ehrlichman, Moynihan was there not so much to provide a link to the Kennedy Past, but to serve as a much-needed buffer against the ominous threat of Kennedy Present—the last surviving brother. They knew this threat was a matter of paramount concern within the Oval Office during the first six months of Nixon's Presidency—before the world ever heard of Mary Jo Kopechne or a small island off Cape Cod called Chappaquiddick.

It was not recognized at the time, and wasn't recognized publicly by many even later, but Chappaquiddick and Edward Kennedy's behavior there was a decisive event for the Nixon Presidency, for after Chappaquiddick the restraint provided by the daily thought that Nixon might have to face Kennedy for re-election was gone. Not for good, as it turned out. But gone for a long while. And with it went the early Nixon administration goal of trying to be more centrist than conservative in domestic policy. Yes, there were other factors in the shift to conservatism. And, yes, it *might* have happened sooner or later in the first term anyway. But, beginning with Chappaquiddick and Kennedy's handling of the tragedy, Nixon and those close to him veered toward the political right. Their hearts had been there all along, but many of their actions had not. Haldeman, especially, strongly felt a sense of relief and release.

Looking back on it, Moynihan's days may have been numbered from then on. There were other factors involved here, too, but that was no small one in determining how Moynihan and his welfare-reform ideas were eventually to fare. Central to understanding the significance of Chappaquiddick is remembering how much political clout Ted Kennedy wielded during those months before it occurred.

Bobby Kennedy's assassination in 1968 had unleashed a fresh torrent of emotion joining with the old river from Dallas to form a mighty confluence. The reservoir for all this resurgent Kennedy fervor was the last of the brothers; having picked up the "fallen standard," he would now bear the burden of legacy and carry the legend forward.

By 1969, his period of private mourning over, Teddy was coming on like a tidal wave. Public-opinion polls showed him so far out in front for the 1972 Democratic nomination that it was embarrassing for other party luminaries whose names were listed as also-rans. His legions were everywhere. Even within the Senate, where both his brothers had been notably weak in their days as backbenchers, he had enough strength to depose one of the Southern grandees, Russell Long, as majority whip. Simply to have made such a challenge against the sacrosanct Senate establishment was an audacious act, and his victory over Long stunned and dazzled official Washington. Party leaders, young and old, were in his hip pocket, and his support on the grassroots level was both broad and deep. He was constantly on the go, speaking out everywhere on issue after issue. Indeed, he carried about him the aura of a shadow government, a thriving and palpable government-in-exile, just waiting to take over.

This too was the period when it was most fashionable to dismiss Nixon as a caretaker President, a one-term fluke, who would be well-advised in '72 to do as Coolidge did and choose not to run, rather than face the fury of a Ted Kennedy onslaught.

All these facts were duly noted at the White House, and there were days when the entire place seemed to be in the grip of a morbid obsession, not unlike the mood aboard the *Pequod* when Ahab was at the helm. Nixon didn't clump about with a piece of whale bone for a leg, but then he had no need for a graphic reminder of the permanent wound the Kennedys had inflicted on him. Everyone remembered. His great nemesis, *his* Moby Dick, was still Out There, churning up the waters, making waves, moving relentlessly toward him for another confrontation. Hence, there could be no rest for captain and crew members alike, until the Kennedy menace had been met and defeated. Just as Ahab's mariners were under orders to bring in every report no matter how slight of the White Whale's whereabouts, so the people at the White House were put on the alert to take note of everything Kennedy did or said. They were to pass it on to the top, to First Mate Haldeman. There was a tight-lipped intensity about this Kennedy obsession that permeated the White House in those days, as well as a deep sense of apprehension. In their own way, the Kennedys seemed as indestructible as Moby Dick. One of them gets killed, and another pops up to take his place. This one is slain, and a third brother emerges, stronger than ever. Even worse, beyond him there was a whole new generation coming up, ready to carry the legacy forward. The President could hire a Moynihan, talk about "bringing us together," hint about federal aid to parochial schools, and make other moves to try to drain off some of the Kennedy strength here and there. But there seemingly was no end to the Kennedys, no escaping them. Thus the dread sense of inevitability: Kennedy Kennedy Kennedy Kennedy. The very name beat against the White House walls like a jungle drum of impending doom.

Then came deliverance.

It is surely nothing more than a bizarre coincidence that man's first landing on the moon and the Chappaquiddick accident occurred on the same summer weekend, though who knows what hidden significance future historians may find in that. Nixon, yielding to a characteristic weakness for hyperbole, chose to call the scientific triumph "the greatest event since Creation." (An ill-advised claim, if only because it got him in dutch with his good friend and spiritual comforter Billy Graham.) Wherever the moon landing ranks on the list of Big Happenings since Eden, there is no doubt that the event that weekend which had the most telling impact on America's political future was the other one—the plunge off that bridge on Chappaquiddick Island.

The official White House reaction, of course, was an expression of sympathy—"for the girl's family and for Senator Kennedy as well." But behind the scenes, in the Haldeman-Ehrlichman world, the air was filled with jubilation over what had happened to their enemy. Here, at last, was a Kennedy "tragedy" of a different sort, one they could sink their teeth into. At the time of the two assassinations, decorum had required even the most virulent Kennedy haters to wear false masks of piety, to participate in the agonized mood of the moment. But this time a Kennedy had stumbled and fallen in such a way that they could afford to smile a bit, although it *was* terrible about the girl's death. There was a quality of smugness in their glee, stemming from the comforting conviction that this sort of thing would never, could never, happen to their man.

So there it was: all of a sudden Moby Dick, the great sperm whale, was beached and gasping for survival. As the impact of Chappaquiddick set in, it became apparent that Teddy Kennedy would not dare run for the Presidency in 1972; or if he did, and the Democrats were crazy enough to nominate him, he would be on the defensive, from beginning to end. The one and only issue would be Kennedy's personal morality. Haldeman and his band of media men would see to that.

Oddly enough, in some respects, however, the incident only served to intensify the Kennedy obsession in the Nixon White House.

Thus it was that Tony Ulasewicz, the sardonic gumshoe on the White House payroll, was assigned to keep the heat on, to dig through the Chappaquiddick muck, to seek interviews with girl friends of Mary Jo Kopechne in an effort to find out anything more that might further humiliate Teddy. Every political pundit worthy of the name was giving his assurance that Kennedy was out of it, as far as 1972 was concerned. But the obsession at the White House ran so deep that they weren't about to take any chances; they had to be absolutely sure he was not just on the ropes, but was truly down for the count.

In their more sanguine moments, when they were able to rise above their Kennedy fixation, Haldeman and Ehrlichman and other political strategists at the White House were almost amused by what the nature of the opposition was apt to be in '72, with Teddy on the sidelines. About all that was left of Humphrey, in their view, was his impressive larynx. Goldwater's quip about Humphrey in 1964 was still current. "Hubert Horatio Wind, who speaks at three-hundred-and-twenty words a minute, with gusts up to three-hundred-and-eighty." No problem there. Ed Muskie, the only other Democrat the White House then considered even a possibility for the nomination, was dismissed as a bland moderate who would fail to ignite the voters —a rather accurate assessment, as it turned out. George McGovern had not yet emerged as a practical candidate; his appearance would come much later.

From this point on, the major concern at the White House, in looking ahead to '72, was not with the orthodox Democrats so much, but with George Wallace and what he might do as a third-party force to take votes away from what John Mitchell and others were calling "the new Republican majority." In other words, the political picture had changed dramatically. With Kennedy seriously wounded, there was no longer any real threat from the left. Now the main problem was on the right, where all those Wallace people were waiting to be convinced that they had a friend in Richard Nixon.

The White House now went out of its way to adopt openly and with vigor the divisive, inflammatory approach that would embroil it in controversy after controversy all through the months ahead. Soon the administration would be engaged in its bitter dispute with the Senate over the Haynsworth and Carswell Supreme Court nominations. Both Southerners, their names were sent to the Senate on the recommendation of Southern Strategist Mitchell, and the obvious motive was to attract new supporters in the heart of Wallace country. (At this time, Nixon was trying to send *them* a message.) And, in the fall of '69, the malcontents on the right throughout the country were given a huge, juicy bone to chew on in the form of Spiro Agnew. His lively fusillades against the media and other "Eastern elitists" who indulged in effete snobbery (essentially the group that Wallace himself liked to characterize as "pointy-head intellectuals") were carefully orchestrated by the White House. The Veep's major speeches, the ones with the real muscle in them, were composed by Nixon's top conservative speechwriter, Pat Buchanan, and the whole Agnew operation went forward under the overall guidance and direction of Haldeman, and, through Haldeman, the President.

As this new, pugnacious mood took hold of the White House that first autumn, Pat Moynihan, it appears upon reflection, became a marked man. As far as Haldeman and Ehrlichman were concerned, Chappaquiddick had taken all the wind out of his sails. The whole rationale behind Moynihan's presence at the White House, the reason for his influence on the President, was to protect the administration's left flank, to shore up the lines of defense there against what everyone had assumed would be the inevitable Kennedy assault. Welfare reform was merely the most ambitious example of this strategy, this "dishing it to the Whigs," as the Tories in Disraeli's time called it. After Chappaquiddick, there was no longer any need for such nonsense. By the fall of '69, Haldeman and Ehrlichman felt free to move against Moynihan, to cut him down.

Still, they had to proceed cautiously. They could not afford to be brazen about it. For one thing, Moynihan still had all the momentum of welfare reform going for him. The great wave of public approval for the program was then at its crest, and Moynihan's name was popping up everywhere as the golden boy of the new administration, the guiding genius behind Nixon's innovative domestic policy. Then, too, he continued to get along well with the President personally. With his quips and easy banter, he still had the gift of making Nixon laugh. But even here Haldeman could detect that the Moynihan charm was starting to wear a little thin. That gave Haldeman and Ehrlichman some encouragement, and with the post-Chappaquiddick mood working in their favor, they stepped up their subtle attacks on Moynihan's obvious shortcomings.

Ever since the spring of 1969 when he had been given the green light to step into the domestic area and help coordinate policy, Ehrlichman had been coming on at a steady pace. He was basically a plodder, a straight-ahead runner. Actually, he didn't need much in the way of speed or swivel-hip moves, not as long as he had Haldeman running interference for him. An irony worth noting is that Ehrlichman's first major contribution in his new assignment, the one that earned him a pat on the head from Nixon, was to put together the final version of the welfare-reform package. He incorporated all the various elements—the basic Moynihan proposal along with George Shultz's "workfare" additions—and strengthened some of the language in an effort to mollify conservative objections. Then, during the in-house debate that broke out in the early summer weeks, he gave every appearance of standing solidly in Moynihan's corner against those like Burns and Agnew and Romney who tried to talk the President out of approving the measure. Because of his role in that squabble, Ehrlichman, unlike Haldeman, acquired an early reputation as someone who was at least willing to listen to liberal and experimental programs. There was some justification for this. Ehrlichman in general was—again, unlike Haldeman—undoctrinaire. He was open to experimental ideas. He sometimes expressed his frustration when nobody came up with innovative proposals. For example, he pressed hard for new approaches to vocational training. And supported enthusiastically several suggestions that he got.

It is also true that in some instances his appearance of sympathy for programs not consistent with a conservative Republican bent was a case of his simply being astute enough to go with the grain, to go with the flow of power—which at that moment was moving in Moynihan's direction.

In the aftermath of Chappaquiddick, however, the flow began moving in the opposite direction, and by November it was coalescing around Ehrlichman himself. Haldeman had done an excellent job laying the groundwork, suggesting to Nixon and officials in various administration posts that Ehrlichman be used as their contact with the President. That month Nixon announced the elevation of Ehrlichman from White House counsel to Assistant to the President for Domestic Affairs. Now he had the title and rank to go with the job.

Now he was officially the domestic counterpart of Henry Kissinger. But, since this was essentially a Haldeman operation, it goes without saying that Moynihan also received a "promotion." He was given the lofty and imperious title of Counsellor to the President—that alone should have tipped him off, since for the past nine months he had been watching, with wry amusement, the steady disintegration of Arthur Burns in that role. (Or it might have occurred to him to check with Herb Klein, who would have been happy to enlighten him on the subject of Haldeman-style promotions.)

But whatever illusions Moynihan may have had at the time, they were soon dispelled; for from this point, he was effectively boxed out of the decision-making process. All that now remained to finish the job was to sabotage his welfare program, and it was decided the best way to accomplish that would be to discredit him with his own people—the Harvard crowd and other Kennedy liberals. In the early weeks of 1970, the aforementioned Moynihan memos began to be leaked, unexpectedly and inexplicably, to the press. The *New York Times*, the newspaper Nixon at that time hated most, was a prime recipient of these leaks. At least one of the memos was circulated with Nixon's comments on it.

Haldeman himself had direct responsibility for such memos, though few believed that he personally did the actual leaking. Who did remains a mystery. A few of Moynihan's friends suspected Haldeman aide Tom Huston; others thought it was Patrick Buchanan. But it was difficult for many who knew the inside workings of the White House to believe that any such memos could or would have been leaked without Haldeman's wanting them to be. Possible, but not probable. At the very least, he allowed it to happen.

Regardless of who did the leaking, at a time when Moynihan should have been devoting all his time to drumming up liberal support for the welfare-reform bill, he was busy trying to explain to black leaders that "benign neglect" really didn't mean what they thought it meant; or doing his best to assure former Harvard colleagues and other friends from academe that no, sir, he certainly didn't have any of *them* in mind when he referred to the college professors who had toppled Lyndon Johnson from office. In the meantime, welfare reform went on to defeat, and soon thereafter Pat Moynihan left the Nixon White House.

Thus a new course was set. What had started out as a euphoric reaction to Chappaquiddick soon crystallized into a hard and bitter determination to poison the atmosphere with the politics of spite and vendetta—to wage unceasing war on Congress, the press, and, as we shall see, even members of their own Cabinet who dared question the wisdom of the new strategy. This resulted from the concentration of power in the hands of men who, because they had no background experience themselves in the world of Washington—or in government on any level—chose to transform the White House into an embattled fortress, sealing it off from what they regarded as an alien city around them, a city infested with hostile groups seeking to bring harm to them and their President. Yet, because so much of the poison was bottled up within those walls, it was inevitable that it should spread inward, and that they themselves should become its ultimate victims. The new tactics—the sharp veering away from centrist politics, the bitter resolve to attack and divide, and the tight concentration of power—were brought on, at least in part, by what happened at Chappaquiddick. That experience was harrowing enough for the people directly involved: for the family of the young woman who died, and for the U.S. Senator who accidentally caused her death. Yet, beyond that, it may be said that Chappaquiddick helped to unleash the forces that, in time, would make a wreckage of Richard Nixon's Presidency.

Fifteen

THE poison infected even the best of them, as we learned when evidence revealed that Henry Kissinger had agreed to the wiretapping of his subordinates and his friends in the press corps. It supposedly had been done in the interest of "national security," just like so much else: the raid on the office files of Daniel Ellsberg's physician, for instance. The official justification is worthy of consideration. But it must be weighed against other possibilities, including the one that Kissinger and Nixon also thought the taps to be in their personal best interest. For example, consider that from the moment

Kissinger first came to the White House, he found himself under enormous pressure to prove that his dedication and first loyalty were to those within the walled castle and not to the trendy social set he cavorted with on the outside. For as he moved through the White House during those first months, quietly building his own empire and cultivating a cordial working relationship with the President, he constantly came under Haldeman's baleful eye. It is true that Haldeman didn't find Kissinger's presence there quite as unsettling as Moynihan's. (On a scale of ten, in rating a record of previous nonsupport of Richard Nixon, a close association with Nelson Rockefeller was worth about a seven; as a Kennedy man, Moynihan qualified for the full count.) But Kissinger was basically from the same world. Like Moynihan, his points of identity were Harvard, Manhattan, and Georgetown, the three intellectual centers of the liberal Eastern Establishment. That alone was enough to make him suspect.

Then, in addition, Haldeman had trouble coming to terms with Kissinger's rather exotic background. His Jewishness may have been a factor here, though, in truth, Kissinger was not especially ethnocentric—certainly no militant Zionist, as Golda Meir has had occasion to find out. The most distinctive thing about him, the discordant note that hit Haldeman in the face every time Kissinger opened his mouth, was the fact that he was a *naturalized* citizen, or as the retired executives in their blazers sitting around the yacht club back home in Orange County might put it less euphemistically, he was a foreigner. This was what set Kissinger so much apart from the Legionnaires and Chamber of Commerce types who, in Haldeman's view, formed the core of Nixon's constituency. What could he possibly know about the Silent Majority out there in the heartland? And what would go through *their* minds when this European egghead talked to them about Communism and such things? Here was a man who, as a spokesman for President Richard Nixon, said "ve" for "we" and "zis" for "this." *Real* Americans, from places like Ohio and Indiana, knew how to pronounce the *w* and *th* sounds. We might note that during his first three years in Nixon's White House Kissinger's television appearances were largely confined to silent film only; he almost never spoke on camera. Media man Haldeman had a hand in that decision. (Kissinger himself apparently was of two minds about whether he should or shouldn't be heard a great deal on radio and television: Haldeman helped him settle on a "no" answer.) So there it was: Kissinger was Rockefeller-Harvard-Jewish, and talked like the father of the Katzenjammer Kids. In sum, his credentials were almost as outlandish as Moynihan's.

But the great difference was that Kissinger didn't make himself vulnerable in any of the ways Moynihan did. For example, he was more than a match for Haldeman and Ehrlichman in the area that accounted for so much of their success with Nixon: efficiency and organization. And he was a real workhorse. When the heat was on, he could out-Prussian all of them, even the classic grind himself—the man in the Oval Office who for years has attributed so much of *his* success, going all the way back to college days, to the fact that he does his homework more thoroughly than others. Kissinger could not be faulted on that score. His work habits were impeccable.

Nor did he play the intellectual snob. In reality, Kissinger was if anything even more arrogant than Moynihan, and he too had a flair for irreverent wit. But he took great pains, especially in the beginning, to keep those attributes under wraps, although he did allow them to surface in his private talks with Nixon on those occasions when he sensed they would have a positive effect. Kissinger also was adept at dancing the President around the historical-analogy maypole. His model was Metternich, rather than Disraeli, and there must have been times, after back-to-back meetings with his two Harvard profs, when Nixon felt as if he had been cut adrift somewhere in nineteenth-century Europe. But outside the Oval Office Kissinger didn't flaunt his intellectualism. He didn't go in for long, pontifical lectures in the Arthur Burns manner, nor did he antagonize other members of the White House staff the way Moynihan did, with sly putdowns and obscure name droppings. Indeed, he made every effort to play down his professorial side, concealing it behind a mask of affable deference and unfailing courtesy.

A one-time member of Kissinger's White House staff, who admires his former boss as a "genius," says of Kissinger's relationship with Haldeman: "Henry kissed Haldeman's ass—regularly in the beginning, less as time went by, but always some. He did it because he knew he had to. He recognized early Haldeman's power, and his potential for considerably more power." He even treated the Beaver Patrol with a modicum of respect, and given the sophisticated circles he was accustomed to traveling in, that was a real triumph of iron discipline over temptation. In short, Kissinger did not shoot sparks off like a volcano. Instead, he did his best to blend in with the other stalks in the cornfield, and they in turn, flattered by the show of respect he accorded them, responded in kind and welcomed him as one of their own. Well, almost one of their own. He *did* talk funny.

Kissinger knew his immigrant status was a problem, and in the area of patriotism he pulled out all the stops. He was determined to prove that he was as true-blue American as the rest of them; that his pulse also quickened whenever he heard the blare of a Sousa march, and that he too felt a surge of patriotic pride when he went to see *Patton* and other war movies. At one point, it's true, he did draw the line. He was one of the few in the Nixon White House who declined to go along with Haldeman's Rotary Club inspiration that it would be a nice touch for their image if everyone, from the Chief on down, wore little flags in their lapels so the rest of us would be sure to know what country it was they were governing. The flags also were intended as a message to the voters, suggesting to them subliminally that a vote against the Nixon White House would be a vote against patriotism. Kissinger's sensibilities were just a bit too refined for that.

Also, he declined, publicly at least, to engage in any hate-the-press campaigns. There have been, from time to time, various stories about Kissinger privately indulging Haldeman's loathing of reporters, and some of them may be true. But most of Kissinger's own personal dealings with journalists, even those critical of him, always have struck most reporters as models of fairness and respect.

Yet, in many important respects, he played the Haldeman game in accordance with the prevailing rules. He was determined not to have his loyalty questioned—either as an American or as a Nixon man (one and the same, as far as Haldeman was concerned)—and if this meant he had to conceal the truth, dissemble, condone wiretaps, then he would. He might feel a twinge of conscience now and then, but he would do it. He would be the good American, as it came to be defined at the Nixon White House; and that enabled him to win even Haldeman's grudging acceptance.

So, as the troops moved into the second year of Nixon's Presidency, the power structure at the White House was locked into place. Henry Kissinger was secure in his post as Special Assistant for National Security Affairs. John Ehrlichman was settled in as his domestic counterpart, and Bob Haldeman, as the man who tightly controlled access to the Oval Office and served as manager of the overall operation, enjoyed more administrative power than either of the other two. Moreover, as Ehrlichman's patron, he could also take a direct hand in domestic policy decisions. Now that the three of them had consolidated their positions on the inside, the next move was to assert their primacy over the Cabinet.

For Haldeman and Ehrlichman, this meant zeroing in on certain key targets and ignoring others. For example, they did not concern themselves with the ultimate fate of Bill Rogers at State or Mel Laird at Defense. It was never their intention to become intimately involved in foreign policy, for they realized that, whatever their area of competence, it did not extend to the subtleties of global diplomacy. That, they understood, was Kissinger's field of expertise, and therefore Rogers and Laird belonged to him. By this time, they had seen enough of Kissinger's behind-the-scenes maneuvering to know that he already had taken much of the play away from his two Cabinet rivals in regard to the Vietnam war and on other issues as well. The dramatic assault, the full-scale usurpation, had not yet begun (1971 would be the year for that), but as they observed the skillful way he was gathering his forces, they knew it was only a matter of time before he would overrun both Rogers and Laird. This was still another reason why Kissinger was able to form an alliance with the Haldeman-Ehrlichman axis. As the foreign-policy man, he did not come into their line of fire, the way Burns and Moynihan had. In terms of power, Kissinger was moving on a parallel rather than a collision course. He might be, in Haldeman's eyes, a shifty foreigner who was a little too chummy with Harvard liberals and Washington journalists, but Haldeman could at least derive comfort from the fact that he was *their* shifty foreigner. That is, he did his thing from within the White House, where he could be closely watched.

Nor was the name of Treasury Secretary David Kennedy on their "hit" list. Haldeman and Ehrlichman were aware that Kennedy's lackluster performance had been a disappointment to Nixon, and by the early months of 1970 they knew that the economy was a serious problem, and was threatening to become a critical problem. But they also knew of the President's plan to bring Labor Secretary George Shultz into the White House to take charge of the newly-created Office of Management and Budget. And they correctly assumed that, once ensconced there, Shultz would assert his authority over the administration's economic policy—that he would become, in effect, an economic Kissinger. This was just fine from their point of view. For, like the President they served, Haldeman and Ehrlichman had no real grasp of the complexities of the Dismal Science, and they did not want to get bogged down in a morass of economic problems. Hence, they were more than willing to let Shultz shoulder the burden of Nixonomics. In taking on that responsibility, he would pose no serious threat to their power since he also would be moving on a parallel rather than a collision course. What's more, he too would be based inside the White House, and would therefore be under constant scrutiny.

So they left it up to Kissinger and Shultz to bring State, Defense, and Treasury into line, while they concentrated on the rest of the Cabinet. Yet, as they drew up their list, Haldeman and Ehrlichman realized that there were some department heads who, because of their narrow jurisdiction, were already so far removed from the center of power that they weren't worth fussing over; they could be dealt with in a perfunctory manner or, in some cases, simply ignored. For example, they saw no reason to disturb the serenity of Postmaster General Blount as he went about the task of phasing his giant bureaucracy out of the Cabinet. The conversion of the Post Office Department into a quasi-private government corporation to be called the Postal Service was moving along on schedule, and by 1971 the transition would be complete. No need to tamper with that operation.

Then there was the post of Labor Secretary. By tradition, it had never amounted to much in a Republican administration, but during Nixon's first year in office it took on an inflated status because of the President's high regard for George Shultz. However, Haldeman and Ehrlichman were confident that once he moved on to his new job at the White House Labor would recede into the bureaucratic backwater, where it belonged. And they were right: Shultz's successor at Labor, someone named Hodgson, quietly settled into the role of a functionary and made no discernible effort to horn in on the big policy decisions.

They adopted a similar "let-sleeping-dogs-lie" attitude toward Clifford Hardin over at Agriculture, a decision that also made sense, for at that time farm problems were not perceived as a major concern. In many respects, Hardin was lucky. Although he served in the Agriculture post for nearly three years, the great controversies that engulfed his department (e.g., the Russian wheat deal and soaring food prices) erupted after he had been replaced by Earl Butz. Hardin's one big moment came in the early part of 1971, and it went almost unnoticed at the time. He was the man who staunchly resisted all pressures from the dairy industry to raise the price of milk. It was his refusal that prompted the dairymen to take their case to the White House. As it was later revealed, Nixon personally ordered Hardin to grant the price increase, though perhaps one should not too quickly assume that there was any connection between that decision and the fact that the dairymen, at or about the same time, pledged some two million dollars to the President's re-election campaign. Nor should one necessarily make a connection with the fact that it was just a few months after the milk squabble that Hardin was replaced at Agriculture.

The reference to campaign contributions quite naturally puts one in mind of Maurice Stans. As Secretary of Commerce, he took over a Cabinet post that had been on a long and steady decline ever since its heyday in the 1920s when Herbert Hoover used it as a springboard to the Presidency. Stans did nothing during his three years there to reverse the trend. But then he wasn't put there to help shape policy, or anything like that. Stans's real value to Richard Nixon was as a campaign fund raiser. He had an almost supernatural gift for putting the arm on potential contributors—or "fat cats," as they're known to the cognoscenti. At the mere sound of Stans's voice, checkbooks would fly open and the requested figures would urgently be scrawled in. (Big figures, too, with lots of zeros.) His impressive performance in the '68 campaign was, of course, just a dry run for the awesome feats he would accomplish to fill the Nixon coffers for 1972. And in the interim the post of Commerce Secretary, with its natural pipeline to the lairs of fat cats, was an ideal place for him to maintain old contacts and develop new ones. (One of these contacts, alas, was with a financier of dubious reputation named Robert Vesco, and through that association both Stans and John Mitchell would eventually be brought to trial in federal court. Both were acquitted on all charges growing out of Vesco's secret campaign contributions.)

So, for the most part, these minor Cabinet officers were left alone to carry out their routine assignments. As long as they didn't try to see the President on their own initiative, or otherwise make nuisances of themselves, they could count on not getting any static from the White House. Later on, after they had built up their empire, Haldeman and Ehrlichman would move to impose their direct authority on these smaller departments and other government agencies as well. But first things first, and in the early months of 1970 all their attention was directed toward the five major domestic departments, and the Cabinet officers who had been appointed to run them: John Mitchell (Justice), Robert Finch (HEW), George Romney (HUD), John Volpe (Transportation), and Walter Hickel (Interior). Their immediate and most obvious targets were those favorite Presidential whipping boys, the three ex-Governors. Of this trio, let us start with their most celebrated victim.

Sixteen

At the time of his appointment, there was no reason to suspect that Wally Hickel would go on to become the angry rebel in Richard Nixon's Cabinet. One of the seven self-made millionaires to be given a portfolio, he seemed to blend in snugly with the other Horatio Alger types. Just another Republican entrepreneur Nixon had hired to give his Cabinet a respectable, board-of-directors look. The fact that Hickel had made his pile as a builder and land developer aroused the concern of environmentalists, and their darkest suspicions were soon confirmed. In his first news conference after being named to run Interior, Hickel came on like a cartoonist's version of an earth-gouging developer, utterly insensitive to the needs of conservation. First, he disclosed that he didn't see much point in "conservation for conservation's sake." Then, as he tried to step out of that one, he went in up to his knees from the environmentalists' viewpoint, with the warning that "if we set standards too high, we might even hinder industrial developments." And finally he came up with a touch of mysticism worthy of comparison with the famous Zen Buddhist line about the sound of one hand clapping. "A tree looking at a tree really doesn't do anything," he proclaimed.

Because of this performance and his background in Alaska as a man who had aimed many a bulldozer at trees caught looking at each other but not doing anything, Hickel had a hell of a time getting his nomination confirmed. The Senate Interior Committee gave him a thorough going-over, and he wasn't cleared for duty until after the inauguration, and after the rest of the Cabinet had been sworn in. Taking note of this at Hickel's own swearing-in ceremony, Nixon reached for an appropriate cliché, and vowed: "So if I may present him now with the Biblical scripture, 'the last shall be first' as far as this administration is concerned." The words were prophetic and would later be remembered with great irony.

To everyone's surprise, perhaps even his own, Wally Hickel underwent a genuine conversion—and soon he was displaying all the zeal of a convert. In deeds as well as words, he became an ardent defender of conservation. For example, he blocked the construction of a huge airport near the Florida Everglades, and cracked down hard on oil companies responsible for oil spills off the coast of California and in the Gulf of Mexico. These decisions were well publicized, in large part because they coincided with the ecology movement, which was then all the rage. (The peak would come in April of 1970 with the celebration of Earth Day.) But unfortunately Hickel's emergence as the administration's "good guy" in the fight against pollution did not endear him to the White House. The loyalists there felt he was using the fashionable issue to build up his own political following, especially among college students, who at the time were very much "into" ecology. Then, too, the oil companies and other victims of Hickel's policies were grumbling, and with their solid Republican connections (though some were Southern and Western Democrats), their grumbles quickly reached the Oval Office. And beyond that he had become an irritating nuisance in other ways. In his pushy, combative manner, he openly began to criticize the President's economic game plan, intimating his disapproval of other administration policies as well. So, by the early months of 1970, Hickel was viewed by the White House as the antithesis of a loyal team player, and even before he wrote his famous letter of protest, it was decided by the President, with encouragement from Haldeman and Ehrlichman, that when the time came for a little housecleaning he would be the first to go.

Hickel wrote his letter to the President in the spring of 1970, at a time when the White House was under heavy siege. In hindsight, the period stands out as the low point of Nixon's first term, for by the spring of '70 the strident and divisive policies undertaken the previous fall had begun to reap a bitter crop. Here are just some of the events that unfolded during those weeks:

—Early in April, the Senate rose up in indignation and rejected G. Harrold Carswell, just as it had rejected Clement Haynsworth five months earlier. Thus Nixon became the first President in this century to be dealt the humiliating rebuff of having two consecutive Supreme Court nominees turned down by the Senate.

—On the last day of April, the President, his spirits bolstered by having just seen the movie *Patton*, announced the decision to send U.S. troops into Cambodia, at one point choosing to justify it by saying, "I would rather be a one-term President than be a two-term President at the cost of seeing America become a second-rate power." This, of course, was just what everyone was waiting to hear: how the military escalation might affect *his* political future.

—The Cambodian invasion (or "incursion," to use the White House euphemism) touched off a storm of protest. Except for two big antiwar demonstrations the previous fall, the administration had been quite successful, up to this point, in blunting the edge of Vietnam protest. But now the rage and frustration which had been simmering just beneath the surface were once again in full eruption. All of a sudden the mood was reminiscent of Johnson's last two years in office, and as was the case then, most of the anger came boiling up from college campuses.

—Reacting to the student reaction, Nixon, in a spontaneous interview given as he emerged from a Pentagon briefing, referred to "these bums . . . blowing up the campuses."

—Four days after the Cambodia announcement, on May 4, National Guard troops were sent to the campus of Kent State University in rural Ohio to put down an antiwar demonstration. During the confusion they opened fire on the students, killing four of them.

—In response to Kent State the White House had no trouble deciding where to pin the blame. The killings "should remind us all once again that when dissent turns to violence it invites tragedy," read the official statement issued in the President's name by Ziegler. Many of Nixon's own staffers, especially the young ones, were shocked at what they thought was the insensitivity of the statement. Some refused to believe that the President had seen the statement before it was issued, much less written it. Speculation was rampant that Ziegler (never known as a writer) wrote it in haste, or that he had written it with help only from Haldeman. The speculation was never confirmed.

Later in the week, the grieving father of one of the Kent State victims appeared on nation-wide television. He recalled that shortly before his daughter was killed she had told him how much she resented being characterized as a "bum" by the President of the United States.

—The Kent State tragedy opened up fresh arteries of protest and outrage, and the following weekend an estimated 100,000 persons converged on Washington for a mass demonstration outside the White House. At the time of the Vietnam Moratorium the previous October, the cry of the antiwar groups had been an almost plaintive "give peace a chance." But now, on this Saturday afternoon, the protesters gathered in front of the Washington Monument exploded with a fury that seemed even to surpass their earlier hatred of Johnson. "Fuck Richard Nixon," they shouted over and over again. "Fuck Richard Nixon . . ."

There were a few older, veteran professional agitators in the midst of this, playing upon what they knew to be deeply-felt convictions held by many, if not an actual majority, of the nation's college youth. But Haldeman and his minions, from their offices inside the White House, encouraged the President in his belief that only a tiny minority of college-age young people shared the protesters' opinions, putting most of the blame on older agitators. Nixon's men refused to acknowledge even the possibility that Nixon, his actions, and some of those people around him had heightened polarization on the issue through at least the appearance of insensitivity.

Watching those young Americans that afternoon, it took a supreme act of will to recall that just one year earlier the promise of the new administration had been to "bring us together" and "lower our voices." It was in the midst of this cheerful atmosphere that Wally Hickel wrote his letter.

Actually, Hickel had been trying to get his message through to Nixon for several weeks. Because his new role as high priest of ecology put him in close touch with college groups, he was aware of the deepening resentment toward the Nixon administration that was taking hold on the campuses, especially in the months since Agnew had begun his tirades against student protesters. Hickel was genuinely disturbed by the situation and tried to set up a private meeting with Nixon to discuss the problem. By this time, however, in early 1970, Haldeman's Wall was firmly in place; for the Interior Secretary, in particular, it was impregnable. As a matter of fact, he had trouble even getting through to Haldeman or Ehrlichman, much less the President. So, when Kent State happened, Hickel decided he had let the matter slide long enough, and two days after the killings he fired off his letter to Nixon. He accused the administration of setting out "consciously to alienate . . . our young people," and he strongly implied that much of the problem was the President's own isolation. He urged Nixon to "consider meeting on an individual and conversational basis with members of your own Cabinet"—a rather unsubtle slap at the Wall. Hickel then signed it—"Faithfully yours, Wally"— and sent it off, while through his office a copy of the letter got out to the press.

At the White House the next day, everything hit the fan, and soon Haldeman was on the phone to Hickel. "I have the letter, Wally," he said in an icy tone, "but it's already on the AP wire."

A few days later, during that weekend, when Hickel's friends the young people were assembled outside the White House to pay homage to the President in their vigorous way, Haldeman called the author of the now-famous letter at home. This time, he dispensed with the first-name amenity. "Mr. Secretary," he began, and then proceeded to inform Hickel that he was *not* invited to the White House religious service the next day, the ultimate ostracism, as far as Nixon's inner circle was concerned. Hickel, fully aware that this qualified as cruel and unusual punishment, demanded to know if it was Nixon's personal wish. "The President was in the room when the decision was made," replied Haldeman, with finality.

Yet, depriving Hickel of his spiritual sustenance at the Sunday services was about as far as the White House was prepared to go at this point. The troublemaker from Alaska would have to be sacked —there was certainly no question about that—but not right away. The problem was that all the furor over the letter had made him a bigger hero than ever among college students, other anti-Nixon groups, and even among some Republicans. So, with the midterm election coming up in the fall, the last thing the White House wanted was Hickel barnstorming the country as a martyred Cabinet officer, speaking out against the President. As LBJ once said, in explaining why it would have been impolitic to fire J. Edgar Hoover: "Better to have him inside the tent pissing out than on the outside pissing in."

So it was decided that the Hickel problem would be resolved by what Ehrlichman began describing, in private, as an "interlocutory decree"—i.e., there would be a divorce, all right, but it would not become official until after the election. The only trouble was, the party being divorced was not informed of the arrangement; nor, for that matter, was anyone else outside the inner circle. In fact, once the strategy was agreed on, the White House began an elaborate charade to convince the outside world that Hickel was still in good odor, that Nixon continued to have the highest personal regard for his outspoken Interior Secretary. Why, to hear them tell it, there just wasn't anyone the President would rather sit around and chew the fat with than good ol' Wally. And this snow job was performed on Hickel himself. A week or so after he wrote the letter, he was invited to the Oval Office for that private meeting he had so eagerly sought, and as he passed through the Wall, the atmosphere couldn't have been more cordial. But, because of all the fuss the letter had caused, Hickel was still wary. So his first question to Nixon was: "Mr. President, do you want me to leave?" Nixon, seemingly stunned by such a crude and offensive suggestion, threw up his hands and replied: "Now that's one option I've never considered." (If you are keeping score, there's another statement for your "inoperative" file, for the truth was of course that Nixon had already given his blessing to the "interlocutory decree.")

The stratagem worked. The flareup over the letter was soon forgotten, and before long Hickel found himself back in the deep freeze. There he remained until after the midterm election, when it became safe to finish him off. Yet even then the White House made an effort to avoid letting people know what really was happening. John Mitchell was assigned to inform Hickel that it would be a good idea if he resigned, quietly. But the Alaskan bulldog would have none of that. "The only man who could ask me to quit would be the President," he told Mitchell. This only infuriated Haldeman and Ehrlichman all over again, for they understood just how deeply Nixon detested such unpleasant personal confrontations. But Hickel was leaving him no choice in the matter, so finally, on Thanksgiving Eve, the Interior Secretary was summoned to the Oval Office for the last time. There, with Ehrlichman standing at the President's side (to bear witness, to stiffen his resolve?), Nixon asked for Hickel's resignation. At last the deed was done.

For Wally Hickel, the method of execution had been a long, drawn-out process, a Chinese water torture. Now came Haldeman's specialty: the guillotine. The next working day, Haldeman sent one of his hatchet men, Fred Malek, over to the Interior Department to mop up. Setting his scaffold up in an empty office, Malek called in six of Hickel's top deputies and told each of them, one by one: "We want your resignation, and we want you out of the building by five o'-clock." His basket filled, he then returned to the White House and presented the six heads to Haldeman. Just like that, Hickel's department was decimated.

In cutting down Hickel, Haldeman and Ehrlichman clearly had specific approval from the President. They may not have had it when they first went after him but at least they eventually got it. But, in their maneuvering of other less-notable and not-quite-so-high-ranking people in and out of jobs, they often appeared to operate on their own authority. Malek's quick strokes with the axe at Interior on Hickel's subordinates had the look of just such an operation.

Sometimes—and this appeared to be one of them—Haldeman and Ehrlichman acted out of a subtle mixture of knowing what the President's intentions, gripes, concerns, and fears were and the assumption that he probably wouldn't object. Other times they acted in the belief that they knew him well enough to know what he wanted even before he did. Haldeman's maneuvering of former Kansas Congressman Robert Ellsworth off the White House staff early in the administration appeared to have been one of those cases.

There were also times when Haldeman or Ehrlichman or both appeared to operate simply on their own authority, getting rid of people with whom they personally had problems. Haldeman's firing in 1973 of long-time Nixon friend and admirer Bob Taylor—although that is not how it was made to appear, a firing is what it was—seemed to have been such an instance. Taylor was head of the White House Secret Service detail. He had disputed Haldeman on how much protection the President needed, when, and where. And he had talked back to Haldeman when what Taylor believed to be principle was involved.

There were, certainly, many other times when Haldeman and Ehrlichman could truthfully say they were only "carrying out orders"—explicitly indicated by the President. But Hickel left Washington convinced that the idea for firing him had not originated with Nixon.

Named to replace Hickel was Republican National Chairman Rogers Morton, a team player if there ever was one. With Morton at the helm, the Interior Department soon faded into the shadows and drifted further and further away from the center of action. This is not to say that the legacy left by Hickel's aggressive policies in the conservation field was altogether ignored. But from this point on all the initiative on the ecology front would come, not from Morton's office at Interior, but from the newly-created Environmental Protection Agency (established in the summer of 1970) and the energetic Hoosier picked to run it, William Ruckelshaus. There was, of course, no crime in that—Ruckelshaus, in fact, was regarded as one of Nixon's better appointments—but it stands as just another example of how executive power in Richard Nixon's Washington was systematically drawn away from its traditional source, the Cabinet, and replanted in ad hoc groups set up by the White House.

Hickel's insistence on making a public spectacle of himself by refusing to bow out quietly had the side effect of saving George Romney's job. He too had been slated for dismissal right after the midterm election, for by the fall of 1970 no one in the administration was more out of tune with the prevailing mood in the Nixon White House than the Secretary of Housing and Urban Development.

Romney had come into the Cabinet with a strong sense of personal mission, fueled in part by his natural zeal and evangelism. As Governor of Michigan, he had been deeply shaken by the riots that erupted in the black ghetto areas of Detroit in the summer of 1967. That experience convinced him that drastic measures were needed to save America's major cities, which he saw disintegrating into enclaves of black poverty and despair surrounded by affluent, lily-white suburbs. So he came to Washington with a resolve to make his department the focal point for the new administration's domestic policy. True, HUD was a new Cabinet post (having just been established three years earlier) and therefore did not have a tradition of power behind it. But, since Romney was the best known of all the Cabinet appointees, he assumed that he had been given HUD because Nixon shared his belief that the crisis of the cities was the chief domestic problem facing the country. Hence, it was only natural that the new President would want a man of his stature to take charge of Housing and Urban Development.

Grossly overestimating his mandate (lack of self-esteem was not one of Romney's problems), Romney came on like a tiger in the early weeks of '69, arguing for the continuation of LBJ's Model Cities program with such force and passion that Nixon felt he had been pressured into accepting something he really didn't want—and, as he later confided to Haldeman, he resented it. In the months that followed, Romney persisted in his pressing demands for more housing and other costly programs for the cities. This alone was enough to make him an irritant, as far as the White House was concerned, but what really sealed his doom was his proposal for an ambitious housing program that would bring racial integration to the suburbs. That was an ironclad no-no, for it struck right at the heart of what might be called the Northern Flank of the Southern Strategy.

The Nixon hard-liners (Haldeman, Ehrlichman, Mitchell, *et al.*) understood only too well that the Wallace constituency, which they hoped to graft onto their own to form the new Republican majority, was not to be found exclusively below the Mason-Dixon Line. As avid students of the white backlash that had been crackling across America ever since the days of the civil-rights movement, they knew that in the North, as well as the South, there were plenty of disgruntled blue-collar workers who complained, on the one hand, that the "niggers" were too lazy to work, then, on the other, that the "niggers" were out to take away their jobs. And the hard-liners also knew that in the white-collar, middle-class suburbs, North as well as South, there were related fears, although generally expressed with more gentility. There, the concern was over the "colored" and what would happen to their neighborhoods and real estate values if the "colored" were allowed to move in. The code phrase for all this around the White House was one that Ehrlichman, in particular, used to spout with relish: "It'll play in Peoria." That would be his comeback time and time again, when asked to defend a policy decision that had aroused the ire of black groups or white liberals and moderates. "No sweat," he'd say. "It'll play in Peoria." To clarify, it should be explained that Peoria, the pride of central Illinois, had been singled out for this citation because it was one of the few cities of any size that Nixon carried in 1968. Thus, Romney's proposal to build federal housing projects for blacks in the midst of white suburbia was clearly viewed as the sort of thing that would *not* play in Peoria. And, the more he pushed it, the more the White House came to regard him as not just an irritant who wanted to waste money on the cities, but as a genuine threat to their basic political strategy.

To make matters worse, there was his combative personality, his Mormon fervor. Romney was never content to discuss the race problem simply in pragmatic, political terms; for him, it had to be a moral issue, a religious crusade. But neither the Quaker sitting in the Oval Office nor the two Christian Scientists stationed outside his door appreciated Romney's sermons on the subject. They didn't care to be told that, as high government officials, it was their Christian duty to help channel some of the blessings of white America toward the blacks and other minority groups. So, during the months leading up to the '70 midterm election, it was decided that as soon as Hickel was disposed of Romney would be the next to go.

But Hickel's refusal to play docile and take his medicine without protest fouled up the plan. His public firing touched off another furor, and in that atmosphere the White House didn't dare risk following it up with a second stormy dismissal. A discreet effort was made to induce Romney to step down quietly (once again John Mitchell—"Mr. Bad News"—served as intermediary), but when word came back that the Housing Secretary did not want to resign and would probably raise a squawk if he was pressured out, Haldeman and Ehrlichman gnashed their teeth, but held their fire. For they knew that in the aftermath of Hickel that's all they needed: the impassioned Mormon bringing the wrath of Brigham Young down on their heads.

So instead Romney was simply put on ice for the remainder of the first term. He was kept well outside the real councils of influence, out where his subversive schemes for moving blacks into white suburbs could do little harm. In fact, the freeze had been in effect for months, long before the midterm election. As early as the summer of 1970, Romney was already so far removed from the decision-making process that he confided to a friend, "I don't know what the President believes in." Then, in a tone of disillusionment and disgust, he added: "Maybe he doesn't believe in anything."

As for the third ex-Governor, John Volpe, he too had fallen out of favor at the White House by mid-1970, but not to the extent of being a candidate for early dismissal. Volpe's saving grace was his genial personality. While viewed as a chatterbox and a glad hander, he nevertheless did not grate on the President or Haldeman and Ehrlichman in the same way Hickel and Romney did. That enabled him to hang on to his job as Transportation Secretary, although steps were taken to rein him in and keep him under wraps.

Like Romney on Model Cities, Volpe was able to talk the President into approving a controversial project (SST) in the early weeks of 1969 when Nixon felt besieged by overzealous Cabinet officers. But that wasn't his only triumph. A few months later, even after Haldeman and Ehrlichman had moved into the breach, Volpe persuaded the President to go along with his plan for saving the nation's intercity passenger railroads through a new program of federal subsidies. (Originally called Railpax, the name was later changed to AM-TRAK.)

In contrast to the blustering, hard-sell approach of a Romney or Hickel, Volpe's weapons were cajolery and seduction. He was not quite the polished master of these arts that Pat Moynihan was, but he did have a knack for exploiting areas where the President was inclined to be soft and sentimental. For example, in the case of SST, he shrewdly appealed to Nixon's desire to see America stand as "number one" in the world in just about everything. Volpe's argument, simply put, was that, since Britain and France and the Soviet Union were moving into the new field of supersonic transport, then by cracky, the United States should have its *own* SST, and a better one. Arthur Burns, then in his brief role as domestic overseer, denounced the SST as an extravagant folly, and other White House advisers joined him in opposing it. But Nixon succumbed to the notion that somehow America's prestige was at stake and gave SST his blessing—though later, after heavy opposition mounted in Congress and elsewhere, he would regret that decision.

If anything, Volpe was even more shameless in the argument he put forward for the rail subsidies. He evoked romantic images of America's past when passenger trains gave people the opportunity to travel about and see their wonderful country. Despite his disappointment over not being picked as Nixon's running mate in 1968, Volpe must have been paying attention the night of the acceptance speech in Miami Beach when the nominee conjured up a vision of himself as a lonely boy in Yorba Linda lying in bed at night listening to train whistles and dreaming of faraway places. Volpe's chief adversary on this one was none other than Ehrlichman (apparently trains hooting in and out of Santa Monica never rang his bell all that much), but that didn't matter. For this was one of the rare times that a Cabinet officer with limited clout was able to carry the day in a head-to-head clash with Ehrlichman.

But that was it for Volpe. If the President was unable to resist such sentimental appeals, then Haldeman and Ehrlichman would resist them for him, for there was no telling what the smooth-talking Transportation Secretary might be selling the next time—electric cars, perhaps, or bicycles built for two. Volpe had also hurt himself in his promotion of AMTRAK because it put him in the position of opposing the interests of the oil-automotive-highway-construction complex. But more damaging by far was his habit of arguing with Haldeman and Ehrlichman, especially Ehrlichman, and his frequent criticisms of the young and inexperienced members of the White House staff. For example, he once said, "I sweet-talk some top executive to leave his one-hundred-thousand-dollar-a-year-plus job to come down here, and he ends up having to go over to the Office of Management and Budget and do a fertility dance before some kid bureaucrat over a couple of hundred thousand dollars for a new program." So Volpe also was consigned to the administration's living graveyard, along with Romney and others who continued to hold fancy titles even though they had been stripped of any major function or responsibility. But he had the satisfaction of seeing at least one of his programs go through. AMTRAK, approved by Congress in 1970, began operating the following spring; and, although it got off to a rather shaky start, it went on to become a moderate success. SST, however, went down to defeat. It was killed by Congress in May, 1971, at a time when White House relations with Capitol Hill were at such a low ebb that many Republicans joined with Democrats in shelving the project. When a Democratic supporter of SST taunted Volpe about this, he dropped his affable manner and replied: "They weren't voting against SST. They were voting against John Ehrlichman and his German Mafia in the White House."

So much for the fate of the three men who gave up state governorships to accept positions in Richard Nixon's Cabinet. They came
in as outsiders and, having failed dismally to establish positive personal relationships with the President, they remained outsiders. And
that, of course, was what made them such easy targets. Haldeman
and Ehrlichman knew all along they could move with impunity
against this trio of Cabinet officers. But they had no such advantage
working for them when it came to dealing with the two most important members of the domestic Cabinet. For, whatever there was to
be said about Robert Finch and John Mitchell, they clearly were not
outsiders. That was the one thing—perhaps the only thing—they had
in common.

Seventeen

THERE was no doubt from the beginning that Finch or Mitchell would become the dominant figure in Nixon's domestic Cabinet.
George Romney may have had his dreams of grandeur, but to more
detached observers it was evident that, because of their intimate
relationship with the new President, Bob Finch and John Mitchell
would be the men to watch. During those pre-inaugural days at the
Hotel Pierre, most of the smart money leaned toward Finch. He was
the winter book favorite.

For one thing, he was vastly more experienced than Mitchell. It
was a point often overlooked in the power struggles that followed,
but while Finch had devoted almost all his adult life to politics and
government, Mitchell was quite new at the game. His stint as Nixon's
campaign manager in '68 was his first significant venture into politics,
his first departure from the world of Wall Street and his lucrative
practice as a bond lawyer. And, although he yielded to Nixon's urgent
plea to take on the post of Attorney General, he really didn't want
the job. He had no particular interest in Washington and the inner
workings of the federal government. But Finch was just the opposite.

He was eagerly looking forward to the challenge of a high position in the new administration, and one reason he asked for Health, Education, and Welfare was because he thought it offered the best opportunity in terms of his future career. For unlike Mitchell Bob Finch was a man with strong political ambitions of his own.

For a long time he had lived entirely in Richard Nixon's shadow. Back in the early Congressional years, when they had met and become friends, he had been the young protégé, just out of college. It was on Nixon's urging that Finch went back to school to get his law degree, and while enrolled at USC he wrote a campaign pamphlet entitled *The Amazing Richard Nixon.* By the time of the 1960 campaign, when he first surfaced to national attention, his identity was so closely bound to Nixon's that he was often described as the Vice President's "alter ego," just as Ted Sorensen was seen in that role vis-à-vis Kennedy. But the great difference, all along, between him and someone like Sorensen or Haldeman was that Finch hoped not only to serve his leader but to emulate him—to follow in his footsteps as an active player, charting his own political course. So in the early 1960s, having served his apprenticeship, Finch began to concentrate on his own future in California politics. By 1966, he had built up enough of a following for himself so that in running for Lieutenant Governor on the Ronald Reagan ticket, he outpolled the popular conservative by some 100,000 votes. At last, he had something going for him besides his long association with Nixon. At the age of forty-one, the former protégé and alter ego was making it on his own.

So Bob Finch's own political star was rapidly on the rise by the time 1968 rolled around. Still, he did not yet feel independent enough to say yes when Nixon, in one of the most generous gestures of his long career, chose to express his gratitude for their twenty years of friendship by asking Finch to be his running mate. Finch was deeply touched by the offer and there were tears in his eyes when he turned it down on the grounds that he could not put Nixon in the position of having to defend the ticket against the inevitable charges of "cronyism." Later, after Nixon had settled on his eventual choice, Finch would chide himself for having been so fastidious. Although in many ways a modest man, he at least had a high enough opinion of himself to realize that he would have been better for the ticket, and for the country, than Spiro Agnew. Still later, Nixon inquired if the man he once had to prod into going to law school would like to be his Attorney General. But Finch said no to that, too. In recent years, he had focused his attention on the issues of social progress, and what government could do in that area. And, since he hoped that would be the prime concern of Nixon's domestic policy, he chose to take on the sprawling bureaucracy of Health, Education, and Welfare. "HEW is where the action is," he said at the time. He was right about that. His mistake was in assuming that he could handle it.

Bob Finch was never the impassioned liberal he was often reputed to be during his months of travail at HEW. But, when he started out, he gave every sign that he was determined to be, at a minimum, reasonable and progressive—a leader who would not knowingly make enemies of blacks and poor people. His major sub-Cabinet appointments alone seemed to reflect an almost gleeful desire to arouse the wrath of conservatives, and arouse it he did. For the number-two position of Under Secretary, he brought in a liberal Republican assemblyman from California named John Veneman, who for the past two years had been a bitter foe of Governor Reagan's policies in the state legislature. (Reagan, in fact, tried to block Veneman's appointment, but to no avail.) The post of Assistant Secretary went to one-time black militant James Farmer, and Southern Republicans, in particular, were infuriated by that choice, for they remembered with rancor Farmer's so-called "freedom rides" in the South when he was head of the Congress of Racial Equality (CORE) in the early 1960s. For Assistant Secretary of Education, Finch picked James Allen, a New York liberal who had built up a national reputation as an ardent advocate of school busing. And to head the sensitive Office of Civil Rights he called on Leon Panetta, another liberal Republican from California who was deeply committed to the aggressive enforcement of school desegregation.

These appointments would not have raised an eyebrow if the President's name had been Kennedy or Johnson or even Nelson Rockefeller (then still in his liberal phase), but they hardly seemed appropriate for a Nixon administration. Yet, in Finch's view, they were not only appropriate but necessary. Toward the end of the '68 campaign, he told reporters traveling with Nixon: "This is the last election that will be won by the un-black, the un-poor and the un-young." In other words, if Republicans truly hoped to become the new majority party, they would have to move to the left and reach out to groups they had alienated in the past. This, of course, ran directly counter to the Southern Strategy motif that would eventually dominate the administration's outlook. And, in no time at all, Finch's liberal strategy, and the men he hired to put it in practice, would help bring about his undoing.

He ran into trouble right from the start, but during the early months, when the trend was toward a centrist approach with its overtures to the left, Finch had his triumphs as well as his setbacks. He and Pat Moynihan were natural allies, and in the process of working toward the same goals, a warm friendship developed. ("Bob Finch is an absolutely sweet man," Moynihan proclaimed in one of his Irish moods.) Together, they fought the good fight for welfare reform. Then, on another delicate front, Finch and Moynihan teamed up to counsel Nixon into adopting a calm, even tolerant attitude toward student dissenters. Largely because of their efforts, there was no Presidential talk, in 1969, about "bums" on college campuses. Yet, even in the midst of these early successes, Finch was taking his lumps on the issue that had brought him into direct conflict with John Mitchell.

Ever since the Supreme Court's landmark decision in 1954 declaring racial segregation in public schools unconstitutional, effort had been made to enforce the "law of the land." But it had not been easy. During the Eisenhower and Kennedy years, almost all of the burden fell on the courts, with the result that failure to comply was rampant. Then in 1964 came the passage of the Kennedy-Johnson Civil Rights bill, which authorized the executive branch to cut off federal funds to school districts that failed to show progress in ending segregation. With this act on the books, the various court rulings now had the threat of real muscle behind them. Under Johnson, the Department of Health, Education, and Welfare set up guidelines in 1966 to enforce desegregation, and the pace suddenly accelerated. And, by the time Nixon assumed office in 1969, many school districts throughout the South were at the point of showdown: either they would have to submit to the HEW guidelines or they would lose their federal money. Taking over HEW, Finch left no doubt about his intentions. "We're going to be hard," he told his liberal appointees. "We're going to stick to the guidelines."

Mitchell, however, had other ideas. As the stern guardian of the Southern Strategy, he knew that Southern Republicans and Wallace

Democrats were just waiting, with their arms crossed, to see what the new administration would do on this issue to countermand the evils of Johnson, the great Judas Iscariot of Southern segregation. And Mitchell was determined to convince them that Richard Nixon was basically on their side. So, in the early weeks of 1969, he and his allies began to move against Finch and the HEW liberals. Their goal was to water down the guidelines and postpone the existing deadlines for enforcement; in other words, encourage the South to return to the delaying tactics that had been commonplace before the Johnson years.

This was the moment of truth for Finch. He might have been able to avoid the troubles that later beset him if, right then, he had put it to Mitchell in no uncertain terms: namely, that (a) he did not intend to budge one inch on the school issue, and (b) if Mitchell didn't stay out of his hair, then he would go public with the charge that the Attorney General of the United States was trying to prevent him from enforcing the law. If Finch had taken that kind of stand, Mitchell just might have caved in, for there were many who felt, even then, that he had a soft underbelly beneath his gruff exterior. And, while he liked to take advantage of his special relationship with Nixon to push others around, he must have known that such strongarm methods could easily backfire if applied to Finch, who, after all, was known to be an even closer personal friend of the President.

But Mitchell was never put to that test. That was not Bob Finch's way of doing things. He did not have the stomach for hard and open confrontations, especially those that might embarrass his friend in the Oval Office. Nor was it just a case of lacking the courage of his convictions, for in truth the convictions themselves were not that strong. As Haldeman and others who knew him well were aware, he *was* indecisive. He was at all times far too agreeable in acknowledging the other fellow's position, and while this is admirable in a panel moderator or talk-show host, it is not the best way to get ahead in power politics. On school desegregation and similar issues, his instincts clearly leaned toward the "liberal side," but there was no real depth to his commitment. All this made him easy prey for a man like Mitchell, who by contrast enjoyed throwing his strength into a good tough scrap (especially when he sensed weakness in his opponent), and whose inflexible mind seldom succumbed to the nuances of self-doubt.

So, instead of meeting Mitchell's pressure with a force of his own, Finch followed his natural bent for compromise and accommodation. And, in a series of meetings over the spring and summer of 1969, he steadily back-pedaled away from his earlier vow to "stick to the guidelines." With Mitchell calling the shots, some school districts had their guidelines softened, while others, faced with imminent enforcement, were granted postponements. Thus by August, when the administration went into court to win a delay for thirty-three school districts in Mississippi which were under orders to desegregate that fall, the thrust of Mitchell's message was getting across to segregationists throughout the South: go ahead and stall, and we'll do all we can for you on this end.

The only trouble was that message also was coming through loud and clear to veteran civil-rights lawyers, who heard it as a call to arms. If Finch was reluctant to fight, they could hardly wait to take Mitchell on, and the Mississippi case gave them the opportunity. Now, for the first time since the 1954 decision, the NAACP entered a major civil-rights case against the federal government, and in October the Supreme Court handed down a unanimous decision that left no further room for devious maneuver. Not only did it reverse the Mississippi delay ruling, but it said all school districts were under an obligation to desegregate "at once." So, after all the machinations, the administration was driven back to Finch's original position. It now had no choice but to "stick to the guidelines," and indeed in the months ahead it would finally begin to enforce desegregation in the South at a pace worthy of comparison with that of Johnson.

But, if Mitchell's heavy-handed tactics failed to undermine the push toward school desegregation, they had a crippling effect on the reputation of Robert Finch—especially within his own department. His various concessions leading up to the Mississippi court case convinced many HEW professionals that, while his heart was in the right place (and there were some by now who even questioned that), he just couldn't be trusted to hold up under pressure. He was viewed, as one irreverent staffer put it, as "a nice guy with no balls." Finch's top deputies—his own appointees—remained loyal to him personally, but even they did not extend that loyalty to others in the administration. Hence, they were often openly critical of Mitchell or the White House or, at times, even the President himself. And Finch, caught in a web of conflicting loyalties, wound up trying to appease both sides, which only heightened the impression that he was more interested in keeping peace in the family than in taking a stand on principle.

His situation was made even more difficult by the fact that after one year on the job he was proving to be a poor administrator. His chronic indecisiveness betrayed him here as well. Even in areas that did not involve controversy, he was inclined to ponder and procrastinate instead of taking direct action to move matters forward. He came under sharp criticism, both from within and without HEW, for being an erratic administrator and poor manager. So, by the end of 1969, Finch had fallen way back from the high promise of the early weeks when he loomed as the man most likely to become the kingpin of domestic policy in Richard Nixon's Washington. There was, by this time, no longer any chance of that, and with his own department beginning to slide out of his grasp, the worst was yet to come.

Finch's vacillating behavior as HEW Secretary came as no surprise to Haldeman and Ehrlichman. Although they still felt a lingering sense of gratitude toward Finch for all he had done for them a decade earlier, when he was Nixon's top lieutenant and they were just recruits, they long since had come to believe what the HEW pros were now concluding: that Finch did not have the backbone for leadership and tough decisions. In fact, they had fallen into the habit by this time of referring to their old campaign ally as "the Pasadena Hamlet." Finch was aware of this, and had he been on his toes he could have come back with a snappy quid pro quo by calling *them* Rosencrantz and Guildenstern. But that was part of his problem; he did not have their gift for palace intrigue.

Haldeman and Ehrlichman were careful not to become openly involved in the bruising struggle between Finch and Mitchell over school desegregation. They knew they might only jeopardize their own position with Nixon if they took sides against either one of his close friends in the Cabinet. But in private they supported Mitchell, partly because their own sympathies leaned toward his Southern Strategy point of view, but even more so because, knowing both men, they were certain the Attorney General would emerge the clear victor in terms of personal power. They also believed that Finch had brought all his troubles on himself by appointing what they viewed as so many liberal firebrands to key sub-Cabinet posts.

Haldeman and Ehrlichman knew there was no need to be concerned about Finch's own cautious liberalism, which they dismissed as more emotional than ideological. The real problem was with his top deputies, who kept pushing him to advocate policies that could not be reconciled with the administration's overall position. They were the ones who had to be disciplined. So, in the fall of 1969, after Finch had been worked over by Mitchell, Rosencrantz and Guildenstern moved to cut up Hamlet's department, beginning with Leon Panetta, the thirty-year-old lawyer who had been brought in to run HEW's Office of Civil Rights.

All along Panetta had been the most outspoken foe in the administration of the plan to slow down school desegregation. Aside from his moral objections, which were considerable, he thought it was both bad politics and weak law to pursue such a course. And, being endowed with a peppery manner, he was unusually caustic in his criticisms. At the White House he became known as a "zealot" and a "hothead," and by the fall of '69 Haldeman and Ehrlichman, working in league with Mitchell and his faction, were putting pressure on Finch to get rid of him.

This was probably Finch's last chance to demonstrate his resolve to control his own department. If ever there was a time for the "nice guy" to stand up and show that he had guts, this was it—even if it meant going to his friend in the Oval Office with the threat that if Panetta was forced out then he himself would resign in protest. That, of course, did not happen, although at first Finch did resist the pressure, in his own quiet way. At one point, he sent a carefully-worded memo over to the President listing the reasons why he thought Panetta should not be dismissed. That modest effort won the young lawyer a few more weeks on the job, but in no way did it discourage the forces that were out to get him; indeed, it all but convinced them that Finch would *not* go to the mat over Panetta, just as Haldeman had suspected all along.

So, after a brief lull, the White House resumed its pressure, citing "new evidence" gathered by its agents at HEW and elsewhere that Panetta, an unrepentant type, continued criticizing administration policy. Faced with this new anti-Panetta campaign, Finch began to waver . . . and waver . . . until it soon reached the point where Haldeman knew the final move could be made without even bothering to clear it with Finch. Thus in February, 1970, the White House

announced that the President had accepted Leon Panetta's resignation. The fact that Panetta had not submitted his resignation was
airily dismissed as a minor point of semantics. (Panetta later wrote a
book dealing with his brief career in the Nixon administration which,
with a typically sardonic touch, he entitled *Bring Us Together*.)

Now Bob Finch began his final descent. In the spring of 1970, he
went plummeting into the abyss.

The Panetta firing was intended to teach everyone a lesson: criticism from within the administration would not be tolerated. Yet,
although the screws from the top were tightening, there still were
those who failed to get the message. (Wally Hickel, for example, in
the spring of 1970 was obviously listening more to voices rising up
from the campuses than to those rumbling out of the White House.)
And over at HEW, the scene of Panetta's crimes, there was a growing
spirit of rebellion. Now, more than ever, Finch was caught in a
squeeze between the grim authoritarians at the White House and the
mood of insurgency taking hold within his department. Responding
to the latter pressure, he agreed to a general meeting with HEW
workers in March to thrash out the problems and make it clear
exactly where he (and therefore the department) stood on desegregation and other issues. But the meeting was canceled when Finch
became ill from dysentery picked up on a recent trip to Mexico.
Eventually, the confrontation was rescheduled for May 18; and given
the rancorous mood in Washington at that time because of Cambodia
and Kent State, it promised to be a lively session.

By now, the long months of struggling to cope with conflicting
pressures were taking their toll. Finch was on the verge of physical
and emotional exhaustion. A long-time chain smoker, he had made
an effort to kick the habit when he took over HEW because he felt
that, as the man in charge of the nation's health programs, he should
set a proper example. But, by the spring of 1970, he was back on
three packs a day, trying nervously to puff his way through his or-
deals. By then, the rumor mill was churning that he was hitting the
bottle so hard it was hitting back. In truth there was even less basis
for the gossip about Finch's drinking than there had been in Moynihan's case. His "excesses" in that area largely consisted of such modest transgressions as squeezing in a third martini at Washington dinner parties, thereby inducing the frowns of protocol addicts, who
sternly believed that more than two cocktails on such occasions
smacked of exhibitionism.

The problem was that Finch *looked* as if he were drunk or hung over most of the time. He often appeared to be bleary-eyed and unsteady in movement, as though he had the "shakes" so commonly associated with a lush. However, this ravaged demeanor was the result of his state of utter nervous exhaustion, and not caused by excessive drinking.

The timing of his collapse was like something out of Sophocles. On May 18, 1970, about an hour and a half before his scheduled showdown with the rebellious HEW workers, a nerve ailment brought on by all the unrelenting pressures caused his arm to go numb. He was taken off to Walter Reed Hospital for treatment of exhaustion. Under Secretary Veneman stood in for Finch at the meeting, and when he read his boss's statement supporting the President's action in Cambodia, a chorus of boos and hisses erupted. Finch was drowning, and all that remained was for the White House to throw him a rock.

By this time, the President began to express concern over what was happening to his former protégé. Richard Nixon really cared about Bob Finch, the man. One day, during this troubled period, the President personally telephoned Finch's office no fewer than seven times. Before and after Finch went to the hospital, the President swore and agonized over the HEW job and what it had done to Finch. Finch was determined to stay. But for him it was over. The President saw his removal of Finch as an act of mercy. Until then, he had not been concerned enough to support Finch in the various struggles that had led to his collapse.

Nixon often had ridiculed Finch in private for allowing himself to be "humiliated" by being imprisoned in his own office by the Welfare Rights organization people, George Wiley and Beulah Sanders. The President complained that obviously Finch was not in command. Many of Finch's friends, and his wife, were convinced that Nixon had not been told much, if anything, about the struggles as they developed. Not having been told, he didn't know; his ignorance was a combination of his isolation and of Haldeman's keeping things from him. About some of Finch's difficulties, and about the full extent of his problems, this may have been true. But the President eventually had come down on Mitchell's side in the school-desegregation fight.

Now, though, he expressed worry about "poor Bob." Haldeman too was suddenly solicitous about all the problems Finch was having, and as usual he had just the right remedy. He proposed to Nixon that their good friend from the old campaign days be rescued from his vale of torment at HEW and brought into the White House to serve as—what else?—Counsellor to the President: that lofty post with Cabinet rank which had brought Arthur Burns such glory, and which was now being used as a chute to slide Pat Moynihan out of Washington. The President thought that was a capital idea.

The execution came in early June, thus making Finch the first Nixon Cabinet officer to be relieved of his command. Naturally, every effort was made to conceal the knife in Finch's back. In his announcement, the President described the deposed Secretary as "my oldest and closest friend within the administration," and then he lapsed into his favorite verb tense, the pluperfect inoperative: "I regret losing him at HEW, but I need him here." Finch, standing at Nixon's side, did his best to make the charade plausible, even tossing off a lame quip. "It's a higher calling," he said, "but a lower salary." The stricken look on his face, however, made it plain that underneath he was really saying: *"Et tu, Richard?"*

In just a few weeks it became evident what Finch's "higher calling" was to be. Along with his fellow Counsellor, Moynihan, he was put on short rations, left to scrounge for whatever scraps there were to be found on the back burner. Moynihan, who had no interest in service if it didn't involve power, would soon say to hell with it and return to Harvard. But Finch lingered on to the end of the first term, a humiliated and largely forgotten figure. From time to time, he would be seen around the White House in quiet conversation with his good friend from happier days, Herb Klein. The two of them together made a poignant scene, like two old doughboys from World War I at an American Legion hall struggling to make sense out of the hip, nuclear lingo of today's modern veterans. Finch and Klein simply could not connect with the spartan severity of the world around them. They stood apart, frozen in the visions of yesteryear, irrelevant mementos from Richard Nixon's past. And, when they left, at the end of the first term, their departures were scarcely noticed or commented on. For Finch, in particular, this was a cruel fate, for he had lost all the bright promise of his own political career that he had brought with him to Washington in 1969. True, there was always the chance that once back in California he might recapture it, but there was nothing in his record of service to the Nixon Presidency that could be cited to bolster a future candidacy.

A rather sour reward, then, for two men who had devoted so much of their lives to helping Nixon reach the White House. Yet in Bob Haldeman's view their reward was not exactly undeserved. And should have been expected. He did not hate them. Indeed, in some ways he was personally fond of them both. But he believed they had proven themselves to be what he had long thought: a bit slow, a little too wishy-washy and not quite big-league material—politically, they lacked the "killer" instinct. He held them to be most responsible for Nixon's traumatic defeat to Kennedy back in 1960. When you're a true believer, there are some things you never forget or forgive.

Finch's successor at HEW was Elliot Richardson who, in his crisp and cool style as well as his aristocratic Boston heritage, gave every impression of being Richard Nixon's version of McGeorge Bundy. Richardson brought to the post an impressive set of credentials, which included an earlier stint at HEW as Assistant Secretary during the Eisenhower years. In the 1960s, he had held high elective office in Massachusetts, first as Lieutenant Governor, then later as Attorney General. Prior to replacing Finch, he had served as Under Secretary of State in the Nixon administration. Unlike Finch, Richardson had proven to be a good administrator, which was one reason why he was given HEW: aside from ideological conflicts, the department was very much in need of a strong hand.

Haldeman and Ehrlichman, however, were wary of Richardson. For one thing, he was a favorite of Kissinger's. While at the State Department, he had the reputation of being the one official there whom Kissinger fully respected and trusted. He saw Kissinger often, and had assumed the role of interpreting Kissinger to the department, and vice versa. Kissinger spoke highly of Richardson to Nixon. He already was angling to have Richardson take over the Defense Department, which did not endear Kissinger to Laird. Kissinger finally got his wish when Laird left the Pentagon after the end of the first term. But in 1970, when Richardson's name was mentioned as a successor to Finch at HEW, Haldeman and Ehrlichman were much more worried about him than was Laird. They didn't know him well, and they didn't exactly know what to make of him. He was too Eastern, too Ivy League, and too close to Kissinger for them to be immediately comfortable about him. There also was the consideration that he might develop into a threat to them. They could not be sure he would not challenge their authority. The President, however, was—with help from Kissinger—sold on Richardson.

It was more than his administrative skills that enabled Richardson to succeed where Finch had failed. There was also his acquiescence, his unfailing willingness to play the game in accordance with the existing rules. When he took over HEW, he had a reputation for being a liberal Republican. Hence, there were some HEW liberals who were heartened by Richardson's appointment, thinking that he would fight their battles for them, that he would be firm and decisive in their defense as Finch had not been. But those who expected that to happen were soon disillusioned. For Richardson quickly settled into a position of subservience to the Haldeman-Ehrlichman axis, emphasizing to his deputies that, regardless of their personal feelings, HEW would be a loyal member of the team. The days of challenging policy decisions made by the White House staff were over.

This, of course, was the same Elliot Richardson who, during the post-Watergate crisis three years later, would take a heroic stand. Then as Attorney General (his *fourth* high-level position in the Nixon administration) he would resign in protest rather than consent to the firing of Special Prosecutor Archibald Cox. It was a gallant episode as Richardson seemed to emulate Thomas More holding to a line of iron principle from which he would not budge, or be pushed. Cox was Richardson's papacy, and he viewed Nixon's decision to sack him in the same way More had viewed the king's claim to sovereignty over the church: an act of usurpation that could not be justified. Like More, Richardson would go to his own beheading rather than give his blessing to that. But, without taking anything away from the character he displayed then, it should not be forgotten that on a number of occasions in the past Richardson, it seemed to some, had compromised and even violated his own principles in order to stay in the good graces of the Nixon White House. If the Cox firing brought him to the point where there were some things he could not stomach, then it was partly because by the time he arrived at that moment he had had his fill.

As Under Secretary of State, he had vigorously supported Nixon's decision to invade Cambodia, even though it was said at the time that he had serious private reservations about the operation. That act of loyalty in the face of heavy protest helped to persuade the White

House power brokers that he would be a safe enough choice to replace Finch at HEW—and Richardson did not let them down. Time and time again, on a variety of issues involving his huge department, he bent his will and preference to conform to the dictates he received from Ehrlichman. The most glaring example came in the summer of 1971, in the aftermath of the Supreme Court's decision proclaiming busing as a "legitimate tool" to end school desegregation. As a sound lawyer, Richardson's first response was to say that in line with the Court's ruling, HEW would move to establish and enforce busing programs in areas where they could help achieve integration. And, aside from what he felt to be his legal obligation, it was known that he personally viewed busing as an effective weapon against the *de facto* segregation that stemmed from rigid housing patterns in both Northern and Southern suburbs.

This, however, was certainly not the view at the White House, where busing was perceived as the flash-point issue—the one on which Southern Strategy and the courting of Northern suburbs met and joined hands. As far as the White House was concerned, it didn't make any difference what the Supreme Court said was "legitimate." The Nixon administration was adamantly opposed to busing, and that's all there was to it. This was spelled out in public statements, and Ehrlichman and others slammed the point home to Richardson in private—in even stronger terms. So Richardson called a news conference and explained that he had been mistaken; HEW wasn't going to follow the Supreme Court's lead on busing after all. In watching him squirm and dissemble that summer day in 1971, as he publicly renounced the strong stand he had taken earlier, one was reminded not so much of Thomas More, but of Galileo recanting.

This was the Elliot Richardson of Nixon's first term. He had come into the administration as a man of class and recognized ability. In sharp contrast to Haldeman, Ehrlichman, and many of their underlings, he had both the background and principles for enlightened leadership. Yet instead for a while he was a yes-man, a Brahmin turned toady. Not until the fifth year of his service to the Nixon Presidency would he finally break out of that role. By then he had the example of Archibald Cox, his former Harvard law professor, to remind him that there was an alternative to compromising one's conscience.

Eighteen

THROUGH the last half of 1969 and into the first half of the next year, Haldeman and Ehrlichman molded the Cabinet to do business *their* way. In the early months, they did not appear to be acting so much for the sake of their own power. There was already some of that, but not much. Nor did their chief motivations seem rooted in ideology. No, from what the two said, what they did, and how they did it, close observers were left with the impression that they acted mostly out of their intense desire to protect the President, plus their impatience (and Nixon's) with dissent of any kind. Sometimes the President himself decided how much insulation he wanted and needed. But these times became fewer and fewer as he insisted over and over that, in general, he wanted to deal personally only with what he called *"big* policy" (he said it with that emphasis). So Haldeman and Ehrlichman with increasing frequency decided on their own when and how much to protect the President, in the belief that they knew what he wanted as well as what was best for him.

By the summer of 1970, one man in the Cabinet stood alone, the only member of Nixon's Cabinet whose power and influence were comparable to that of Haldeman and Ehrlichman at the White House —John Mitchell. Mitchell had several things going for him that set him apart from the other Nixon intimates. There was, for one thing, his presence as an "older man," which helped to reinforce the aura of strength that emanated from his somber and laconic manner. Almost all of Nixon's political friends from the California days— Finch, Klein, Haldeman, etc.—were younger-brother types who had always looked *up* to Nixon for guidance and approval. But Mitchell was different. Although actually eight months younger than Nixon, he generally gave the impression of being older and more mature. And, since he seemed to exert such a steadying influence on Nixon, he came across, if not quite as a "father figure," then certainly as an "older brother figure," one who seemed a little wiser in the ways of the world and far more secure about his own identity. This was, in fact, the basis on which their close friendship had been formed in the first place.

The two met in 1963, shortly after Nixon moved to New York to begin, at age fifty, his new career as a Wall Street lawyer. He had never felt especially welcome in New York, either as a national candidate or, going way back, when he first approached the city as a young law-school graduate, and was unable to land a job with an established firm. And, with his confidence bearing the more recent scars of his defeats in the political arena, he was more than a little apprehensive about the new world he was entering. At the time, no one was more at home in that world than John Mitchell. The Wall Street legal fraternity was his domain and he understood it in all its complexities. As they became acquainted, Mitchell lent a helping hand to acclimate Nixon, to guide him through the difficult period of adjustment. As their friendship developed, Mitchell proved to be a patient and sympathetic listener, the sort of fellow who would lean back and puff on his pipe in silence while Nixon opened up, in his brooding way, about his problems, past and present. In a sense, then, Mitchell's role in the early New York years was not unlike the one Haldeman had played in the aftermath of 1960, when he had massaged Nixon's ego during the period of planning and research for *Six Crises.* But the similarities were more apparent than real. For Mitchell was no hero worshiper eagerly striving to wedge his way into the inner sanctum of Nixon's political life; the support he gave Nixon was not that of a devoted sycophant, but rather that of a calm mentor, a senior adviser, counseling a new man in town on how to ply the tricks of *his* trade.

Nixon, therefore, came to lean on Mitchell's strength and judgment, and this habit of dependence carried over into the Presidential years. At Cabinet meetings, Mitchell seldom had much to say. Concealing his views behind a poker face and a steady swirl of pipe smoke, he would sit there, impassive and inscrutable. But more alert observers soon began to notice that, when Nixon was presenting a case for something or other, he would often glance out of the corner of his eye in Mitchell's direction. If the Attorney General grunted and nodded his balding head, the President would usually press on, and with increased enthusiasm. But if Mitchell grunted and looked away, or stopped puffing, then Nixon would backtrack a bit, or sometimes change the subject altogether. Mitchell watchers quickly discovered that it was futile to try to interpret the grunts themselves; it was the subtle head movements that went with them that betrayed his reaction. In time, toward the end of the first term, Nixon would come to rely much less on Mitchell's stolid approval, and finally, as Watergate and other scandals closed in on the Attorney General, the President would abandon him altogether—to the wolves, as it were. But during the first two years no one in Nixon's official family was more formidable than Mitchell.

For one thing, Nixon and Mitchell consulted frequently in person and almost daily on the telephone. The President also often called Mitchell at night. This continued even for a while after the Watergate break-in in June, 1972. By the time the election was over that year, however, Nixon was seeing Mitchell seldom and talking with him by phone less and less.

So it was the nature of their personal relationship that accounted for Mitchell's privileged status as a confidant and all-around adviser, whose opinion was sought on a wide range of issues. (This included foreign policy. Mitchell was a major factor in the President's decision to approve the offensive into Cambodia.) But, beyond that, there were specific qualities he brought to the post of Attorney General, not the least of which was his forbidding presence. With his dour, implacable mien, so suggestive of stern parental authority, he served as the perfect symbol of the tough law-and-order message the White House was determined to convey. Even more important, from an operational point of view, was Mitchell's willingness to play the front man, to become the lightning rod for controversial policies and decisions that, more often than not, originated with others.

A case in point was the famous Southern Strategy. Although it became inextricably linked to his name, Mitchell actually was not the one who formulated that strategy. It was essentially the brainstorm of Kevin Phillips, a young conservative lawyer who worked out of Mitchell's campaign headquarters in 1968 and who, a year later, published a book elaborating on the thesis to include Wallace voters in Peoria and other Northern flanks, as well as those based in the Deep South. (Titled *The Emerging Republican Majority*, it promptly became the New Testament around the Nixon White House.) But Mitchell clasped the Southern Strategy to his bosom and made it his own. Thus, when it was attacked by critics, a group that included several fellow Republicans who considered it unseemly for the party of Lincoln to be avidly courting racist supporters of Wallace, he was the one who took the heat.

This was also the pattern when the time came to translate strategy into tactics. Most of the original impetus behind the effort to slow down school desegregation came not from Mitchell, but from a middle-echelon White House assistant named Harry Dent. Dent, who worked directly under Haldeman, was a protégé of South Carolina Senator Strom Thurmond, and his very presence in the White House stemmed from a series of deals Nixon had made with Thurmond at the '68 convention in order to hold Southern support behind him for his nomination. The White House always denied this, but it was obvious that there was little reason for him to be there except to serve as "Uncle Strom's" eyes and ears. Dent, who was very much a hustler, did everything he could to enlarge his role into something more than that, but the original connection was still there. It was Dent who came up with the basic formula for watering down the desegregation guidelines, especially as they pertained to his— and Thurmond's—native South Carolina. Yet every effort was made to play down Dent's contribution, to keep him well behind the scenes, deep within the bowels of the Executive Office Building next door to the White House. Haldeman saw to this in what he thought was Nixon's best interest, if not on direct instructions from the President. For the administration did not want to give the impression that its racial policies were being set in accordance with the approval of so notorious a Southern segregationist as Strom Thurmond.

Mitchell, therefore, was the ideal man to carry the ball out front, in the critical contests with Finch and the HEW liberals. He could give what was basically a policy designed to satisfy the South the respectable gloss of a Northerner's advocacy. Even more important, as Attorney General he was able to imbue the desegregation slow-down with the cut and force of seeming legality. But from the beginning the legality was fraudulent. Leon Panetta wasn't the only administration lawyer who argued that the Dent-Mitchell tactics were in violation of existing laws. Some of the lawyers in Mitchell's own Justice Department tried to warn him that if he persisted on such a course the courts would be sure to rule against him. Brushing aside their objections, Mitchell did persist, however, and in its unanimous decision on the Mississippi delay case the Supreme Court slapped him down.

Mitchell's attempt to undermine school desegregation was just one in a long string of legal and tactical setbacks that characterized his performance as Attorney General. Some of the others were:

—The Haynsworth and Carswell nominations. Although he personally recommended both men, his investigation of their credentials was so slipshod that it failed to turn up critical flaws in their judicial background—flaws which made them sitting ducks for Senate opposition, thus bringing on their public humiliation, and a defeat for the President.

—His insistence that the government had an inherent right to wiretap domestic subversives without court supervision; like his approach to school desegregation, that stand was also unanimously rejected by the Supreme Court.

—His prosecution of prominent antiwar groups, such as the "Chicago Seven" (Tom Hayden, Abbie Hoffman, *et al.*) and the "Harrisburg Seven" (Daniel Berrigan's clique), on evidence so flimsy that neither case could produce a sustained conviction.

—His suit against the *New York Times* over publication of the Pentagon Papers, which went to the heart of the First Amendment and which led to still another repudiation by the Supreme Court.

As the setbacks began to accumulate, it became fashionable in certain legal circles to contend that John Mitchell's arrogance was exceeded only by his incompetence, and his apparent ignorance of the law. The problem, however, was not Mitchell's lack of legal background, but the precise and narrow nature of that background —and the attitude toward politics and government he derived from it.

The point to keep in mind about Mitchell is that prior to his association with Nixon he had never been involved in national politics or the world of Washington. And he had been little involved if at all with courtroom law. His entire career had been devoted to his legal specialty, state and municipal bonds. This brought him a nice living (to the tune of two hundred grand a year) but it also brought him into regular contact with public officials on a level that did not exactly inspire an ennobling view of politicians and the governmental process. Bond issues are often resolved in the back rooms of statehouses and city halls, where the pervading atmosphere is one of private deals and accommodations, sly winks and furtive handshakes, and on occasion, inevitably, a greased palm or two. (When Spiro

Agnew's shenanigans in Maryland were publicly revealed, John Mitchell was probably the least surprised man in America; without implying anything illicit on his part, one can assume he was well aware, from first-hand knowledge, that that sort of thing went on from time to time.)

Over the years Mitchell had become cynical—he would call it pragmatic—about the way law and government really worked, and this, quite naturally, was the attitude he brought with him to Washington when he became Attorney General. Venerators of the Constitution such as Sam Ervin and Hugo Black might prate on about the inherent majesty of law and justice as the cornerstone of our democratic system, but Mitchell was inclined to sneer at such talk as high-minded twaddle. He, after all, had cut his teeth in the "real world," where one learned to view the law as an instrument to be manipulated for financial gain or political power. To him, then, the office of Attorney General was a logical extension of his role as campaign manager; having worked to elect Richard Nixon President, he now would use his legal guile and authority to enhance the President's chances for re-election. Thus the cynical selectivity of his pose as Mr. Law and Order. Black militants, student protesters, and anti-war groups would be prosecuted to the fullest extent of the law because they fell into the category of political enemies (and indeed, as seen through Mitchell's eyes, dangers to the Republic). But toward certain Southern school districts, toward generous campaign contributors, like Robert Vesco and ITT, and finally toward at least some of the outlandish schemes of G. Gordon Liddy, Mitchell would be the model of permissiveness. Thus, too, his decision to quash a grand-jury investigation of the Kent State killings because the votes were on the side of the National Guardsmen, not the slain students. And thus his various moves to drag the administration into court on cases that were legally weak but politically shrewd. In short, John Mitchell's limited background and his own special concept of justice helped to move his department and the whole administration in these directions.

Yet through it all Mitchell knew exactly what he was doing. Legal and constitutional scholars may have deplored his actions and questioned his competence, but as far as the White House was concerned he was the ideal Attorney General. How much more difficult it all would have been if another kind of man had been in that post. On the issue of school desegregation, for example, an Attorney General who was the least bit concerned about his own legal reputation or felt an obligation to safeguard the integrity of the Justice Department almost surely would have gone to Nixon and said, in effect: "Mr. President, we just can't do this. The law won't permit it." Such a stand, taken by his Attorney General, would have severely limited Nixon's options.

For there is no doubt that Mitchell's tactics met with the President's personal approval. On the question of race, in particular, Nixon himself seemed to be playing both ends against the middle. Regardless of what Thurmond or Harry Dent or the rest of his Southern friends may have thought possible, Nixon had enough experience and political savvy to realize that there was no way his administration could repeal or circumvent the civil-rights laws that were on the books. Yet, by going through the motions, by giving his approval to legal maneuvers that were certain to be repudiated by the courts, he could turn to Southern Republicans and Wallace Democrats and say: Well, we tried to help you folks out, but *they*—the courts—wouldn't let us. Then later when, with the Supreme Court and Congress pointing a gun at his head, he ordered the enforcement of laws passed during Johnson's administration (the Voting Rights Act, for example, and the law allowing the cutting off of federal funds to school districts adamantly refusing to speed integration), he would try to win credit from blacks and white liberals for bringing about desegregation in the South. When you're playing that kind of game, it helps to have an Attorney General who is not encumbered by an excessive regard for integrity or the fine points of law.

Later, when the scandals broke and all the indictments came raining down, people would ask: What happened? How did everything get so far out of line? The answer is that the law too often was viewed as something to be twisted or ignored or, at times, even violated if there was a political edge to be gained. During the early years, it is true, the abuse of law took on fairly innocuous forms, and no one seemed to mind all that much. There was a tendency to tolerate the zeal for wiretapping, since nobody then dreamed it would lead to an elaborate plan to "bug" the opposition party as part of a criminal effort to sabotage the democratic process. Nor were there many who charged "obstruction of justice" when the Kent State probe was suppressed, though that should have been the tipoff as to how Mitchell and the White House felt about covering up crimes that threatened to be politically embarrassing. In retrospect, then, we can see that all the later crimes, the brazen felonies that brought the Nixon Presidency to its knees, grew out of a fundamental disregard for the law that took root in the first two years. It may never have been intended that such an attitude take hold. Those responsible may have believed that they could control any excesses, any outright violations of legality which might take place, so that it would not become a dangerous tendency in government. They may have believed that, sparingly used, occasional disregard for the law would not be dangerous for them, for what they were trying to accomplish in the way of a counter-revolution, or for their country. But, if so, they were dead wrong. The attitude took root and grew deep. And the two men most responsible for allowing that attitude to become dominant were the bond attorney who served as the nation's chief law-enforcement officer, and his former Wall Street partner, the lawyer who sat in the Oval Office.

During this early period, Haldeman and Ehrlichman generally looked upon Mitchell as an ally, a worthy partner in power. To some extent, of course, this merely reflected a prudent respect for Mitchell's own clout with the President, but there was more to it than that. Haldeman, in particular, recognized Mitchell's value in image terms, the stern presence he brought to his role as Mr. Law and Order. And, having suffered through 1960, when unflattering (and, at base, unfair) comparisons were drawn between Kennedy's heroism and Nixon's more modest war record, he also took delight in the fact that Mitchell had been Kennedy's senior officer in the Pacific, the commander in charge of several torpedo-boat squadrons, including the one that contained PT–109. (Mitchell himself was fond of saying, with characteristic disdain, that he scarcely knew Lieutenant Kennedy since he was, after all, "just one of the junior officers.")

Then, too, both he and Ehrlichman appreciated Mitchell's value as a front man, not only in his official capacity as the one who took the heat and provided legal cover for actions and decisions that provoked criticism, but also in a more personal sense. They soon discovered that in their own unrelenting drive for power they were able to use Mitchell as a convenient buffer in the various moves to cut down other Cabinet officers, like Hickel and Romney and, above all, Finch. Yet, even during this time, though they worked together in relative harmony, the alliance between Mitchell and the Halde-man-Ehrlichman team was a fragile one, marked by undercurrents of friction and distrust. This presented no great problem as long as they joined forces against common rivals and/or administration offi-cers they considered to be unworthy; but once the Cabinet officials they were out to get were either purged or brought to heel, their guns slowly shifted position until they were trained on each other.

The first signs of serious discord surfaced in the Mitchell-Ehrlich-man relationship. For example, Ehrlichman thought the checking-out of the Haynsworth and Carswell backgrounds had been sloppy. He criticized Mitchell for that, and Mitchell, to put it mildly, didn't like it. As time went on, and Ehrlichman steadily tightened his con-trol over the full range of domestic policy, he began, inevitably, to encroach more and more on Mitchell's territory at Justice. Ehrlich-man became directly involved in trying to make J. Edgar Hoover and the FBI more responsive to the President's wishes. He plunged into law-enforcement aspects of handling antiwar demonstrators. And he is believed to have helped ride herd on negotiations for the paroles of Teamsters Union leader James Hoffa and others Nixon wanted out of prison. Ehrlichman moved on his own some of the time, but more often he was operating with, at very least, tacit approval from the President—or Haldeman's word that Nixon approved.

Soon Mitchell could scarcely conceal his loathing for the lawyer from Seattle. Mitchell was quoted by friends as saying privately, "John is getting too big for his britches." Perhaps the only thing that prevented him from forcing the issue into an open and stormy show-down was the fact that by 1971, when the pressure from Ehrlichman began in earnest, he already was preparing to leave the Cabinet to take over publicly as manager of the '72 re-election campaign.

Ehrlichman also began to suggest (as he had about Finch before) that Mitchell was not running his department as efficiently as he should, that Mitchell's sense of command was all right but that it was not permeating as well as it should down through the ranks. Also, Ehrlichman, while personally amused by Martha Mitchell, consid-ered her an embarrassment, and reportedly had been overheard saying so.

For his part, Mitchell was beginning to be bored with his job. When Martha—who cared for Ehrlichman not one whit—demanded why her John didn't *do* something about him, whack him down to size, Mitchell responded along the lines of Rhett Butler's famous words to Scarlett O'Hara: "Frankly, my dear, I don't give a damn." He adored Martha, but he had reached the point where he just didn't think squabbles with the likes of Ehrlichman were worth the time and trouble. Mitchell's whole tone and demeanor were, by then, giving the impression he was tired of it all. He kept his title at the Justice Department for the remainder of the year, but increasingly he appeared to his co-workers there to be coasting. Secretly he was already gearing into the work of putting together the Committee to Re-elect the President. Before he officially stepped down as Attorney General in February of 1972, however, he got from Nixon the right to name his own successor—his chief deputy, Richard Kleindienst. Ehrlichman had no objection, for he knew Kleindienst was no Mitchell and he was confident that the new Attorney General could be easily lassoed into the corral to take his place alongside Richardson and others as a compliant member of the domestic Cabinet.

But now Mitchell had another problem, for the switch from Attorney General to campaign manager moved him directly into Haldeman's line of fire. Haldeman was determined to run the re-election campaign himself through his operation at the White House, and in the early months of 1972 he and Mitchell entered into a fierce struggle for power that soon evolved into a struggle for survival. Mitchell believed he had made a deal with Nixon for near-total authority over the re-election campaign. Haldeman was determined that Mitchell would have no such thing. As a result, upper tiers of the Nixon team began to split into Mitchell forces and Haldeman forces. Mitchell and Haldeman—never really close—were envious and suspicious of one another. These feelings fed upon themselves, and spread.

As the struggle between Mitchell and Haldeman grew and deepened, the course was set which eventually provoked the forces that would carry all of them to their Watergate ruin. As it turned out, Haldeman won the first round, and Mitchell was the first to be sacrificed. The arrests at the Watergate break-in, involving people from the Committee to Re-elect the President, coupled with the ominous yammerings of his impulsive wife, were enough to force Mitchell into an abrupt resignation as campaign manager. Ten months later, when the walls came tumbling down and Haldeman and Ehrlichman joined Mitchell in exile from power, all three men must have had reason to recall with sober regret a decision made back in the days of comparative innocence when relations between them were still fairly cordial. At the time, the decision had seemed so inconsequential that hardly anyone outside the inner circle took notice. But June, 1970, is a date to remember. For it was then that Haldeman and Ehrlichman, in looking around for someone to move into the post of White House counsel that Ehrlichman had vacated the previous fall, accepted one of Mitchell's protégés at the Justice Department, an ambitious young lawyer named John Dean. More than anyone else, Dean symbolized the tenuous link between Mitchell and the White House power brokers, the extremely thin layer of trust on which their relationship was formed. So perhaps it was only fitting that when the day of reckoning came he should have been the one to blow the whistle.

Nineteen

THE road down and out for John Mitchell was long and slow. Of all the men who came to Washington with Richard Nixon, he seemed the least likely not to survive. He was considered by many, and considered himself to be, an untouchable. He had "Don't Tread On Me" tattooed all over him. All through his heyday as Attorney General, Mitchell played the public heavy with such glowering conviction that he was fully recognized, throughout the country, as a man of great importance. The reams of articles written about him during the first two years of Nixon's Presidency invariably described him as "the President's most trusted adviser" or "the second most powerful man in Washington." It is true that by 1970 Mitchell was sharing his role as abrasive front man with Spiro Agnew, but unlike the Attorney General, Agnew had no real power to go with his rhetoric. He was purely a marionette who had been sent out onto the national stage to dance the White House tune. Yet between them they performed a useful service. For the clouds of dust stirred up by Mitchell and Agnew provided a smokescreen that helped to conceal from public view the strings being pulled from within the White House—as well as the men who were pulling them. Although by this time Haldeman and Ehrlichman ranked on a par with Mitchell in overall power and influence, they remained shadowy figures, at least as far as the general public was concerned. They had begun to make an impression in Washington, especially on those who had frequent and direct dealings with the Nixon White House.

It was during the spring and summer of 1970 that the various nicknames started to catch on: Hans and Fritz, the Berlin Wall, and the Palace Guard. Sometimes Kissinger would be lumped in with them to form the Teutonic Trio, and others like Ziegler and Shultz could claim inclusion whenever reference was made to the White House Germans, the Katzenjammer Kids, or All the King's Krauts. But, insofar as such terms were intended to characterize the inflexible and authoritarian atmosphere at the White House, they were clearly directed at Haldeman and Ehrlichman. (Victor Gold, Agnew's press secretary at the time, chose to eschew the Germanic line altogether, preferring instead an Iberian conceit. Borrowing from Cervantes, by way of the Broadway musical based on *Quixote*, he dubbed Haldeman and Ehrlichman "the Knights of the Woeful Countenance.")

Always there was the tendency to speak of them in tandem, as a *pas de deux*. It was as though "Hans" had no identity apart from "Fritz," and vice versa. The point is that for a great many people it was simply easier to think of them as a composite figure, as though they naturally fused into a single entity and became, in effect, a persona known as "Hehrldeman." They came to Washington together, rose to power together, and as others in the government learned of their existence, it was almost impossible not to focus on the striking similarities we have seen: fellow Christian Scientists, abstainers from liquor and tobacco, Eagle Scouts, UCLA classmates, their joint background as campaign advance men, their fierce loyalty to Nixon—and, not to be overlooked, their deep devotion to each other. They never flaunted their friendship all that much, at least not in a demonstrative way. Still, there is one moment that stands out in memory. On Inauguration Day, 1969, shortly after Nixon had taken his oath and given his speech, Haldeman and Ehrlichman could be seen behind the reviewing stand, shaking hands and hugging each other and smiling over the sheer joy of it all. Haldeman, in particular,

had a big, toothy smile that made him look a little like Bobby
Kennedy, who also used to smile as if he were responding to a dental
command. And the expression on both their faces said, "We did it,
by God, we finally did it!" The scene makes for a vivid memory
because it was so atypical. Even those who saw them regularly and
under informal circumstances say it was not their natural style to
behave like that with each other.

But they were together constantly, both at work and at play.
Despite their Prussian schedules—ten to fourteen hours a day—they
did allow time for recreation. But, in keeping with their zeal for
super efficiency, even their leisure was rigorously planned and
blocked out. They disciplined themselves to have some fun now and
then, though usually on schedule, within tightly specified "time
frames." And they shared an interest in a number of pastimes and
hobbies.

For example, they were both camera bugs—especially Haldeman. Whenever the Haldemans entertained, their guests were invariably treated (or subjected) to a viewing of home movies, many of
them taken during his recent travels abroad. But in this case the
pictures were not the usual ones of the host's family: the missus or
Momma or some "Uncle Fred" posing self-consciously in front of the
Leaning Tower of Pisa. The star of Haldeman's private film festivals
was Nixon—the President in action, at home and overseas. One of
the select few who always accompanied Nixon on his many trips
abroad, Haldeman was indefatigable in his efforts to record it all on
film. Those who regularly traveled with the Presidential party became accustomed to the sight of him hovering on the edge of a crowd
scene, his eye pressed to the view finder of the fancy movie camera
he purchased in a Bonn PX in 1969. By the time he left Washington,
he had put together an enormous film collection of the Nixon Presidency. So, along with his more official duties, Haldeman served as the
President's cinematic Boswell.

Ehrlichman also used to bring his camera along when he traveled
with the President, but he was neither as enthusiastic nor as skilled
in his picture taking. In fact, he sometimes gave the impression that
his interest in the camera was rather half-hearted, as though he were
only indulging in the *cinéma vérité* bit out of a "monkey-see, mon-
key-do" deference to his friend and patron. This would not have
been out of character; for even after he staked out his own position

of power in the White House, Ehrlichman continued to take his cue, on matters large and small, from the man who had made it all possible.

There was the same tendency to play follow the leader when it came to music. Although Haldeman loathed almost everything about the counter-culture, he was, surprisingly, attracted to the music of the "now generation." In fact, he himself did a little strumming on the guitar for relaxation. In general, he preferred the country sound of Nashville to the folk and rock groups, with their reputation for being heavily into drugs. One of his big favorites was Johnny Cash, and he was instrumental in arranging an appearance by Cash at the White House, though along with others he would express disappointment over Cash's refusal to sing "Welfare Cadillac," a hot-selling putdown of "welfare chiselers." Yet, when the rock world went on its religious kick, Haldeman was among those leading the applause. He was practically a walking advertisement for *Jesus Christ, Superstar,* and when *Godspell* was running at a Washington theater, he went to see it three times. So, naturally enough, Ehrlichman also made a point of seeing it three times, though here again there were signs that his ardor for the show was a little forced. But at least he had the jump on Dwight Chapin. One day, during the *Godspell* run, Haldeman sharply reminded Chapin that he had not yet seen the rock musical despite the fact that he, Haldeman, had urged him to do so. Chapin did not have to be prodded again. He went to see *Godspell* the very next night, and the following morning he dutifully reported to Haldeman that he agreed it was a terrific show.

Also, during their years in Washington, Haldeman and Ehrlichman succumbed to the tennis boom. They weren't especially good at the game, but what they lacked in ability they tried to make up in determination, zeal, and resourcefulness. A woman who used to play against Ehrlichman on occasion recalls that almost every time she hit a shot close to the base line he would holler "out" and claim the point for himself, even though she often had the feeling the ball was really in bounds and should have been her point. (In the Watergate summer of '73, when Ehrlichman made his bellicose appearance before the Ervin Committee and prompted Senator Daniel Inouye to utter his famous whisper—"What a liar!"—which the microphones picked up and sent out on television across the country, this woman, remembering those shots to the base line, would say to her friends that she understood exactly how the Senator from Hawaii felt.)

Yet, because of their heavy work load and the constant press on their time, they had to abandon or severely curtail some of the pleasures they had enjoyed in the past. Ehrlichman tried to keep up with his hiking, his "huffing-and-puffing," but he just didn't have the time any more for the long weekend back-packing trips he had relished as a Boy Scout and later during the Seattle years. And every so often he would confide to friends in the White House how much he missed all of that. And Haldeman, who used to sail a great deal back in his adman days when he was living in Newport Beach, in the heart of Orange County, pretty much had to give that up. Indeed, even during those earlier years, when he did have a lot more leisure time, he sailed in a style suggesting a man going through a brisk close-order drill. Friends from Newport Beach say he would often just get in his boat and proceed in a crisp, straight line to a predetermined point, then abruptly turn around and sail right back again. Not exactly the way it's done as a rule, but at least he could put himself on record as having given himself an outing.

Their social life in Washington was confined almost exclusively to their immediate families and the small circle of friends and subordinates who had come with them from the West Coast. The two families were especially close, as they had been over the years, going back to their courtship days at UCLA. During warm weather they would often get together at either Ehrlichman's home in suburban Virginia (Great Falls) or Haldeman's in suburban Maryland (Kenwood) to take part in that great triumph of California living—the outdoor barbecue. "I would say the barbecues ranked right up there with the home movies," recalled a White House acquaintance. "They definitely preferred the simple pleasures of home and hearth. But they enjoyed themselves, in their way. I mean, don't get the idea that all they ever did was sit around and read Mary Baker Eddy."

Despite that reassuring disclaimer, it was commonly acknowledged that the life styles and social attitudes of both men were affected in no small way by what they believed was their firm adherence to the tenets of Christian Science. Much later, when Watergate brought their probity into question, they responded with characteristic self-righteousness. They came to Washington self-righteous, and the quality seemed to grow proportionately with their increase in power.

There should be no misunderstanding: Haldeman and Ehrlichman really believe in the creeds and ideals of the Boy Scouts of America and Christian Science. On the other hand, it is something else again to try imposing one's beliefs on others, and to stand in harsh judgment of those who cannot or will not accept such an imposition. At any rate, throughout the first Nixon term, before it was fully revealed that Haldeman's and Ehrlichman's own feet were made of clay, their codes and beliefs—religious and otherwise—were forces to be reckoned with. For, as they acquired power, the pair moved to impose their moral values on others. In the process they established a mood of stern public piety that infected the entire White House.

Haldeman was the chief inspiration behind the Sunday-morning religious services at the White House, and he tolerated no dissent from those who questioned them as possibly being counter to a political heritage founded on the separation of church and state. At first, when the plans were unveiled, it was assumed that these services would be primarily small private prayer gatherings for the benefit of the President's family and a few close friends. But they immediately took on political overtones and the status of official events. Cabinet officers and other members of the administration were given to understand that attendance was expected, that if they were among those invited who failed to show up they would suffer a serious fall from grace in the eyes of the moral guardians at the White House. One therefore skipped a White House worship service at one's peril.

Nor was it enough to be merely a dutiful Sunday Christian. Members of the administration were expected to lead missionary lives seven days a week, fifty-two weeks a year, and both Haldeman and Ehrlichman were quick to form harsh judgments of those who did not measure up. These included judgments of some of the people closest to and working hardest for the President himself, including Nixon's long-time personal secretary, Rose Mary Woods.

In their first days at the White House, when they were still setting up shop, Haldeman tried one of his power plays on Miss Woods in an effort to dislodge her from proximity to the President. He even preceded the stick with the carrot by first sending her a dozen roses. But the ploy didn't work. For the next day, when he sent Larry Higby around to suggest that she would be happier in more spacious quarters across the way in the Executive Office Building, Miss Woods refused to cooperate—though she did tell Higby to thank Haldeman for the flowers. But, having failed to get Rose Mary out of his hair, Haldeman then set out to undermine her morale in a number of petty ways, such as leaving her name off the list of those authorized to accompany Nixon on his foreign travels. (That didn't work, either; she always got to go.) And before long the gossip was going around about *her* drinking. Here again, as with Finch and Moynihan, the rumors were grossly exaggerated.

All this was contemptible enough, but what made it worse was that the two public White House teetotalers seemed to be motivated as much by expediency as by their professed moral revulsion. It just so happened that those who acquired reputations for being fond of the sauce were always people who already were out of favor, for other reasons. On the question of booze, Haldeman and Ehrlichman were not above applying the old double standard, if it served their purpose.

For example, by all accounts, the one member of the Cabinet who really did know how to put it away, on a regular basis, was Mitchell. His was Dewar's, and visitors to the Mitchell home were impressed by the gallon jug he kept near his desk mounted in a wooden frame for easy pouring. Here clearly was a man who liked to keep an ample supply on hand and in a place where he could get at it, with a minimum of effort. But, in the days when they were all getting along as partners in the pursuit of power, Haldeman and Ehrlichman generally excused Mitchell's drinking on the grounds that he could handle it, that he could take a few belts and it wouldn't affect him that much. That is, he did not go around with a hungover look on his face the way Finch did during his period of travail at HEW. Nor did he ever dance a dreamy tango with himself, as Rose Mary Woods supposedly had done one night in California. This was basically true: Mitchell *was* known to be a stoic drinker, the strong and silent type who could grunt with as much authority when he had had a few as he could when he was cold sober. But such distinctions were also irrelevant, if indeed their objections to the demon rum were moral ones.

For a long time, Haldeman and Ehrlichman were even willing to tolerate Martha Mitchell's antics. They had no illusions about the condition she was believed, rightly or wrongly, to be in when she made her famous late-night telephone calls, like the one to the newspaper editor in Arkansas urging him to "crucify" Senator Fulbright for having voted against the Carswell nomination. But, since her heart was in the right place, they made allowances. Besides, she wasn't an administration official, so it didn't really matter all that much. Later, of course, when they turned on the Mitchells, they would move to discredit them for their drinking as well, even going so far as to imply that Martha was so deep in her cups she had lost touch with reality. But her touch was just fine. In fact, the problem was that it was right on the mark: she had gotten a strong whiff of Watergate and she didn't like it. And in her spirited, blabbermouth way, she let it be known that she didn't like it. So it became imperative that she be dismissed as a lush and a kook.

During their years of power, Haldeman and Ehrlichman also kept a vigilant eye out for any signs of sexual misconduct. This was one of the things they had against Kissinger: his reputation as a "swinger" and, even worse, the fact that he seemed to take such delight in it. Of course there were limits as to how puritanical they could be. Kissinger was, after all, a divorced man (at that time), so allowances could be made. Still, it was a constant source of irritation to them. Everything about his life style seemed an affront to their most cherished values of home and family. There simply was no way they could form a common bond with a man who preferred squiring actresses to fancy restaurants over the pleasures of backyard barbecues with a wife and kiddies.

But it was the married personnel who really had to watch their step. The pastime known as "getting a little on the side" struck at the heart of the Nixon morality, as it was defined by Haldeman and Ehrlichman, and the married men who came under their aegis were given to understand that the primrose path was off limits to them. They might risk a dalliance now and then, but always with the knowledge that, if caught, they would face dire consequences. As a result, the few affairs that did flower in that atmosphere were entered into with a certain morbidity, like two fatalists settling down to a grim game of Russian roulette.

One morning in London, during a Presidential visit to Europe, one of the middle-level White House staffers connected with the Beaver Patrol emerged from his hotel room in the company of a young woman who also was employed at the White House. She was not, however, the young man's wife, and as they stepped out into the hall they encountered the familiar face of a White House reporter. Now, there are some men who know just how to handle a situation like that. Certain Englishmen, in particular, bring to such moments an admirable touch of aplomb. However, Little Beaver's way of putting everyone at ease was to recoil in terror. ("He looked like Dracula reacting to the Cross" was how the reporter later described it.) And for days, even weeks afterward, the poor fellow went around in a state of palpable dread, as though he were staring into his open grave. He seemed to be convinced that it was only a matter of time until word of the incident got back to Haldeman, and he would then be cast out of Eden, into the darkness, there to live out his days in bitter disgrace.

So the Haldeman-Ehrlichman reign was characterized by a spirit of Cromwellian rectitude that, in many ways, was even more oppressive than their rigid political dogma. This may explain why the name of someone like Joe Namath found its way onto the White House Enemies List. The New York Jet quarterback has never been known for his outspoken political views. Instead, it may well have been Namath's life style that elevated him to the status of Prominent Enemy. His chortling boasts about how he liked to prepare for a game with a bottle of Johnnie Walker Red in one hand and a shapely blonde in the other openly flouted the all-American Boy Scout, breakfast-of-champions image that was taken so seriously at the Nixon White House. How could the youth of America look up to someone who, when asked about the condition of his injury-scarred knees, would reply, "They only hurt when I make love"—and then *giggle* about it. Yes indeed, Broadway Joe had to be regarded as a menace to Flag and Country.

Yet ultimately to Haldeman and Ehrlichman it was all part of the same disease. The enemy was liberalism in both senses, political *and* moral, and for the most part they associated heavy drinking and loose sex with the political left. Thus their smug, I-told-you-so reaction to Chappaquiddick. That incident, as they saw it, was precisely the sort of thing that would befall the Kennedys and their ilk. And they looked upon Washington as a hostile and alien city in part because, in their judgment, it reflected the moral permissiveness that had been allowed to flourish during the Kennedy-Johnson years; and beyond that because it was situated in the hated East, the region that, again in their view, was the haven for all the forces that were tearing down America: hippies on drugs, pushy blacks, left-wing radicals as well as the Establishment groups that encouraged them, like the Kennedys and the national media.

This attitude, so deeply ingrained in the Nixon White House, finally surfaced to public attention at the time of the Watergate hearings. In his concluding remarks before the Ervin Committee, Ehrlichman described the pitfalls that awaited those who left their homes in Middle America to pursue a government career in Washington. "Be prepared to defend your sense of values when you come here," he warned in the stern manner of an Old Testament prophet. "You'll encounter a local culture which scoffs at patriotism and family and morality just as it adulates the opposite."

All that statement did was reveal how absurdly out of touch he and Haldeman were with the "local culture." Scoff at patriotism? Hardly, for in truth the numerous national monuments that give Washington its physical and spiritual identity are as revered by the home folks as they are by the thousands of tourists who come streaming in every year at cherry-blossom time. Indeed, a great many Washingtonians, especially those who work for the government, live there precisely because they honor the national heritage and want to be a part of it, in however small a way. And they would say to a Haldeman or Ehrlichman that there is at least as much "patriotism" to be found on the steps of the Lincoln Memorial looking out over the war dead buried at Arlington as one could hope to find in a hundred Seattles or southern Californias.

As for the second part of the gripe, it would be difficult to name a major metropolitan area that is more firmly rooted in family values than Washington and its quiet suburbs. The city's social life, while active, is also sedate, revolving almost entirely around the private dinner party, which is about as family-oriented as you can get, and where the genteel rules of protocol call for moderation in drinking and early departures for home. Washington is notorious for being an early-to-bed, early-to-rise city, much to the dismay of visitors accustomed to the night-life glitter of Manhattan or Chicago or Miami Beach. This is part of the small-town Southern flavor it has managed to retain despite its rise to eminence as a world capital. As a matter of fact, most people who know Washington tend to regard it as a Southern rather than an Eastern city—or as John Kennedy once

described it, in a reversal of the old cliché: "a city of Southern efficiency and Northern charm." In mores and temperament, it has far
more in common with Atlanta than with New York or Boston.

Haldeman and Ehrlichman never understood this because they
never took the time or made the effort to discover the real Washington. They came to town with their preconceptions and, like Bible-
belt fundamentalists encountering Darwin, they refused to consider
the evidence around them. They clung to each other and to a small
circle of mostly West Coast friends as if convinced that they and they
alone were islands of purity in a sea of radicalism and moral degener-
acy. With the haughty disdain of Victorian Englishmen forced to live
among the Hottentots, they took care not to mingle with the natives
except in the line of duty. Oh, every now and then they would risk
contamination by accepting a dinner invitation provided the guest
list was heavily sprinkled with Nixon Republicans. Yet even then
they were usually on their guard. A woman recalling Haldeman's
behavior on one such occasion says that during pre-dinner cocktails
"he stood by himself off in a corner with a glum expression on his
face, eyes darting, looking for all the world like a Secret Service
man."

Yet, throughout their years in the White House, there were those
who felt that their uptight attitude stemmed not so much from moral
disapproval as from a sense of inadequacy; that their disdain was a
defense mechanism, a convenient shield they put up to conceal the
fact that they really were intimidated by Washington. Unlike Kissinger or Moynihan or even Mitchell, all of whom moved with ease
through the city's social circuit, Haldeman and Ehrlichman often
gave the impression that they weren't at all sure they could cut it.
For, while Washington can be characterized as a Southern city in
mood and manner, it is hardly a provincial outpost. It may not have
the cultural diversity of New York or the intellectual tradition of
Boston, but in its own field—government and politics—it runs a very
fast track. Those who take part in Washington's social life are expected to read, to stay abreast of what's happening, and to maintain
a minimal level of sophistication. And Haldeman and Ehrlichman
may well have feared that what passed for brilliant conversation in
Seattle or Orange County would have earned them only a C+ in
Georgetown.

Richard Whalen, a conservative intellectual who worked as a

speechwriter for Nixon in the '68 campaign until he quit in disgust over the heavy-handed way Haldeman and Ehrlichman were running things, addressed himself to this point in his book, *Catch the Falling Flag*. In that account of why he became an early Nixon dropout, Whalen wrote: "We were under the heel of men basically unsure of themselves, second-raters playing over their heads and fiercely resentful of anyone who dared approach them at eye level." This insecurity, and the defensive attitude it engendered, stayed with them all during their years in the White House.

But, if they were "fiercely resentful" of the Washington world around them, the feeling was more than mutual. As they took over the levers of power and began to push their weight around, Haldeman and Ehrlichman made enemies everywhere: on Capitol Hill, throughout the bureaucracies, and, covertly, in and around the White House itself. Even the Secret Service, those dutiful, faceless bodyguards who are schooled to behave at all times with decorum and to avoid the slightest hint of personal or political bias—even they were unable to conceal their loathing. As early as 1970, long before Watergate revealed to the rest of the country the poison that had taken root inside the White House, a Secret Service man confided to a friend: "You know what we say to each other now, don't you?"

"No, what?"

"Come the revolution, be sure and save two bullets: one for Haldeman and one for Ehrlichman."

When asked what the decision would be if a choice had to be made, if at the end there was only one bullet, the response came without a flicker of hesitation: "Haldeman. Definitely. One round left, it goes to him. The other guy has moments when he's not so bad. But Haldeman, never."

It is true that the millions of Americans who saw them in action for the first time at the Watergate hearings were left with a different, if not opposite impression. In front of the television cameras Ehrlichman came on as the scowling heavy while Haldeman, who followed him into the witness chair, was all smiles and agreeableness. But that impression was misleading; another example of devious role playing. For, during their years at the White House, it was Haldeman who inspired the greatest fear, partly because he was the more powerful of the two, but also because he was perceived as meaner, harder, and more unyielding. There was some "give" in Ehrlichman, a few touches of shading here and there. Not much, but some. Even his physical appearance suggested a softness, a flexibility, that was lacking in Haldeman and his brigade of trim, heel-clicking Beavers. To begin with, there was his round, open face and ample brow (like Mitchell, he had little use for a comb), which conveyed an affable manner, at least on the surface. It was a full face, in caloric terms, with jowls in the cheeks and under the chin, and the creases around the corners of his eyes and mouth indicated a man who liked to smile and laugh a lot. (Which was true: unlike Haldeman or Nixon, Ehrlichman was known around the White House for his sense of humor.) When animated by conversation, his eyebrows, in particular, became expressive. He was, to be sure, no threat in this department to Sam Ervin, whose eyebrows are said to have an energy and life force of their own, but Ehrlichman's were more mobile than most. And, when on the listening end, he had a habit of cocking one eyebrow in a quizzical pose, which again was not unappealing since it gave the impression that he was intrigued or at least interested in the point being made, the question being asked. Only in repose, and especially when he put on his half-moon reading glasses, did his features take on the severity of the stern martinet that represented the darker side of his nature. For the most part, however, he greeted the world with a warm and friendly face.

Ehrlichman also was the only member of the West Coast group to sport a sizable belly. He brought the bay window with him to Washington, and during his years at the White House it steadily expanded, which is one reason why he missed the hiking and camping of Seattle days. His girth, plus the fact that he preferred to slouch rather than sit in chairs, gave him a rumpled, unkempt look. So, even though he dressed in the conservative, conventional style dictated by Haldeman, he did not measure up to the sleek, spit-and-polish appearance of the others. And there were two other sartorial deviations that distinguished him from the former admen: he went in for what the Marine Corps calls "high-water" trousers, meaning those that end at the ankle, revealing plenty of sock, and he had a fondness for wearing loafers, a residual quirk from his UCLA days.

In other ways as well, there was a certain casualness about Ehrlichman that set him apart from Haldeman. While both men placed a high premium on efficiency and long working hours, the mood around Ehrlichman's office was a lot more relaxed and informal.

Even though one of the taboo areas, the Seattle Christian Scientist was not above looking up from a conversation to gaze admiringly at a well-turned calf or richly-endowed bosom. In fact, one day, as his eyes fastened on a passing secretary, he remarked to an aide that she had a "nice walk"—a cautious euphemism, perhaps, but as the aide remembers it there was no mistaking his point. And Kenneth Cole, who was his top deputy on the Domestic Council, was impressed by Ehrlichman's little gestures of thoughtfulness, such as the time he sent boxes of Mother's Day candy to the White House telephone operators.

There was, too, his sense of humor. He had a passion for political cartoons, which he splattered over the walls of his outer office. Needless to say, they reflected the prevailing White House bias: attacks on the bureaucracies, Congress, bearded radicals, "welfare chiselers." As for his own attempts to be funny, they were often light-hearted enough (routine office jokes and the like), but it was also in this area that one caught a glimpse of the vindictive streak that ran through his personality. For there was unmistakably a snide quality to his humor that was not at all attractive. He liked to make cutting remarks at the expense of others, and then smirk so that everyone would know how pleased he was with himself. His descriptions of Finch as "the Pasadena Hamlet" and Moynihan as "our Oscar Wilde" are two examples of this. Yet when Moynihan, himself a putdown artist of the first rank, responded in kind by rasping out Ehrlichman's name in guttural, Katzenjammer German, the smirk would vanish from Ehrlichman's face to be replaced by a resentful glower. In this respect, he fit the classic definition of a bully: he wanted the rules written so that only he be allowed to dish it out.

The harder side of his personality also came to the fore in the tough-guy, street-corner lingo he affected from time to time. It was as if he were determined to prove that although an Eagle Scout and a devout Christian Scientist, a man who didn't drink or carouse, he was, nevertheless, no Casper Milquetoast—that he could still rabbit-punch with the best of them. Whenever he tossed off his remark about how "it'll play in Peoria," he adopted the brusque, tough tones of a James Cagney or Tony Curtis. "Give him the shaft" was a favorite order, directed at those he didn't like. He liked to describe his initials, which were so often needed to approve documents, as "my chop mark." A member of the administration who was angry or upset about something became the recipient of a "stroking" call, while another who might be feeling depressed or insecure would receive a "puffing" call.

As time went on, Ehrlichman steadily improved on the jargon until, toward the end of the first term, he became quite the dude, a real hipster. Thus, at the time of the Watergate coverup (assuming John Dean has quoted him accurately), Ehrlichman told Dean to "deep six" the briefcase found in Howard Hunt's safe. Not simply throw it in the river, but "deep six" it, man. And finally at the very end, in his last weeks on the job, he made the breakthrough into poetry with his suggestion, again to Dean, that the pathetic FBI figure, L. Patrick Gray, be abandoned to "twist slowly, slowly in the wind." Not even the gifted Jimmy Breslin, writing about Marvin the Torch or his favorite bookmaker, could have expressed it any better.

By the time of his Watergate testimony, Ehrlichman had long been accustomed to choreographing a great deal more than the destruction of poor Pat Gray. Through much of the first term, there was a conscious effort, on the part of the White House, to play down his importance, to give the impression that he was merely the "coordinator" of domestic policy, a sort of middle man or conduit between the President and the domestic Cabinet. But in truth he was the man at the heart of the decision-making process in domestic affairs, and in some ways his power was even greater than that of Kissinger. Because Nixon himself was obsessed with foreign policy, he took a direct hand in decisions affecting it. On Vietnam, on the China question and all the rest of it, Nixon worked closely with Kissinger on much of the overall planning and on some of the day-to-day details, and the policies that emerged had his clear imprint on them as well as Kissinger's. But the domestic side was something else again. More often than not, policy decisions in that area bored Nixon, and as part of his resolve to devote as much time as possible to foreign policy, his pattern on domestic questions was simply to indicate what he wanted in broad, even vague terms, and leave it up to Ehrlichman to work out the specifics.

Sometimes Nixon would do the indicating to Haldeman, who in turn instructed Ehrlichman. Other times, and increasingly as his own power grew, Ehrlichman would get the word directly. In either circumstance, Haldeman usually supervised and often otherwise personally helped in working out details. He already was, and had been for a long while, a kind of surrogate President for administration and communications.

Now, through Haldeman, John Ehrlichman became, in effect, the surrogate President for domestic affairs, whose operational authority in particular exceeded that given Kissinger in the foreign sphere. When Ehrlichman took on that role, he was inclined to defer a bit to the Cabinet and other agency heads. But, as time went on, he came to regard them, collectively, as an irrelevant nuisance, and he would openly complain about the way Cabinet officers were always trying to waste his or the President's time with their "show-and-tell sessions." In short, he was the one who issued the orders on domestic policy and it was the job of the Cabinet members to fall in line; as we have seen, those who failed to grasp that message were sure to suffer the consequences.

Yet, for all his authority, Ehrlichman produced precious little in the way of innovative policy. There was nothing on his end to match the impressive contributions Kissinger was making in the foreign-policy area. The most ambitious domestic proposal, welfare reform, had been, of course, Moynihan's creation. The problem was that while he and Haldeman had a clear understanding of what the Nixon White House was *against* they were never quite certain what it should be *for*. As a result, domestic policy under Ehrlichman's reign was essentially negative, both in tone and substance. He was against integrated housing in the suburbs, but he had no alternative remedy of his own for dealing with the plight of the cities. And, while he was against busing, he did not offer a realistic solution for coming to terms with *de facto* school segregation. The flippant slogan about Peoria that he cherished so much was nothing more than a political excuse for *not* having a policy rather than a policy itself.

There were, to be sure, some positive achievements along the way. For example, there was some progress made on the environmental front. It is perhaps significant that this happened to be one of the few issues that Ehrlichman, with his background as a land-use lawyer in the ecology-conscious Pacific Northwest, knew something about, and to which he was sufficiently committed to make a strong follow-through effort. Also, in the last months of the first term, Congress finally got around to passing the revenue-sharing bill, which represented the Nixon administration's most coherent philosophic goal: to reduce the swollen power of the federal government in relation to the states. So far, it is true that revenue sharing hasn't had much impact; it hardly has brought on the "new American Revolution" Nixon envisioned when he proposed the plan to funnel money and power back to the states and local communities. But the potential for long-range effect is there, especially if some future administration moves to adopt the revenue-sharing principle and carry it forward.

These modest successes, however, were more than overshadowed by the major setbacks in Nixon's domestic policy. Welfare reform, national health insurance, and SST were just some of the programs that Nixon cited as being among his top priorities, but which failed to win approval in Congress. And much of the blame for that must go to Ehrlichman. It was bad enough that because of his total lack of experience in Washington he didn't understand how Congress worked. What made the situation infinitely worse was that he chose to compensate for his ignorance by adopting an attitude of arrogant disdain toward Capitol Hill. "The President *is* the government," he liked to say, indicating what he truly thought of the Founding Fathers and their checks and balances. And as a corollary to that he once dismissed Congress as that "bunch of clowns," a notion influenced, in part, by his belief that Capitol Hill was awash in demon rum. (Yes, *that* again.) In private conversations, he would paint lurid pictures of how certain Senators and Congressmen had staggered into a session and slurred their way through a speech. None of this had anything to do with the way the House and Senate actually went about their business, but it helped to deepen the hostility between Congress and the White House that so characterized the Nixon Presidency. And bills like welfare reform and national health, which, because of their merit, had chances to gain broad bipartisan support, despite Democratic majorities in Congress, failed at least in part because of the hostility Ehrlichman aroused in Congress. Thus, for all his power as Nixon's domestic czar, Ehrlichman never learned to use it in a positive way. His favorite word was "no" and his favorite Presidential weapon, in dealing with Congress, was the veto. The end result was the most undistinguished performance in domestic policy of any administration since the pre-Roosevelt days of Coolidge and Hoover. That was John Ehrlichman's legacy—that and the Plumbers Unit, the secret White House police force set up under his supervision which eventually gave us the Ellsberg burglary and the Watergate break-in.

As Ehrlichman steadily increased his power and became known among the Washington cognoscenti as the overlord of Nixon's domestic policy, the question would sometimes be asked: Why? Why Ehrlichman instead of Burns or Moynihan or Finch, all three of whom were far more qualified, on the basis of experience, than this obscure zoning lawyer from Seattle who had never before held a government job of any kind on any level. The answers generally given focused on two of his more obvious qualities.

Invariably, reference was made to his efficiency, one of the most highly esteemed virtues in the Nixon White House. He was always well organized, and in his dealings with the President, he was not pontifical (like Burns) or meandering (like Moynihan) or indecisive (like Finch). Instead, he was known to be feisty and forceful; he was good at cutting through the bilge and getting to the nub of a problem, and then spelling it out in the kind of direct, straight-to-the-point language Nixon preferred to use in private. Ehrlichman was knowledgeable too about how to get publicity under the guise of "news." He had a reasonably good sense of what would "sell," and how to sell it. Also, he understood the interest which the President and Haldeman shared in form, in "image," the appearance of things as opposed to the substance of them.

Then, too, there was his loyalty, or super-loyalty. It was a special kind of loyalty, as restricted as it was intense, and Ehrlichman himself was always the first to acknowledge it as such. On more than one occasion he admitted that, although he considered himself to be a lifelong Republican, he had never been that committed to his party or to a conservative ideology. Instead, his loyalty was to one man— Richard Nixon—and the President, affected by his own deeply-rooted insecurities, valued this kind of personal loyalty more than anything else. That was the supreme virtue at the Nixon White House, and Ehrlichman was someone who had it, in spades.

But these attributes and others were just so much frosting. The prime source of Ehrlichman's strength was his relationship with Haldeman. His efficiency was an extension of Haldeman's efficiency, his loyalty an extension of Haldeman's loyalty, and his power an extension of Haldeman's power. Even if he had been twice the bungler he was in his role as Nixon's top domestic policy man, he would have remained secure in that post simply because he was Haldeman's best friend and could count, at all times, on Haldeman's protection. Therefore, the real answer to the question "Why Ehrlichman?" is to be found in the answer to the far more intriguing question "Why Haldeman?"

Twenty

IF HALDEMAN had any "give" or softness in him, he kept it well under wraps. There were no cartoons on his office wall. No one could ever recall him gazing with pleasure at a young lady's "nice walk," much less commenting on it in a vaguely lecherous way. Nor was he ever known to give candy to the White House telephone operators. The closest he came to such a gesture was the time he sent the flowers to Rose Mary Woods; but that was a bribe, a tactic aimed at setting her up for eviction from the White House, rather than an act of thoughtfulness. In Haldeman's case, the severity of his reputation was more than matched by the severity of his appearance and personality.

In a way, the rigid crew cut said plenty. It was always closely cropped—"right down to the wood," as they say in Marine Corps boot camp—and it gave him the intimidating look of a drill instructor. It also served to emphasize his distaste for the florid hair styles that were part of the counter-culture revolution of the sixties. During his years in Washington, Haldeman's eldest son, Hank, who was in high school at the time, succumbed to the hippie influence and let his grow to below shoulder length. That not only caused problems in the family, but it reinforced Haldeman's hostility toward the pernicious "local culture." (In an attempt to change his image slightly, after he left the White House and returned to California, he let his own hair grow out a bit—though just a bit. He still kept it Beaver Patrol short.)

To go with the brush, he had a drill instructor's build, lean and hard. In contrast to Ehrlichman, there was no fat in his face or belly.

He jogged and exercised regularly to stay trim, and although Ehrlichman sometimes went out to lunch, thus braving contact with the outside world as well as the caloric assault on his figure, Haldeman usually followed Nixon's own ascetic preference for lunch: cottage cheese and pineapple, which he would eat in his office. A college football coach, looking them over, would have assigned Haldeman to the end position, while Ehrlichman, who was a natural guard when he first came to Washington, soon swelled into a tackle.

Next to the crew cut, Haldeman's most distinctive physical feature is his eyes (as opposed to Ehrlichman's eye*brows*). He has large, vividly blue eyes, their color enhanced by the deep tan he was careful to maintain at all times. There were some who described them as "icy blue," and with good reason. The intensity he could bring to a glare of disapproval was something his many subordinates came to dread. Even in routine conversation, he would often fix one with a hard, piercing stare, as though he were trying to see through the person to the hidden truth behind what was being said. In this regard, Haldeman was the antithesis of his boss and hero. To those who observed him over the years, Nixon became noted for the difficulty he apparently had looking anyone straight in the eye; he usually focused on shirt collars or Adam's apples. Even the Russians privately commented on this at the time of his visit to Moscow in 1972.

The glacial stare and drill instructor's bearing blended in well with Haldeman's curt and frosty manner. Whereas Ehrlichman generally made an effort to put people at ease, Haldeman was brusque and businesslike and frequently impatient for the person he was with to get to the point, to skip the amenities. He did not encourage levity or casualness, at least during working hours; on those rare occasions when something did strike him as funny, he would laugh or smile briefly, get it over with, then snap right back to the serious business at hand.

He had his own distinctive approach to language. It may have lacked the panache of Ehrlichman's efforts to come on as a kind of corpulent Cagney, but it had a deeper and far more pervasive influence on the Nixon White House. Haldeman and his J. Walter Thompson cohorts brought with them to Washington their adman's lingo, and soon everyone around the White House was popping off about "input" and "low profile" and "the bottom line," and how they were all going to "stonewall it" or "hard-nose it out." In the Haldeman-

Ziegler-Chapin argot, news briefings became "information opportunities." Plans were not carried out, they were "implemented."
There were no deadlines as such, but everyone operated within
tightly scheduled "time frames." Instead of perfection, the ultimate
goal was a "zero defect system." People who had rapport with each
other were said to "track well." And, as the entire world found out
during the Watergate hearings, last month or a year ago June or
whenever was always "at that point in time."

With his trim, Ivy League suits, his button-down white shirts, and
his narrow, muted ties, Haldeman's sartorial "point in time" was the
gray-flannel fifties. And not only did he expect others who came
under his direct control to dress in a conservative style, but he was
almost a fanatic on the subject of grooming. He somehow managed
to tolerate the way Ehrlichman went around looking like an unmade
bed, but others were judged more harshly. One junior staffer, who
sensed that he had fallen out of favor with Haldeman, eventually
learned through the grapevine that the chief complaint against him
was that he did not keep his tie on straight.

This passion for neatness carried over into every aspect of Haldeman's work, from the meticulous appearance of his desk and office
to the orderly notes he made on his yellow legal pads. The terse
memos he frequently sent to other staffers were almost always
printed, as though his fastidious nature could not bear the scribbled
look of handwriting. Many of these messages also revealed just how
stern a taskmaster he was. Once Jeb Magruder sent him a memo
spelling out an "idea" he had for something or other. Haldeman
promptly sent it back with the printed reply: "Your job is to do, not
to think." Another time a staffer sent a memo to Haldeman and got
it back with the cryptic notation: "TL²." When he finally worked up
the courage to ask what that meant, Haldeman glared at him a
moment, then snapped, "Too little, too late."

The fear Haldeman inspired throughout the White House was
awesome to behold. Two of his protégés, Dwight Chapin and Larry
Higby, rode to work with him each morning in a government limousine, and there were occasions when, on arriving at the White House,
one or the other or sometimes even both young men would emerge
from the limousine looking pale and cowed, almost on the verge of
tears. What it meant was that Haldeman had used the ride in from

the Maryland suburbs to read the riot act to one of them (or both) for something he, or they, had done or had failed to do the previous day. There was the time Gordon Strachan was awakened in the middle of the night by Haldeman, who called to chew him out for some minor slip-up. Strachan soon fell back asleep, and when he woke up the next morning, he thought perhaps the call had been a nightmare —that is, until he checked with the White House switchboard and was told that yes, indeed, Bob Haldeman had telephoned his home around three o'clock that morning.

Nor was it just the immediate underlings on his personal staff who lived in fear of Haldeman's power and the way he used it. One time a high-level aide to the President asked a reporter to include a favorable word about Haldeman in a story he was putting together. The reporter protested that his story had nothing to do with Haldeman, and that there was no legitimate reason even to mention him. The high-ranking aide grimaced and said, in a beseeching tone: "Say something nice about him anyway." What both the topsider and the junior staff members understood, only too well, was that Haldeman had the raw power to destroy them, at least as far as their careers in the White House were concerned, and that he would not hesitate to do so. Klein and Moynihan and the various Cabinet officers were merely the most celebrated victims. For every big fish Haldeman harpooned, there were any number of small fry forced out of the administration because they incurred his displeasure. And, for all of them, there was no way to appeal over Haldeman's head, except to go the Wally Hickel route and force a public confrontation—and everyone saw what happened to him. "Bob's a great winnower," Dwight Chapin once said in dutiful praise of his mentor. He was referring to Haldeman's ability to handle the mounds of paperwork that piled up on his desk each day. But the remark also was an apt description of the way he treated people.

Chapin's comment about the paperwork was very much to the point, however, for Haldeman's iron control over "input" was an integral part of his power. Virtually every memo or document sent to the President had to go through Haldeman, and he had the authority to pass judgment, to decide what was worthy of Nixon's personal attention and what was not. Often, if a memo didn't meet with his approval, he would send it back to be revised. And, as a general rule, even those documents that did penetrate the sanctity of the Oval

Office were heavily edited by Haldeman, boiled down to the "gist," to use his favorite word for it. "A great winnower," to be sure, but as every editor knows, the entire meaning of something can be changed by deleting or compressing a few sentences here and there.

And there were times when not even the "gist" of a message reached the President. For example, once a request came up through White House staff channels urging Nixon to telephone a mortally ill Republican Senator. When it reached Haldeman's desk, the super efficiency expert decided that since the Senator was in that bad a shape he probably wouldn't be able to talk very well over the phone anyway, and thus it would make more sense to hold off and place a call to his widow—later. So, instead of passing the request on to Nixon, he sent it back down through the channels with the memorable command: "Wait until he dies."

The idea of *two* telephone calls for one dying Senator apparently offended his sense of efficiency. The cardinal rule was that the President's time was not to be squandered. Nor, for that matter, was anyone else's. As time went on, Haldeman began assigning his own people to various offices around the White House to serve as watchdogs and informers. At one point, he found a job for Jeb Magruder in Herb Klein's shop because he had convinced himself that Klein's staff was disorganized, goofing off, and dragging its heels. There also had been talk—nothing serious, just gossip—that Klein's office, which was staffed by several unmarrieds, was a hotbed of promiscuity, and he wanted to be fully informed on that as well. ("Your job is to *spy*, not to think" is how that earlier memo to Magruder should have read.) It was partly for the same purpose—providing information to Haldeman—that Haldeman later sent Magruder over to the Committee to Re-elect the President to work as Mitchell's deputy, a move that placed Magruder at the heart of the Watergate operation and started him on his road to prison. By the end of the first term, after he had built up his empire, Haldeman would have his people placed in strategic positions in departments and agencies throughout the executive branch, yet even then he worked zealously to conceal the fact that he was the man who controlled the chessboard. "You never know when Bob pulls a string," a White House insider once confided, "unless you notice who suddenly pops up straight at the other end."

From the beginning, however, his most important power base was his role as sentinel supreme, the man who stood between the

President and the outside world. And, as Nixon secreted himself deeper and deeper behind his Haldeman-supervised protective rings, the efforts of some government officials to make contact bordered on the ludicrous. Once John Volpe, after months of trying in vain to gain access, managed to slip into the Oval Office on the coattails of a visiting foreign archbishop. Others would seize upon the few seconds available at the White House Sunday services to try to set something up. On such occasions, Nixon would always be courteous, and even appear interested, but that would usually be the end of it. A follow-through call the next day would result in the same old story: "I'm sorry, Mr. Secretary, but the President's tied up this week. If you could put it in writing . . ."

Even more galling was the fact that as Haldeman's own power increased he himself became inaccessible. It eventually reached the point where it was not uncommon for a Cabinet officer or Congressional leader, seeking Presidential guidance on some matter, to wind up doing business over the phone with one of Haldeman's young minions, usually Chapin or Higby. ("I'll give Bob your message, Senator, but I can't promise that he'll be able to get back to you today. He and the President . . .") Since they basked in the reflected glory of Haldeman, even the members of the Beaver Patrol felt they had the right to advise high-level government officials on what course of action to take.

Haldeman resented all criticisms of what he considered to be his "zero defect system" of running things. "I get fed up with the 'isolation' argument," he once said. "If everybody who wanted to see him got in, nobody would get in because there wouldn't be room." And in his book on the 1972 campaign Theodore White quotes Haldeman as saying the President "needs input. And seeing people is not the only way, not necessarily the best way. Getting the facts, the opinions, the ideas, is input. . . . The way to make him accessible is to isolate him from the trivia, and that's my job."

The various government officials and party leaders who felt sealed off from direct and personal contact with Nixon did not regard themselves as bearers of trivia, but Haldeman truly could not understand their objections. As he saw it, Cabinet officers and their associates were more administrators than policy makers, and as chiefly administrators they had the White House staff structure he set up and rigidly controlled to meet their needs. If they had a problem, they should take it up with Ehrlichman or Kissinger or George Shultz, the three members of the White House staff who met on a regular basis with the President to work out policy positions. Those who complained of the arrangement and kept insisting that they had to see Nixon himself were, in Haldeman's view, prima donnas, insensitive to the President's great need for privacy.

Toward members of Congress, he was even less patient. He saw no reason why they should have been bothering the White House at all. In a revealing comment to Allen Drury in early 1971, Haldeman said: "I don't think Congress is supposed to work with the White House. It is a different organization, and under the Constitution I don't think we should expect agreement." Aside from the commotion such a remark must have caused at the various grave sites of the Founding Fathers, it could not help but dismay and antagonize Senators and Congressmen in the President's own party, who were doing their best to line up support for programs that Nixon himself had singled out as among the top priorities of his Presidency. But none of this cut any ice with Haldeman. Even more than Ehrlichman, he endorsed the notion that the President *is* the government (though of course both he and Ehrlichman would profess outrage when George McGovern warned, in a prophetic speech after his 1972 defeat, that America was veering dangerously close to a system of "one-man rule"). As far as Haldeman was concerned, the President, being the government, prescribed programs which in his infinite wisdom he deemed best for the country. If certain Senators and Congressmen couldn't accept them on that basis, then they had no business coming to the White House to offer compromises or alternative proposals. Take it or leave it—that was Haldeman's attitude toward Capitol Hill.

Yet, although he often bristled at criticism of the way he ran the Nixon White House, a part of him seemed at times to take pleasure in his reputation as the dread Rasputin poised at the door to the Oval Office. His favorite description of his role was to say: "Every President needs an S.O.B.—and I'm Nixon's." That line, or a variation of it, was one he would repeat time and time again. And when, at one point, he was told that some junior staff members had started referring to him, behind his back, as the "Abominable No-Man," he broke into one of his broad, toothy grins. He liked that, and he did his best to live up to it.

In addition to all his managerial duties and his role as the stern protector of the President's person, Haldeman also was the chief guardian of Nixon's image. As the top media strategist at the White House, he was in firm control of all decisions related to that mysterious and continual process known as the "Selling of the President." Much of the time, this meant making negative decisions. Haldeman took great pains to make certain that the President never found himself in an awkward situation that might reflect unfavorably on the man or the office. But if such a situation did arise, where the President lapsed into a mode of behavior unbefitting the Nixonian stature, then it was Haldeman's job to keep it under wraps so that the public image would not be tainted.

For example, there was the time that several blind men, representing a veterans group, were ushered into the Oval Office for a brief ceremonial visit. As the President came forward to greet his visitors, there followed the kind of inane and stilted small talk that generally reveals Nixon at his most self-conscious. And, at one point, apparently at a loss for something to say, Nixon happened to mention that they were standing on the Presidential seal. (A large design of the seal is woven into the material of the carpet in the center of the Oval Office.) In response to that disclosure, one of the blind men startled the President by getting down on his knees and moving his hands over the carpet. A moment later, he told Nixon that he recognized the Presidential seal from the "feel" of the design.

Nixon, dropping his stiff and formal manner, was fascinated. And the next thing everyone knew (there were a number of people present, including official photographers from the White House staff) there was the President of the United States down on *his* knees, feeling around the carpet with his eyes closed in an effort to share the blind man's experience. It was a touching and human moment, one that revealed a side of Nixon seldom seen outside his intimate circle of friends, and the photographers were quick to recognize it as such. They went into action—click-click, click-click—while off to one side, witnessing the scene, was Haldeman. This was not what the program had called for. And after the session was over an edict was issued through Haldeman's office, that under no circumstances were any pictures showing the President pawing around on the floor with his eyes closed and his tie hanging out to be released to the press for public distribution. In Haldeman's view, apparently, the spontaneous incident lacked dignity; it was not Presidential. He was right in a way: it was merely human.

Then there was the case of the National Retarded Children's Association poster girl for 1970. The association had arranged to have the girl's photograph taken with the President. There was a mix-up about the exact date. At least the Haldeman-Chapin-Ziegler operation maintained that there was a mix-up. All the girl's family knew was that on the day they had been told she would have her photograph taken with the President, it didn't happen. They complained to their home state Senator, Robert Dole of Kansas. Dole, a staunch Nixon supporter at the time, tried to tell the Haldeman-Chapin-Ziegler group: "Listen, whatever the problem, this is turning into a public-relations disaster, if for no other reason than the fact that this poster girl is black. And, well, you know how that may play . . ."

Tilt. White House aides claimed not to have known that the girl was black. There were hurried phone calls between Ziegler's office out front and Haldeman's in the rear. Confusion reigned. Photographers and reporters already had been alerted and had been led to believe by the White House press office that the "photo opportunity" would be coming off momentarily. Word came forward from Haldeman's office: To hell with the press. The picture isn't going to happen today and may not happen at all, ever. The story that the President had refused to have his picture taken with a black retarded child went out on the national wire services. No one who knew him well could believe that the President personally would have made such a decision.

As 1972 approached, Haldeman began to rev up the image machinery for the re-election campaign. This reportedly involved, among other things, an in-depth marketing survey, which came up with the astounding discovery that the name Nixon generally turned people off. It was supposed to have something to do with the X, or the Nix. Anyway, bad vibes. Nobody dared to suggest that the lack of enthusiasm might be attributed, in some remote way, to the man who made the name famous, for that is not how the advertising mind works. It would be like saying one declines to buy a breakfast cereal because he doesn't like the way it tastes, when we all know it's because he's not attracted to the name or the design on the box. So, to get around the problem of X or Nix, Haldeman and his crew of admen came up with the idea that the bumper-sticker slogan for 1972 should be "Re-elect the President." You know, what's-his-name.

They didn't exactly rush into this decision. In the several days of intense, cerebral discussion that preceded it, there were arguments that perhaps the voters should be urged to "Re-elect *Our* President" —or better yet, "Re-elect *Your* President." In the end, however, it was decided that while *the* President lacked a certain warmth, it had more dignity and class. Yet, in their glee over having come up with a slogan that successfully avoided the need to identify their candidate by name, it apparently never occurred to them that the '72 campaign organization would then be called the Committee to Re-elect the President, and that it, inevitably, would be reduced to the acronym CREEP. Oh, well. He who lives by the sword . . .

Haldeman's daily concern over image even included advising the President on his wardrobe. Not long after they settled in at the White House, he suggested that the President wear light-colored suits in the morning (for cheerfulness), then deepen the hue as the day progressed so that by evening he would be appropriately attired in dark blue. He also offered a few tips on ties, such as when dots were in order and the value of stripes on certain occasions. And, of course, as previously noted, the little flag in the lapel was one of Haldeman's more inspirational touches. He was especially attentive to matters of dress whenever the President was planning to go on television, to address the nation or hold a news conference. On these occasions, he served as a combination stage manager and set designer, seeing to it that the right kind of props were on display (like the bust of Lincoln) and that everything proceeded smoothly.

One of Haldeman's more elaborate image endeavors was a project that came to be known around the White House as the "Sea Shot." As part of his overall Kennedy hangup, he had been irritated for some time by the various pictures over the years of the Kennedys sailing on Nantucket Sound or frolicking with their kids on the beach at Hyannis Port. Haldeman sensed that the photographs had been artfully contrived for effect—i.e., the work of a good image man in the Kennedy camp. Yet he had to admit that they generally met with a favorable response; the public seemed to take to the idea that the Kennedys were fond of the sea. So, after Nixon became President, Haldeman was determined to get some of that action for his man.

Nixon, after all, also had been in the Navy, and his two homes at Key Biscayne and San Clemente were proof enough that he too was a man who loved the sea. It was just a question of driving that point home to the public.

Weeks of planning went into the "Sea Shot." It was debated at length whether the event should take place at Key Biscayne or San Clemente, but finally the latter site was chosen because (a) Nixon was a native of California and (b) since there was such a heavy emphasis on Asia in his foreign policy, it was deemed more appropriate that he should assume a Pacific identity. Besides, the Atlantic, washing up against Cape Cod, was the Kennedys' ocean.

The press, as usual, was kept in the dark until the very end. Even on the morning of the great event, no one suspected anything dramatic was in the works when Ziegler announced that there would be a "photo opportunity" later that day. "Photo opportunities" were fairly common occurrences at San Clemente, partly because Haldeman thought it necessary for the President to be seen on television working in California, as protection against anyone thinking Nixon and his large traveling staff might just be loafing out there. They usually meant that a foreign dignitary or some other personage worthy of camera attention had stopped by for a visit. On such occasions, the principals almost always posed for the pictures in the President's office or in one of the gardens outside the Western White House. But on this particular day, in the summer of 1970, the photographers and reporters were not escorted to any office or garden. Instead, they were led up to a great cliff, not far from the Nixon home, which offers a dazzling, panoramic view of the Pacific and the long stretch of beach several hundred feet below.

As the cameramen lugged their equipment up the cliff, there was grumbling in the ranks along the lines of: "what the hell is *this* all about?" One fellow, known for his morbid nature, suggested that this might be it, that "they're luring us all up there to push us off." On reaching the edge of the cliff, they quickly scanned the empty expanse of ocean spread out before them, and somebody asked: "Anyone know what we're supposed to be looking for?" A moment later, all eyes were directed to the distant beach below, and there he was: the President walking along, at water's edge, in solitary splendor. A respectful hush fell over the group, but it lasted only a few seconds. "Good Christ," a raucous voice sang out, "he's wearing *shoes.*" Alas, so he was.

So here was Haldeman's Old Salt of the Sea, traipsing along the beach in an ill-fitting windbreaker, a pair of dress trousers, and *street* shoes. Not exactly the same as the familiar, windblown pictures of JFK shifting to leeward in his boat off Cape Cod, but nevertheless they did get some mileage out of it. The "Sea Shot" made a big media splash—wet shoes and all.

If the "Sea Shot" was, at best, a qualified success, it was because the sporty image envisioned had so little to do with the true nature of the man. Richard Nixon has a number of outstanding qualities— he has a probing analytical mind and driving perseverance, he is an avid reader and a good listener—but he has never been known for his athletic grace or his zest for the outdoor life, whether on land or sea. It may not be true, as Mort Sahl suggests, that he was "born in a blue suit," but to try to present him to the public as a sporty seafarer à la Kennedy was absurd on the face of it.

On other occasions, however, when Haldeman's media talents were applied to Nixon's natural strengths, the results were impressive. For example, the many trips abroad. Questions of foreign policy have almost never failed to bring out the best in Nixon, a sense of self-assurance that so often seemed to be lacking in his approach to domestic affairs and political problems at home. And invariably, whenever he visited foreign capitals, this confidence in his own ability and judgment would surface and deeply impress his various hosts. For all his bowing and scraping at Orly Airport when De Gaulle welcomed him to Paris in early 1969, the truth is that De Gaulle genuinely respected Nixon for his knowledge of history and international affairs, which was more than could be said for Kennedy or other American Presidents who tried to do business with *le général* over the years. What's more, De Gaulle's high opinion of Nixon was shared by many others: by Tito and Ceausescu, by Willy Brandt and Brezhnev—and most significantly, perhaps, by Chou En-lai. Haldeman's job on these overseas trips was to make sure that the strong, self-assured Nixon who impressed world leaders was the image conveyed to the voters back home, and on the historic visit to Peking in 1972 he really pulled out the stops.

Just as the China trip stands out as the high point of Nixon's Presidency, so the media sell that went with it must be regarded as Haldeman's finest hour. From the moment of arrival in Peking, which was precisely scheduled to coincide with television prime time in all four zones back home (10:30 P.M. in New York, 7:30 P.M.

on the West Coast), and on through all the sundry banquets and sightseeing tours, the event was exquisitely orchestrated to achieve maximum effect, to flash all the lights on Nixon's image board.

Even the fact that the day-to-day meetings with Chou En-lai produced little in the way of substantive news played to Haldeman's advantage. The President's merely being in China was the headline story, regardless of what was or was not accomplished, and Haldeman performed brilliantly to get that story across in pictures, to transform it into a TV spectacular. Day after day, the footage was beamed, via satellite, into the living rooms of America: the Great Wall . . . the Forbidden City . . . Chou and the President feeding goldfish in Hangchow . . . the First Lady chatting with cooks in a Peking kitchen . . . a little gymnastics for the *Wide World of Sports* fans . . . some ballet shots for the culture vultures . . . and even a brief glimpse of Mao himself, chortling with Nixon and looking for all the world like some affable grandfather giving his blessing to a long-lost relative. (Shortly before going to China, Nixon said, in a private chat, that he understood why many young people in other countries and even some in America looked up to Mao. Like Ike and De Gaulle, Nixon contended, Mao was perceived by the young as "a father figure.")

And most important of all was the fact that the trip (or "Journey for Peace," as the White House called it) took place in February, 1972, or just at the time the Democratic primaries were heating up back home. Thus the television viewers (i.e., voters) were treated to a dramatic contrast between the President making history behind the bamboo curtain and the peevish squabbling among Democratic rivals in New Hampshire and Florida. In many ways the China visit *was* a campaign story, the champagne launch of Nixon's bid for re-election, and Haldeman made the most of it. As one White House staffer put it months later, after the landslide victory over McGovern: "The China trip was Bob Haldeman's masterpiece, his Sistine Chapel."

His media gifts, then, were a large part of Haldeman's value to Nixon. The debates with Kennedy in 1960 and, to a lesser extent, the infamous "last press conference" in '62 left Nixon with the feeling that television had betrayed him. But, although he loathed the television age and the crass indignities he felt it imposed on political candidates, he recognized that there was no escaping it. Thus in 1968 and afterward, as he moved into his Presidency, he was determined to master the tube and bring it under his control. Haldeman, therefore, was his Merlin, his media magician. If the medium was the message, then it was up to Haldeman to make sure that the right message got across.

Another plus, of course, was his efficiency, his managerial skills. Nixon's own compulsion for neatness and order found a perfect counterpart in Haldeman's meticulous approach to the day-to-day operation, and between them they set an exacting standard for all others to follow. Brilliance and creativity meant little at the Nixon White House, if such gifts were accompanied by sloppiness and lack of preparation. Attention to minutiae and detail took precedence over the large vision, intuitively conceived, with loose ends and rough edges.

But even more important to Nixon than the efficiency expert in Haldeman was the Abominable No-Man role he assumed. For all his early reputation as a hatchet man who loved to go for the jugular of an opponent, Nixon actually has always abhorred unpleasant personal confrontations. Hence, as President, he relied on others—Mitchell, Ehrlichman, but especially Haldeman—to do his ass kicking for him. (During the post-Watergate months of crisis that followed Haldeman's departure, the personable Alexander Haig would be given that unenviable assignment.) To some extent, no doubt, it is true that "every President needs an S.O.B.," as Haldeman was so fond of saying; but Nixon needed one more than most. For example, Lyndon Johnson would never have dreamed of relinquishing that role to a subordinate, not as long as he had the voice and strength to subject a delinquent Cabinet officer to the torrent of obscenities that marked his personal style. But that was not Nixon's style. When in the presence of a few trusted aides, like Haldeman, the discussion centered on people who *were not there,* Nixon could be just as abusive and obscene as LBJ.

But he had no taste for inflicting rough language on his enemies in face-to-face encounters, as the Wally Hickel episode so clearly demonstrates. "I want to get rid of that bastard," the President was quoted as saying privately when it was going on, yet the vacillation that preceded Hickel's firing was largely brought on by Nixon's lingering hope that the stubborn Alaskan could be persuaded by others to resign quietly. Only when it became evident that there was no other way to "get rid" of Hickel was he summoned to the Oval Office for a direct confrontation, and dismissal. Yet, even then, Nixon behaved with courtesy and restraint. Contrast that with Haldeman's demolition approach the next working day when he dispatched Fred Malek to the Interior Department to sack six of Hickel's top deputies.

On these occasions, when Haldeman lowered the boom for Nixon, the President made it clear he did not want to be burdened with the details. All he desired from Haldeman was confirmation that such-and-such a problem had been taken care of; he did not want to know if the victim bled or cried out when Haldeman put the knife to him. And Haldeman, with his subtle understanding of Nixon's complicated personality, usually took pains to shield the President from the sordid realities, to just give him the "gist" of what happened.

And, finally, there was Haldeman's deeply intense and very special brand of loyalty, which, more than anything else, accounted for the great trust Nixon placed in him. To a degree not even approached by any of the other men around Nixon, Haldeman could suppress his own ego and personality and thus give himself entirely to serving the President's will and needs. This ability to play sounding board and self-effacing confidant first manifested itself back in 1961, when the two men first worked closely together on the *Six Crises* project, and by the time they reached the White House their relationship had been honed to the point where Haldeman could grasp the implications of the slightest Nixon gesture—a sudden glance or the flicker of a smile—and respond accordingly. In a real sense, he became an extension of Nixon himself. Or, as a White House staff member once said of Haldeman: "He has no individual entity the way most men do. If he hadn't found Nixon, he would have found someone else." Even his wife, Joanne, was reported to have said after the 1968 victory: "Thank goodness Nixon won because now Bob will have something to devote his life to."

To say that he was constantly at Nixon's beck and call doesn't begin to suggest the degree to which that was so. Haldeman himself was the first to admit that he had no schedule of his own, that he was always ready to jump whenever the President needed him. He was the first person summoned to the Oval Office each morning, and the last one to confer with Nixon at the end of the day. And in between he would be called in several more times, either for more private talks or to be present when Nixon met with other top officials. Moreover, it was a rare evening that passed at home without at least one call from the President to remind him to take care of something or other.

Always, whenever Nixon traveled, there was Haldeman at or near his side. One time, midway through the first term, the President, accompanied by his entourage, flew to the Virgin Islands for a semiworking vacation at the luxurious Rockefeller resort Caneel Bay. In the aftermath of that trip, a close associate of Haldeman told a reporter the following story.

One evening, while at Caneel, Haldeman decided to go sailing with some other members of the White House staff. But just to be on the safe side he brought along his "beeper," a radio device through which the President could signal if he wanted him for something. And, sure enough, the sailing party had gotten only about a half mile from shore when suddenly, "Beep-beep, beep-beep," followed by a voice relaying the message that Nixon needed something.

Haldeman snapped to attention and ordered the boat returned to shore. Immediately everyone began pitching in to turn the boat around, but the effort did not proceed fast enough to suit Haldeman. Soon tempers grew short, sharp words were exchanged, and Haldeman became frantic, going so far as to imply that his shipmates were deliberately stalling to prevent him from making a prompt response to the President's beep signal. And the next thing the others on board knew Haldeman had taken off his shoes and dived overboard. A strong swimmer, he apparently concluded that a brisk crawl stroke would get him back to shore and to the President's side a few seconds sooner. Later, after the crisis was over, he would deal with his laggard shipmates.

While we realize this story sounds a trifle far-fetched, those familiar with the Nixon White House during those years, and therefore familiar with the way Haldeman worked, have never had trouble believing that it happened.

Unlike Ehrlichman, whose loyalty to Nixon was strictly personal, Haldeman's loyalty was rooted in a strong ideological base, which gave it more of a cutting edge. His idea of conservatism, inherited from his wealthy family and nurtured by the anti-Communist fervor of his UCLA days, took on an even sharper intensity during the years he lived in the heart of Orange County. There he was caught up in the militant atmosphere that flourished in the fifties and early sixties, when Orange County Republicans prided themselves on being several degrees to the right of Barry Goldwater. Haldeman's home in Newport Beach was just down the street from John Wayne's. It is an area catacombed with support for the John Birch Society. This is not to say that everyone in Orange County and the surrounding territory is part of the extreme political right, nor even a lifelong Republican. But the strain runs stronger there than perhaps any place else in the country, just as, for example, the Berkeley–San Francisco vicinity has a similar high index of extremists on the far left.

Haldeman has never considered himself an extremist politically. He believes that he and those among whom he grew up represent the real middle or near middle of the American political mainstream. Thus, when in 1972 he accused Congressmen and others with honest differences of opinion with Nixon over Vietnam of "consciously" supporting, "aiding and abetting" the enemy—the constitutional definition of treason—it was hard for him to believe that any intelligent person not committed to the far left could disagree. Loyalty to Nixon, in Haldeman's mind, was synonymous with loyalty to America. And people who did not agree should be considered enemies, not just of Nixon but also of the country.

But, if his ideological views brought an added depth and strength to his loyalty, the loyalty itself was always more personal than political. Faced with a choice, he would bend or relax his supposed conservative principles if, by doing so, it would serve Nixon's purposes. Hence, Haldeman supported completely Nixon's increasing the federal budget deficit by a record eighty billion dollars plus during his first term. Conservatives such as Arthur Burns worried about that. But not Haldeman. He also cheerfully went along with the President's "grand design" to run for re-election in 1972 from the steps of the Kremlin and the Great Hall of the People in Peking. Other conservatives, like Bill Buckley, may have been distressed to see Nixon, the lifelong anti-Communist, consorting with the enemy, and may have resented the fact that such steadfast Cold War allies as Chiang Kai-shek were sold down the Yangtze by the policies of this "new Nixon." Still others might question whether courting the Soviets and mainland Chinese without first fully consulting Japan and

America's friends in Western Europe was worth the risk to America's long-standing defense alliances. And many conservatives as well as liberals in both parties wondered aloud if the President had not perhaps conceded too much for his country's safety in his rush to get a deal limiting nuclear missiles. But no such concerns touched Haldeman's conscience. His faith in the man was so unshakable that he would defend, with ardor, concessions to Communists or anything else that smacked of liberal revisionism—so long as Nixon approved it. And neither Buckley nor any other conservative could convince him that the Richard Nixon he knew and loved would ever do anything to endanger freedom or further the cause of Communism.

The Richard Nixon he knew and loved. Yes, finally it comes down to that: the fact that Bob Haldeman truly loved Nixon. Other Presidents, of course, have been similarly loved by men who worked closely with them. LBJ, though in many ways a hard man, was loved by Bill Moyers and Jack Valenti and others who knew him well. Ted Sorensen and the claque of Irishmen who served on the New Frontier certainly loved Kennedy. And it could be said of Eisenhower that he was loved by just about everyone.

But that could not be said of Nixon. He has had many allies and associates over the years, men who have respected and admired him for his intelligence and political skills. But, with the possible exception of Bob Finch, it is difficult to think of anyone—save Haldeman —who ever indicated, in any meaningful way, that he loved Nixon. He has been too much the loner, too much the private man, to inspire that kind of open affection. Always courteous, often pleasant, at times even friendly in a guarded sort of way, Nixon has never struck many people who worked with him as being lovable. But to Haldeman he was—and no doubt still is—a man to be loved.

Nixon recognized this and, within the limits of his inherent shyness and reserve, responded in kind. Because Haldeman's devotion to the President was undemanding and low key, in keeping with his own Teutonic reserve, Nixon found it easy to accept. Since they were both inclined to be cautious introverts who shared the same supersquare traits at a time when so much of the country was exploding in cultural revolution, they brought roughly the same criteria to their view of America, of the people around them, and of each other. Nixon could relax with Haldeman because Haldeman was so predictable in personality and attitude; from him there was never any threat of being thrown off balance by dramatic excess or jarring surprise.

Other men with more flamboyant personalities, like Pat Moynihan or John Connally, could fascinate Nixon for a time, enrich his imagination, and absorb his interest. But only for a time. Eventually they would wear him down, drain his energies, and make him wary. After a while, he would withdraw from such men, like a turtle pulling its head back into the shell. But with a Haldeman—or an Ehrlichman too, for that matter—he was never in danger of being overstimulated. Hence, they were viewed as ideal associates over the long haul. With them, Nixon always felt in control, and in command.

Haldeman's love for the President flowed in an unbroken line from the youthful passion of his UCLA days, when he first became a true believer in Richard Nixon. And in a way that was the Nixon —the bare-knuckle campaigner, the destroyer of Hiss—he continued to worship, and continued to perceive even through all the layers of "New Nixons" that had been applied, like so much varnish, over the years. He was like a man who, after twenty years of marriage, can look at his wife and still see, behind the wrinkles and touches of gray in her hair, the fresh young beauty he first kissed beneath the willows that summer night so many years ago.

And in moments of stress and crisis Haldeman had an uncanny knack for inducing Nixon to revert to his early, hatchet-man style, for bringing to the surface the "Old Nixon." One example, already noted, was the morning after the 1962 defeat when Haldeman's rage against the press, delivered in the privacy of Nixon's hotel suite, stirred the darker emotions in Nixon and brought on his own display of public wrath—the celebrated "last press conference." And eight years later, as the pressures of another campaign—the midterm election of 1970—built up to a climax, Haldeman would again inspire his hero to adopt the tactics and belligerent manner of his early, Congressional years. The consequences of that inspiration would have a great bearing on all the political disasters that followed.

Twenty-one

FROM the beginning, an active and tough-minded political apparatus was in operation at the Nixon White House, and this too was an integral part of Haldeman's empire. By 1970, three men— Murray Chotiner, Harry Dent, and Charles Colson—were sharing the assignment of protecting Nixon's political flank, or as one White House aide said, in describing their role in the summer of 1970: "Murray, Harry, and Chuck are the original back-room boys, the operators and the brokers, the guys who fix things when they break down and do the dirty work when it's necessary." They were to politics what John Ehrlichman was to domestic policy, what Ron Ziegler was to press relations, and what other members of the Beaver Patrol were to staff management and Presidential image making. That is, they worked directly under Haldeman and were answerable to him.

Chotiner, the old California ally who first tutored Nixon in how to grip the political hatchet to get the most lethal use out of it, was still regarded by many Nixon followers as an embarrassment, a disturbing reminder of the Bad Old Days. But he had been quietly rehabilitated in 1968, when he worked out of Mitchell's campaign office in New York, and later, just as quietly, Haldeman brought him into the White House. Dent, as already noted, was Strom Thurmond's boy, the White House tactician on all matters involving Southern Strategy. As for Colson, the Boston lawyer who joined the White House staff in the fall of 1969, he would go on to become, in the months following the 1970 midterm election, Nixon's top political lieutenant. And in that role he would acquire vast power, on a par with Ehrlichman and just a notch below Haldeman himself in the overall White House hierarchy. But that would come later: 1972 was destined to be Chuck Colson's big year. In the planning for the '70 midterm campaign, Chotiner and Dent were at least as active as Colson.

The number-one ball carrier for the White House in the '70 campaign was, of course, "El Greco"—the pride of Baltimore County. Actually, the White House drive to win more Republican seats in Congress in 1970 had been in progress since the previous fall, when Agnew was first sent out across the country to give voice to the smoldering resentments of the "silent majority." During this period, from the fall of '69 through the stormy campaign weeks of 1970, Spiro had reached the crest of his brief and improbable career. And what a dazzling, mind-boggling spectacle it was, the political career of this one-time supermarket manager. Not since Lon Chaney was in his prime has anyone gone through more changes in personal identity.

In the short span of seven years, Agnew flashed before us first as a liberal or *quasi*-liberal (in 1966, when he ran for Governor of Maryland against a Wallace-type Democrat, he openly courted blacks and white liberals, and it was their votes that elected him) . . . then as buffoon (in his '68 Vice Presidential campaign) . . . then as scourge of the media and student dissenters and other "enemies" of Flag and Country . . . then as golfing pal and all-around crony of Frank Sinatra . . . and, finally, as confessed felon. (Nor did the quick-change artistry end there, for no sooner was he disgraced and out of office than he took on still another role, that of aspiring novelist.)

Even some of Nixon's closest aides at the 1968 convention were stunned when he settled on Agnew as his running mate. The Maryland Governor was almost totally unknown nationally, and it was difficult to see how he could help the ticket. But Nixon himself seemed ecstatic over the choice. "There can be a mystique about a man," he told reporters the day after he picked Agnew. "You can look him in the eye and know he's got it. This guy has got it." (Spiro had it, all right, but he wasn't keeping it stashed in his eye; and it would be years before Nixon, and the rest of us, would find out just how and where he had been getting it.)

Thrust onto the national stage, Agnew promptly began to play the buffoon. He enlivened an otherwise dull campaign by tossing off ethnic slurs, referring to one fellow as a "dumb Polack" and describing a Japanese journalist as "that fat Jap," thus conjuring up the bizarre image of a Samurai wrestler in his traveling party. And, in what struck many as an unconscious parody of Nixon's earlier campaign style, when he ran for Vice President in 1952, Spiro accused

Hubert Humphrey of being "squishy soft on Communism." Long before the '68 campaign was over, Nixon's top strategists were doing their best to keep Agnew out of sight and buttoned up. After the ticket was safely elected, the early plans called for him to fade into the ceremonial irrelevance of the Vice Presidency and have little to do with the real business of government.

So, as the Nixon regime got under way, Spiro settled into the early-retirement style of living that characterizes what John Adams once described as "the most insignificant office that ever the invention of man contrived." Every now and then, according to the evidence later brought against him, he would receive a furtive visitor from his days as Governor, a Baltimore County friend who would come to Washington bearing gifts. For the most part, however, he languished as others before him had languished—"a heartbeat away," yes, but far removed from the emerging action of Richard Nixon's Presidency.

But all that changed in the fall of 1969. As Haldeman and the other hard-liners established control over the Nixon White House and engineered the post-Chappaquiddick shift to the right, they— and the President—decided to make Agnew a part of the action, to unleash him on the country as a respectable, white-collar version of George Wallace. Or as some observers said at the time, Spiro became "Nixon's Nixon," the Veep who traveled the low road for his President in much the same way Nixon had traveled it for Ike back in the fifties. Agnew rejoiced in his new celebrity status (it was nice to become known nationally for something besides ethnic faux pas), and as he continued to delight conservatives and infuriate liberals with his broadside attacks, he kept insisting that he was his own man, and was giving voice to his own views.

This was, at best, only half true. It is conceivable that Agnew sincerely believed in the hard-hitting speeches he made during this period, though it should not be forgotten that three years earlier, when his needs were different, he seemed just as "sincere" in presenting himself to the voters of Maryland as a friend of the blacks. In any event, regardless of how true or deep his own convictions were, Agnew was not, in this role, his own man. His most inflammatory speeches, including the famous diatribe against the television networks, were written by Pat Buchanan, who liked to boast that he was the most militant conservative on the White House staff. What's more, the entire Agnew "blitz," as it was called, proceeded under Haldeman's overall direction. And the White House power brokers couldn't have cared less if Spiro was being "sincere" or not. Indeed, they were even somewhat amused by the suggestion that he had coherent ideas of his own. (When it came to the Veep's intellectual prowess, the prevailing view at the Nixon White House was that he might need a course in remedial reading in order to get through the speeches Buchanan wrote for him.) His job was to follow orders, to assume whatever role he was told to assume. If, for example, they had wanted to push Agnew in the other direction and use him as their liaison with black groups and student agitators, they would have expected him to carry out that assignment with equal vigor and "sincerity," and there is no reason to believe he would not have.

Nevertheless, it is true that as time went on Haldeman and the others began to fear that they had created a Frankenstein. Part of the problem was that many conservatives across the country, whose fervor had been aroused by the Pat Buchanan rhetoric they associated with Spiro, were now rallying around Agnew as their hero, in preference to Nixon. This was most distressing to the White House strategists, for the idea had been to offer Agnew as an appealing alternative to Wallace, *not* the President. Moreover, they were dismayed by the fact that Agnew was getting out of line, especially in what they considered to be the indiscreet life style he was pursuing.

The business with Sinatra was a subject of profound concern at the White House. The top people there were well aware of Sinatra's history vis-à-vis the Kennedys. They knew that JFK had been a Sinatra crony in the pre-Presidential years, and that the celebrated singer had worked his tail off for Kennedy in 1960. And all he asked for in return was a small favor—a trifle, really. He said he'd appreciate it if Kennedy, on one of his first trips to the West Coast as President, would stay at his place in California. No problem, Kennedy is supposed to have told him, and later, after he became President and plans called for a California visit, he was all set to honor his end of the bargain—that is, until he happened to discuss the matter with brother Bobby, who by this time was settled in at the Justice Department. Then, suddenly, plans were changed. As President, JFK never did stay at Sinatra's home, and Sinatra never forgave the Kennedys for going back on their word.

So that story was well known at the Nixon White House, and now here was Agnew constantly being photographed as a weekend guest at Sinatra's place. Even worse, there were disturbing reports, which kept getting back to the White House, that when Spiro visited Sinatra their recreational activities included a lot more than golf. Such rumors may or may not have been based on fact. But Haldeman among others was alarmed about even the fact that such reports were circulating. He and his media cohorts were more than a little fearful that the man the White House had sent out to lead the assault on "permissiveness" was going to stick them with a serious image problem.

As it turned out, Agnew's cavorting around with Sinatra was the last thing they had to worry about. Midway through the first term, when so many conservatives were excited by the prospect of Spiro's eventually succeeding Nixon, one of Agnew's friends told author Richard Whalen: "The Veep isn't interested in being President. He's interested in making money. He feels that he owes his kids an estate, and that he'd better start making some real dough soon." What the aide did not know (we assume) was that in his zeal to make an extra buck Agnew already had crossed the line of legality, and that it was only a matter of time before federal investigators would pick up the scent of the sordid trail of money payoffs. Yet in a way Agnew was lucky; for by the fall of 1973, when the full exposure came, his corruptions would be viewed as just another item in the long list of scandals that were destroying the Nixon Presidency. Getting hit with the Agnew story while the Watergate storm was raging full blast struck many people as little more than a nagging distraction, like coming across a footnote on the Dresden fire raids in the midst of an absorbing book on Hiroshima. The country only had time to give Spiro's downfall a passing glance before shifting its gaze back to the main event.

But all that was part of the unforeseeable future back in 1970 when Agnew was playing the role of moral crusader for all it was worth. By the summer of '70, the Veep had been riding the GOP banquet circuit for nearly a year, and now he was primed for the critical battle ahead: the midterm campaign. The White House propelled Agnew into the '70 campaign on a wave of high expectation. Still smarting over criticisms that by squandering his big lead over Humphrey in 1968 he had blown a golden opportunity to bring a

Republican Congress in with him, Nixon was determined to silence his detractors in the '70 race, which would amount to a referendum of sorts on his first two years in office. Partly because they were so far out of touch with their party and with people of middle income or below, the President and his political strategists were confident that the results would be positive. They predicted that Republicans would gain a few seats in the House, but their real target was the Senate. Many of the Senators up for re-election that year were liberal Democrats who had been washed into office by the Johnson landslide in 1964, and the White House was convinced that a number of them could be knocked off. In his more euphoric moments, Nixon envisioned a net gain of seven seats in the Senate—i.e., enough to bring it under Republican control for the first time since 1952, when a GOP Congress was elected with Ike. But a great deal depended on Agnew's success in driving the White House message home to the voters.

That message was spelled out to Agnew by Nixon himself in one of their rare private meetings. (As a rule, the Veep received his orders through Haldeman and/or Ehrlichman.) The President instructed Agnew to hammer away at the permissiveness theme without letup. The Democrats, he said, must be blamed for everything from campus protest to drugs to pornography to the whole general breakdown of law and order—in other words, the gamut of what came to be known that year as the Social Issue.

This of course was in keeping with the hard-line attack strategy that had been steadily gaining strength and momentum at the White House ever since Chappaquiddick. It reflected not only the views of the President's top advisers, like Mitchell and Haldeman, but also those of his three full-time political operatives: Murray Chotiner, the original cut-and-slash man . . . Harry Dent, who was in charge of trying to woo Southern voters away from Wallace and toward Nixon . . . and Chuck Colson, whose interest centered on the Northern Flank of the Southern Strategy—that is, blue-collar workers who, though traditionally Democratic, were disenchanted with liberal "elitists," such as John Lindsay and Eugene McCarthy, and were now forming the "new breed" of Wallace voters. A minority faction at the White House argued for a broader, more conciliatory approach, concentrating on middle-of-the-road suburbanites. Its chief spokesman was Bob Finch. But Finch, though still personally close to Nixon, was no longer the dominant political adviser he had been in years past. With the hard-liners in firm control, Finch and others who shared his views had been muscled into a secondary role.

A White House team, headed by conservative adviser Bryce Harlow, was assigned to accompany Agnew on his campaign travels. Also on board were two of Nixon's top speechwriters, Pat Buchanan and Bill Safire, and early in September, 1970, they started out on an itinerary that would eventually take them to thirty states. Spiro followed the White House script to the letter. (Once he got the rhythm he even wrote a few Buchanan-type lines for himself. In speech after speech, Agnew lashed out at the "radical liberals" in the Senate (or "radiclibs," to use the shorthand term he soon adopted), and at first his harsh attacks seemed to be paying off. Polls indicated that voters were responding favorably to Agnew's campaign oratory, and several Democratic seats in the Senate were reported to be in real trouble.

But as the campaign moved into October the Agnew blitz suddenly began to fizzle. Part of the problem was Spiro's overexposure: familiarity was breeding indifference, as well as contempt. The Veep had been going at top speed now for over a year, and he was beginning to sound like a broken record. The shock value of his initial tirades was wearing off, and as people mulled over his message, a delayed reaction of resentment was setting in. What Spiro and his White House puppeteers were discovering was that, while a strident scream is an effective way to get attention, when it continues unabated it soon becomes an irritant to some, and a bore to others.

Conservatives, it is true, continued to cheer him on, but that was just so much preaching to the converted. Moderates, independents, and disgruntled Democrats—those whose votes would be decisive in the election—were starting to turn off. For example, labor baron George Meany, who had been supporting Nixon on a number of key issues, such as Vietnam and law and order, publicly accused Agnew of engaging in "inflammatory rhetoric." And he urged all labor-union members to vote Democratic. What prompted Meany's return to the Democratic fold was his rising concern over economic conditions—and on this he was not alone.

By the fall of 1970, "Nixonomics" was in full flower. The inflation wave inherited in part from Johnson was rolling in (since Nixon took office, consumer prices had been climbing at an annual rate of 6 percent), and now there was a sharp recession to go along with it. Unemployment figures had been steadily rising since January, 1970, and by November, 5.6 percent of the labor force was out of work— the highest level since the recessions of the Eisenhower years. So, as the midterm campaign entered its critical phase, the Economic Issue began to overshadow the Social Issue in the minds of many voters. Their concern shifted from crime-in-the-streets to money-in-the-pocket, and in that atmosphere Spiro Agnew's overblown rhetoric came to seem more and more irrelevant. Now it was the Democrats who went on the offensive—the bread-and-butter issue was their ace to play—and as the White House hopes of capturing the Senate and gaining seats in the House began to fade, Nixon threw himself into the campaign in an effort to regain the initiative.

This was a sudden and unexpected move. The whole point of packaging Agnew to serve as "Nixon's Nixon" was to liberate Nixon himself so that he could be purely "Presidential" in the Eisenhower manner—that is, free to glide serenely along the high road, above the partisan squabbles. Thus, when plans were worked out for the '70 campaign, it was decided that the President would not participate in an active sense. He would make two or three "nonpolitical" appearances along the way, and that would be the extent of it. But Nixon's own combative instincts had been aroused by the harsh campaign rhetoric, and so, when the Agnew blitz began to sputter, he decided to plunge into the battle himself—which is something that crafty Ike, so protective of his benign image, would never have dreamed of doing.

The decision was hastily made in early October during a weekend stay at Key Biscayne. What is significant is that the only top political adviser with the President that weekend was Haldeman. And, when some of Nixon's other strategists—notably Mitchell, Finch, and Harlow—found out about his change of plans, they were convinced that he was making a serious mistake. (Mitchell would later grumble that the President barnstormed around the country like a man "running for sheriff.") But their counsel was not sought. Haldeman thought the switch in tactics was a good idea, and that was all the encouragement Nixon needed.

So, in the last three weeks of the campaign, as the President crisscrossed the country, making appearances in twenty-three states, he picked up where Agnew left off, concentrating almost all his fire on the Social Issue. And, whenever hecklers or demonstrators showed up at his campaign stops, Nixon all but welcomed them with open arms; for they provided the perfect foil for his law-and-order, no-permissiveness theme. This direct-confrontation approach boiled up to a climax in the final week of the campaign when a provocative exchange between the President and an angry group of protesters in San Jose, California, touched off a brief flurry of violence. On this occasion, instead of just shouting the usual slogans and obscenities, the demonstrators ended up throwing eggs and rocks at the Presidential limousine as it left the parking lot where the encounter took place. This was just the kind of incident Nixon needed to dramatize his message. In fact, the timing was almost *too* perfect—just five days before the election—and even at that time there were a few cynics who suspected that some members of Nixon's staff had been reading up on the Reichstag Fire. (There was no evidence to support these suspicions, but much later, when Watergate revealed the whole elaborate scheme of campaign "dirty tricks," they would not seem quite so cynical.)

Haldeman, in particular, was ecstatic about what had happened in San Jose. He was convinced that, if properly exploited, the incident would send a wave of revulsion through the country; and that the voters would momentarily forget their economic woes and turn, in massive numbers, to Nixon's law-and-order candidates. So he, as well as others, urged the President to pound away at the Social Issue with more fervor than ever in the closing days of the campaign. And the President did just that.

Two days after the San Jose incident, Nixon gave his toughest speech of the campaign at a rally in Phoenix. Referring to the "terrorists" and "violent thugs" who were trying to "keep me from going out and speaking with the American people," the speech and performance had all the classic ingredients of vintage Nixon: aggressive arm waving, the dark, glowering facial expressions and, of course, vituperative rhetoric. And Haldeman loved it. In his view, the Phoenix speech was just about the greatest thing since—well, since the glory days of the Helen Gahagan Douglas campaign. The only problem was it received minimal press coverage, and Haldeman felt it deserved a mass audience. This was the way to exploit San Jose and the whole Social Issue, and to get people's minds off the economy.

So he went to Nixon and suggested that they wrap up the '70 campaign by televising the Phoenix speech nationally, as an election-eve broadcast over all three networks. The President, usually deferential to Haldeman in media matters, gave his consent and the plans were arranged.

This was a truly incredible decision. The slashing stump speech at the Phoenix rally was appallingly inappropriate for a midterm election-eve broadcast which, almost by definition, should adhere to the soft and soothing formula of the "fireside chat." As a media expert, Haldeman certainly understood this, and it can only be assumed that in the heat of the moment, in his ardor over seeing the all-out-attack idol of his youth back in action, he suffered a startling lapse of professional judgment. To make matters worse, the video-tape copy of the speech that the Nixon staff bought from a local TV station was in black-and-white, and had an extremely poor, scratchy sound track. Bill Safire, who was assigned to edit the tape for the broadcast, passed on this information to Jeb Magruder, who relayed it to Haldeman. But the word came back to go ahead with it anyway.

So, the night before the '70 election, the President appeared on nationwide television giving an abrasive, arm-waving speech in black-and-white, with a sound track that grated on the ears. With media advice like that, who needs enemies? The blunder was compounded by the contrast between Nixon's harangue and the TV broadcast that night by Senator Ed Muskie on behalf of the Democrats. Muskie came on right after the President with a textbook election-eve appeal. Seated behind a desk in a cozy, attractive living room, he spoke in calm, conciliatory tones, quietly urging voters to reject the Republicans' "politics of fear." Muskie was, to use the favorite adjective of his admirers, at his "Lincolnesque" best that night. He also appeared in color and with a flawless sound track that did not make his voice sound like fingernails scraping across a blackboard. The contrast was devastating.

The next day, voters returned their verdict. The Republicans did make a net gain of two seats in the Senate, but that left them five short of the number needed to wrest control of that chamber from the Democrats. And in the House and gubernatorial races, the news was much worse. The Democrats picked up nine seats in the House, swelling their control there to 255 to 180. And the trend that had emerged in the 1960s of electing Republicans to the governorships of key states (Rockefeller, Reagan, Romney, Volpe, Shafer, *et al.*) was sharply reversed as the Democrats came up with a net gain of eleven new Governors.

Still, by recent historical standards, it could have been viewed as a respectable enough Republican showing, since the party in power seldom fares well in a midterm election. But the traditional standards had been blown all out of proportion by the extravagant predictions the White House had made going into the campaign, and by the frenetic, all-out effort put forth by Nixon and Agnew to make those predictions come true. In a way, the most telling impact was psychological. Ever since Chappaquiddick had knocked the Democrats off balance, forcing them to abandon their natural front runner because he had become damaged goods, they had been in disarray, without much in the way of leadership or hope. To a great extent, they too had fallen for the White House propaganda that there was a "silent majority" or "new Republican majority" spreading across the country, just waiting to assert itself. They had gone into the '70 election in a spirit of profound gloom. More than anything else, then, the results of the midterm election re-energized the Democrats and restored their confidence. Once again, they began referring to Nixon derisively as a caretaker President, whose election in 1968 had been a fluke. Convinced that they were out of the doldrums and were now moving on an upward curve, the Democrats began looking forward, with renewed vigor, to the 1972 showdown and the prospect of ending Richard Nixon's political career, once and for all.

All this was duly noted by the various strategists at the Nixon White House. Thus, in the aftermath of the midterm election, they came to the conclusion that drastic measures would be needed to assure their man of a second term as President. And drastic measures are what they came up with.

PART IV

"To Be Thus Is Nothing . . ."

Twenty-two

On THE surface, for public consumption, the Nixon White House went to great lengths to put a positive face on the 1970 election results. "Let's PR it through" was another one of Haldeman's pet phrases, and that was the tactic employed in the days and weeks that followed as the second year of Richard Nixon's Presidency drew to a close. There was a lot of brave talk to the press about having obtained an "ideological majority" in the Senate, a claim scoffed at by Democratic leaders on Capitol Hill. And reporters were told that the President was "delighted" with the outcome. But behind closed doors in the private rooms of the White House—and especially within the Oval Office itself—a far more sober mood prevailed.

Gone was the euphoria that had set in after Chappaquiddick when Edward Kennedy crippled himself as a Presidential contender, leaving behind him a roster of colorless alternatives led by Muskie, who at the time seemed merely dull rather than "Lincolnesque." Now, in the wake of the 1970 campaign, everything was turning sour.

For one thing, Kennedy was starting to haunt the White House again. In his first post-Chappaquiddick test at the polls, he had won re-election by a comfortable margin in Massachusetts. (Much to the disappointment of the White House, Kennedy's Republican opponent in the '70 race—a high-principled Brahmin named Josiah Spaulding—refused to exploit the famous incident.) So now that Kennedy had defused Chappaquiddick at home, there was the distinct possibility that he might change his mind about 1972; and in the wary mood it now found itself in, the White House did not view that as an inviting prospect. Then there was Muskie. Partly because of Nixon's own election-eve folly (his and Haldeman's), the President could no longer afford to take the Senator from Maine lightly. Indeed, Muskie was being hailed as the Democratic hero of the midterm campaign. And White House concern over Muskie's new potency deepened in the early months of 1971, when national opinion polls consistently reported him to be running ahead of Nixon.

What's more, the White House still had George Wallace to worry about. Wallace also had come out of the 1970 election a big winner (after a four-year hiatus, he was back in the Alabama Governor's chair), and there was talk that he already was gearing up for another Presidential run as a third-party candidate. Such a move would automatically kill any hope of putting together a "Solid South" for the Republicans in 1972; in going after the Wallace constituency, Nixon's Southern Strategists would have to settle for leftovers, just as they did in 1968, when they barely squeaked through. For there was no way they could beat Wallace at his own game. Early on in his career, after he lost an election to a rabid segregationist in Alabama, Wallace vowed that no one would ever "outnigger me again," and even the most determined Southern Strategists in the President's camp understood that it would be suicidal to try that approach. The appeal to the Wallace voters would have to be subtle and restrained so as not to antagonize other Nixon supporters who regarded the Alabama governor as a coarse demagogue. And that, everyone at the White House agreed, would not be easy.

So, with Muskie and/or Kennedy threatening from the left, and Wallace looming up bigger than ever on the right, the President and the men clustered around him could almost feel their political enemies closing in on them. "To be thus is nothing, but to be *safely* thus," said Macbeth when, after disposing of Duncan, he discovered that other rivals for the throne were lurking in the shadows. Now, as Richard Nixon moved toward the end of his second year in office, a similar anxiety crept into the White House.

Four days after the 1970 election, the President and his top political lieutenants—Mitchell, Haldeman, Ehrlichman, *et al.*—gathered for a meeting in the wood-paneled living room of Nixon's home on Key Biscayne. Out of that meeting, and others that took place over the next few weeks, came a series of critical decisions, all aimed at making the President "safely thus." One point on which everyone agreed was that Nixon had to abandon the slashing, partisan role he had assumed in the recent campaign. Henceforth, he must revert to the manner of calm restraint that characterized his first few months in office; he must go back to being "Presidential." Nixon concurred in this judgment, but as the most experienced politician in the group, he realized that it would not be enough for him merely to take on a Presidential "tone." Issuing proclamations honoring Motherhood and greeting veterans in the Oval Office might spruce up his image a bit, but they would not get him through the traps that lay ahead. What he needed, and needed most desperately, was a record of performance on which to run. "We have no monuments" was how the President himself ruefully phrased it at the time. He was right.

After two years in office, Nixon's domestic policy had produced next to nothing in the way of positive legislation. His one showcase attempt to build a "monument" in that area was the proposal for welfare reform. But in November, 1970, as Nixon and his advisers were charting future political strategy, the Senate Finance Committee, meeting in a lame-duck session, voted to kill the administration's welfare-reform bill, with Republicans joining Democrats in opposing the measure. Ostensibly, if not otherwise, the President tried again to arouse Congressional support for his domestic programs in his 1971 State of the Union message. Resubmitting the welfare bill, he again claimed it was his top domestic priority; and he also called on Congress to approve his proposals for revenue sharing, for national health insurance, and for protecting the environment. By now, however, it was too late. The antagonisms between the White House and Capitol Hill had been building up over the past year, and in the bitter atmosphere of the '70 campaign they had flared into open hostility. Nixon was enough of a realist to know that for all the talk about an "ideological majority," he could not count on a Democratic-controlled Congress to help him win a second term. Through such acts as the Haynsworth and Carswell nominations and the unleashing of Spiro Agnew—as well as the Haldeman-Ehrlichman view toward Capitol Hill that permeated the Nixon White House—the President had squandered any chance he might have had of running for re-election on a record of strong legislative achievement.

Whatever chance there had been for legislative achievement was at its best in 1969, during the extended honeymoon Congress had provided. It was still alive, barely, in early 1970. Now it was dead. And Nixon knew it. He already had made up his mind to run against Congress in 1972 much as Truman had done in his "Give 'em Hell" 1948 campaign.

So, if there were to be any "monuments," they would have to be found in foreign policy, where he had more authority to act on his own and where his major decisions could take effect without his having to coax new laws out of Congress. In this area, where he was confident of his strength and his ability to apply that strength to maximum advantage, Nixon was ready, by 1971, to be "Presidential" on a grand scale, in a manner worthy of a De Gaulle or Churchill.

All during 1969 and the early months of 1970, the public diplomatic effort toward détente with the Soviet Union centered on the Middle East, and the chief instrument of that effort was Secretary of State William Rogers. But it proved to be a dismal failure. Indeed, its main effect was to exacerbate tensions in the area and ignite the 1970 "mini-war" along the Suez border, dividing Egypt and Israeli-occupied positions in the Sinai desert. Through arduous negotiations, Rogers was able, in the summer of 1970, to nail down a Suez ceasefire agreement, but by then all hope of using the Middle East as a springboard to U.S.-Soviet détente had been abandoned. Still, Cairo and Jerusalem weren't the only roads to East-West accord. A far more exotic route already was being explored.

Even before he became President, Richard Nixon had been doing some hard thinking about China. In a 1968 campaign interview he talked about how any permanent resolution of the Cold War would have to include U.S. recognition of the Communist government in Peking. This was a mildly startling admission from a man who, in his Vice Presidential years, had been an ardent disciple of John Foster Dulles; but by this time Nixon had quietly moved away from the knee-jerk anti-Communism of his early years. In that '68 interview, however, he implied that a major shift in U.S. policy toward China was far down the road, and could only come *after* the various differences with the Soviet Union had been resolved. And that, presumably, was the view Nixon brought with him into the White House. But then, in the early weeks of his Presidency, he gradually came under Henry Kissinger's influence.

Ever since Kissinger's emergence as the diplomatic "Super Star" of the Nixon years, much has been made of the Svengali-like power he is supposed to have wielded over the President's thinking. This notion has especially appealed to people who never liked Nixon, but suddenly found themselves approving of his foreign-policy initiatives. Beguiled by Kissinger's forceful personality and intellectual charm ("Power is the great aphrodisiac!" he once exulted when asked to comment on his reputation as a "swinger"), professional Nixon haters were eager to bestow all the credit on him. But that view represents a gross exaggeration. If anyone at the Nixon White House came close to being a Svengali, it was Moynihan. The Tory Reform conceit, and all the intoxicating blarney about Disraeli that went with it, were entirely his inspiration—which is one reason why it never really took hold. Although Nixon was intrigued by the novelty of Moynihan's thesis, the role of Tory Reformer did not sustain his interest or engage his deep commitment.

But foreign policy was another matter. The subtleties of global diplomacy stirred Nixon's imagination in ways that domestic issues never could. What's more, he was deeply knowledgeable in foreign affairs, in terms of both historical perspective and contemporary realities. As a result, his discussions with Kissinger were on a more even keel and involved a lot more give and take. If Kissinger, the professional scholar whose field of expertise was the European statecraft of the nineteenth century, made a pertinent reference to Metternich, Nixon could move with him on that level and counter with an adroit comment on Talleyrand and the skill *he* displayed at the Congress of Vienna. Touché, and all that. This is not, however, to minimize Kissinger's influence on the President, which was considerable. As Haldeman was adept at bringing out the dark side of Nixon —the scowling and vindictive gut fighter—Kissinger learned how to invoke the statesman in him, the global expert dedicated to exploring new paths toward a secure and enduring peace. But the point is, as they developed an intimate working relationship, the decisions that flowed from their private talks represented a synthesis of complementary views and aspirations.

Between them, then, Nixon and Kissinger arrived at the idea that the time to open up relations with the Communist regime in China was now—or soon—rather than at some point in the far-distant future. At the heart of this secret shift in policy was a shrewd sense of *Realpolitik*. Both men were aware that the "Sino-Soviet bloc," one of the governing clichés of the Eisenhower-Dulles years, was no longer, if indeed it ever had been, consistent with reality. Moscow and Peking had been bitter rivals since the early 1960s. Racial fears and suspicions were part of the reason. So were mutual fears of invasion. Nixon and Kissinger decided that the time had come to exploit that division. The way to shake up the Russians was to make friendly gestures toward the Chinese, which would raise the specter of an eventual Washington-Peking alliance. Thus threatened on their weakest flank, the Soviets would stop horsing around in the Mediter-ranean and get down to the serious business of working out Cold War agreements with the United States. Very *Realpolitik*. Global hard-ball.

So, over the first two years of Nixon's Presidency, a series of elaborate and subtle "signals" were exchanged between Washington and Peking. (Nixon's 1969 trip around the rim of China and on into Rumania was one such "signal.") Then early in 1971, with one eye fixed on history and the other on his need for "monuments" to pre-sent to the voters, Nixon pressed Kissinger to accelerate the "signals" and come up with something solid.

We will have to wait for the official memoirs to learn the full story behind the brilliant statecraft Kissinger conducted through the early months of 1971. During this period, he became a figure of fascination whose movements were shrouded in mystery. Observers around the White House knew he was constantly slipping away for secret meet-ings in foreign countries, and there was a certain Graham Greene aura about these stealthy missions to points unknown: one envisioned trench-coat encounters at fog-enveloped air strips in remote settings like Tibet. It was widely assumed at the time that Kissinger's furtive activities had to do with Vietnam, and there was some of that in the mix. In January, 1972, the White House disclosed that he had been meeting in secret with Hanoi's top diplomat, Le Duc Tho, since the summer of 1969. These meetings were part of a much broader effort aimed at pressuring the North Vietnamese through their allies, but until early 1971, they were kept secret from Americans.

Then in July, 1971, Nixon went on television to make a dramatic announcement: Henry Kissinger, said the President, had just re-turned from a two-day meeting with Premier Chou En-lai in Peking and, at Chou's invitation, he himself would visit the People's Repub-lic of China early in 1972. Once the shock wore off, the general reaction throughout the world was overwhelmingly favorable. And, in terms of domestic politics, the China announcement started Nixon on the road back to the level of popularity he had enjoyed during his first months in office.

In the meantime, Kissinger's big-power chess game continued. In October, 1971, Nixon announced he would visit the Soviet Union the following May, just a few weeks after his trip to Peking. As had been the hope all along, the China breakthrough pried open the gates of the Kremlin. All of a sudden, Nixon was piling up an impressive list of historic "firsts." When he went to Rumania, he became the first President to visit a Communist country since the start of the Cold War. Now he would be the first President ever to visit China, and the first one to go to the Soviet Union since Roosevelt journeyed to Yalta in 1945. These statistical data meant a great deal to Nixon; from the day he assumed office, he had been in the habit of discussing his Presidency in such terms—the most this, the first that—as though he were a baseball player citing his credentials for admission into the Hall of Fame.

The China trip, understandably, aroused the most interest. Ever since the Communist takeover in 1949, Americans had been instructed to regard mainland China as a kind of mass leper colony, and now that the bamboo curtain was finally being lifted, just about everyone was curious to see what life was like in the most populous nation on earth. In substantive terms, however, the visit to Russia was more significant. The signing in Moscow of the U.S.-Soviet agreement to impose limits on strategic weapons was the biggest step taken on the road to disarmament since the Nuclear Test Ban Treaty was negotiated in 1963. It is true that the controversial wheat deal proved to be a blunder and some of the blame for that must go to Kissinger, who was in charge of orchestrating the entire package of trade-and-arms agreements. ("That's his weakness," a Kissinger intimate confided at the time. "Henry's tone deaf when it comes to economics.") Nevertheless, the overall effect of the China and Russia trips was a huge plus for the Nixon-Kissinger foreign policy. When the President returned from Moscow in the late spring of 1972, he had his "monuments."

Still to be resolved, however, was Vietnam. By the spring of '72, Defense Secretary Melvin Laird's plan of gradual withdrawal had made great strides in reducing U.S. involvement in the ground war. When the Nixon administration took over, there were more than

540,000 Americans fighting in Vietnam and U.S. combat deaths were running as high as 300 a week. By May, 1972, the troop level was down to 70,000, and the number of Americans killed was averaging less than ten a week. So far, so good. But the negative side of the picture was that in the fourth year of Nixon's Presidency the war itself, which he had pledged to end—not just wind down, but *end*— was still raging with undiminished fury. In fact, in the spring of 1972, the North Vietnamese launched another major offensive, a move against which Nixon retaliated with full-scale bombing raids on Hanoi and the mining of Haiphong harbor. So, four years after the Tet offensive helped to bring down Lyndon Johnson's Presidency, Richard Nixon, who had just given a convincing performance as "peacemaker" in Peking and Moscow, was still ordering Americans to wage war in Vietnam.

The major flaw in Laird's gradual-withdrawal strategy centered on the prisoner-of-war problem, which by 1972 had surfaced as the most volatile of the issues pertaining to Vietnam. With all his charts and meticulous timetables, there was no way that Laird could with- draw the POWs, either gradually or *en masse*. Their release from enemy prison camps could only come about through a negotiated settlement, and in the spring of '72 the prospects for that looked as bleak as ever. For more than three years, first at the Paris peace talks (which by this time had come to be regarded by many as a sham) and later in the private meetings between Kissinger and Le Duc Tho, the Nixon administration had made a strenuous effort to work out a ceasefire agreement with the North Vietnamese. But always the message from the negotiating table was the same: no progress. Then in the summer of 1972 prospects suddenly brightened.

We may never know how much pressure, if any, Peking and/or Moscow put on the North Vietnamese to induce them to soften their demands in the negotiations with Kissinger. But it surely was more than a coincidence that after so many years of iron-hard intransi- gence Hanoi's demands *did* soften in the weeks following Nixon's visits to China and the Soviet Union. So, in the end, the "domino theory" about Vietnam turned out to be correct after all, though hardly in the way its proponents meant when they first cited it to justify U.S. military intervention in Southeast Asia. Yet, just as the overtures to China forced Russia's hand, so the trips by Nixon to Peking and Moscow clearly had a bearing on the sudden push toward an agreement to end the fighting in Vietnam. By the summer of 1972, Kissinger's personal triumphs with Chou En-lai and Leonid Brezhnev had made him an international hero; and in the months ahead he concentrated all his diplomatic skills on Le Duc Tho. By the time of the fall campaign, it was obvious that Nixon's Democratic opponent, George McGovern, was not going to get very far with the peace issue. The ceasefire settlement would not be reached until January, 1973, more than two months after the election—and only after Nixon ordered more and larger bombing attacks on Hanoi right through the 1972 Christmas season. But, all through the weeks of the Presidential campaign, the news coming out of the negotiating sessions in Paris left little doubt that the loss of American lives in Vietnam was nearing an end—and on Election Day, 1972, the vast majority of Americans voted accordingly.

Yet it is entirely possible that Nixon's foreign policy achievements would have availed him nothing if, by re-election time, the President had not taken decisive steps to ease the economic woes that plagued the country during most of his first term. At that Key Biscayne strategy meeting four days after the 1970 election, no subject was discussed more intensely than the Economic Issue and the beating Republicans had taken on it in the midterm campaign. (Perhaps even Haldeman might have assessed the San Jose rock-throwing incident a little differently if he had heard the comment made by the wife of an unemployed aerospace engineer, one of thousands out of work in southern California. Asked about San Jose, the woman angrily told a reporter: "The kids beat us to it.")

All through the summer and fall of 1970, Nixon had stoutly defended his original economic game plan: the 1969 decision to adopt gradual measures in the fight against inflation. This led to moderate cuts in federal spending and a firm stand against government intervention in the flow of the free market. But the game plan had been largely responsible for the malignant growth of Nixonomics—deepening recession in the midst of rising inflation—and in the gloom that descended on the Nixon White House after the '70 election, everyone agreed it was time for a change. What followed over the next few months, however, was not merely change, but massive upheaval. In his struggle to slay the twin monsters of recession and inflation, Richard Nixon would violate almost every economic principle he had ever embraced. Yet in the process he would succeed in defusing the Economic Issue to the point where the Democrats could not use it against him in 1972—and that, after all, was the idea.

The sweeping decisions Nixon made to lift the country out of the economic morass were set in motion in December, 1970, when he announced the appointment of a new Treasury Secretary, the former Democratic Governor of Texas—and LBJ protégé—John Connally. To appreciate the impact Connally would have on future events, it may help to reflect, for a moment, on one of the minor curiosities of the Nixon Presidency: the utterly self-effacing performance of his first Treasury Secretary, David Kennedy. Ever since Alexander Hamilton, Treasury has ranked second, just behind State, in the hierarchy of Cabinet posts. In Republican administrations, in particular, it has been customary for the Treasury Secretary to assume a dominant role, not only in economic affairs but over the whole range of domestic policy. (Andrew Mellon during the Harding-Coolidge-Hoover era and George Humphrey, under Ike, are two notable examples.) Viewed against this tradition, David Kennedy's two-year career in Nixon's Cabinet was all the more remarkable.

A Mormon banker from Chicago (he was board chairman of Continental Illinois National Bank and Trust), Kennedy had a solid reputation in financial circles at the time of his appointment—though he was, to be sure, something less than a household name. And, as Treasury Secretary, he went on to scale new heights of obscurity. The problem was basically one of temperament and what might be called the senior-executive mentality. He had no grasp for power, in the Washington-political sense, and he was hardly cast in the Prussian mold of indefatigable worker. After making his sub-Cabinet appointments, Kennedy delegated almost all his authority to his deputies and promptly settled into the bankers' hours to which he was accustomed. He attended Cabinet meetings, and he also sat in on special economic sessions, but he seldom asserted himself.

Kennedy's lack of leadership didn't seem to bother Nixon all that much during his first two years in office; he simply turned to other people, such as Paul McCracken and George Shultz, for decisions on economic matters. But now, as 1970 drew to a close, the President decided it was no longer in his best interest to have a Treasury Secretary who stayed so completely in the background. So he went charging off to the other extreme. To a great extent, of course, the

Connally appointment was politically motivated. Nixon had staked a great deal on a Republican victory in Texas in the midterm election, but his candidate for the Senate seat there, Congressman George Bush, had lost. He was determined not to lose Texas in 1972, and bringing a Lyndon Johnson Democrat into his Cabinet reflected that determination. As it turned out, however, delivering Texas to Nixon was the least of the contributions Connally made to the President's re-election.

From the first day he shook things up. The placid Nixon cornfield soon discovered another roaring volcano in its midst. Just as Pat Moynihan was a Kennedy Democrat who had all the Kennedy virtues (wit, charm) as well as the Kennedy vices (social snobbery, intellectual arrogance), so John Connally was a Johnson Democrat who had all the Johnson virtues (physical energy, country smarts) as well as the Johnson vices (explosive temper, megalomania). In one of his first confrontations, he even trampled over Haldeman. Rushing over to the Oval Office one day, he demanded to see the President—"and pronto." Haldeman, unaccustomed to being talked to that way by a "mere" Cabinet officer, fixed Connally with a glare and said: "I'll convey your wishes to the President." Connally, his great bull chest puffing up to the challenge, came snorting back with: "*I* will convey my wishes to the President." For the next few seconds, they were eyeball to eyeball, but it was Haldeman who blinked. Long John Silver conveyed his own wishes. The interesting thing is that Haldeman went on to become one of Connally's biggest boosters. He was among those who pushed hard for Connally to replace Agnew on the 1972 ticket. In the classic bully pattern, Haldeman was the first to knuckle under when faced with a real show of strength.

But, in his drive to bring the policy-making apparatus under his control, Connally saved his best fire for the team of economic advisers the President had been relying on up to that point. He soon fell into the habit of describing Paul McCracken, the diminutive and mild-mannered professor who was the principal architect of the now-discredited game plan, as "a disaster." In one conversation with Nixon Connally reportedly said of McCracken: "The trouble with the little man is not only that he *says* the wrong thing, but he says it so *badly.* He doesn't make any sense."

Connally's chief rival for power, however, was not McCracken, but George Shultz. Back in the spring of 1970, when Shultz was induced to give up his post as Labor Secretary to take over the Office of Management and Budget, it was with the understanding that he would be allowed to chart the course of the administration's overall economic policy; and by the time Connally replaced the acquiescent David Kennedy, Shultz had emerged as Nixon's top economic adviser. Although he had not been in on the original 1969 decision, Shultz generally approved of the early game plan. His own economic views stemmed from two basic principles: (a) the forces of the free market should be permitted to set economic trends with as little government interference as possible. And (b) insofar as it was practical, economic decisions should not be dictated by political concerns. In the bleak aftermath of the 1970 election, Shultz recognized the need to bend that second principle a bit. Hence, he gave his reluctant consent to Nixon's decision to adopt a deficit budget in an effort to curb the sharp and steady rise in unemployment. Deficit spending, the cornerstone of Keynesian economics, had long been regarded by conservatives as the cardinal sin against the sacred precepts of fiscal integrity—and few had attacked it more vigorously in the past than Richard Nixon. Yet, in January, 1971, after preparing his new budget, the President cheerfully confided to a reporter that "I am now a Keynesian in economics," thus rendering "inoperative" twenty years of adherence to economic orthodoxy that Adam Smith himself might have found excessively rigid. In going along with the budget decision, Shultz stressed at the time that it should be about the only departure from Republican tradition; there should be little if any further government tampering with the economy.

This was the situation that prevailed when Long John Silver came galloping into Richard Nixon's Washington. Connally's fundamental view did not emanate from an economic philosophy so much as from a businessman's practical concern (the oil barons he drank bourbon-and-branch with back in Houston were "hopping mad" about economic conditions—especially the beating the stock market had been taking) and, even more so, from his innate political savvy. In his early weeks as Treasury Secretary, Connally took a crash course in economics, and his principal tutor was none other than Arthur Burns. Now in his second year as chairman of the Federal Reserve Board, Burns continued to view the McCracken-Shultz economic policy with mounting dismay. As he had predicted, the once-heralded game

plan, which he had so strenuously opposed back in 1969, was leading
the country into economic peril; and by 1971 he was more convinced
than ever that the only solution was some kind of government action
to hold down the inflationary spiral of wages and prices. As a conservative economist, Burns was well aware that such a move would violate sound Republican principles. But, as he had repeatedly tried to
tell Nixon and his in-house economic advisers, the "old rules just
aren't working the way they used to." Burns long since had given up
any hope that *he* could bring the Nixon White House to its senses;
yet with the arrival of Connally, he saw another way to go. Sizing up
the new Treasury Secretary, he pronounced Connally "educable"—
which, translated, meant that the Texan was more than willing to
accept Dr. Burns's general diagnosis as well as his prescription for a
cure.

By the spring of 1971, Connally was ready. Armed with Burns's
economic sophistication and the enormous strength of his own personality, he proceeded to go to work on Nixon. It wasn't easy. Over
the years, Nixon had been even more adamant in his opposition to
wage and price controls than he had been in his stand against deficit
spending; and since becoming President, he had made it abundantly
clear, on a number of occasions, that he would not even consider
proposals in that direction. Now, in the spring of 1971, with Shultz
backing him at every turn, Nixon firmly restated his position. It was
a matter of principle, he told Connally. He regarded wage and price
controls as the most offensive kind of government meddling in economic affairs.

Connally, for his part, did not mince words. Cutting through the
bull, he put it to Nixon bluntly. Was the President more interested
in principle or in getting himself re-elected? Was it Nixon's desire to
be a one-term President who would go down in history as the Herbert Hoover of his time? Was the President purposely trying to convince everyone that the Republican party deserved its reputation as
the party of economic disaster? Such questions, of course, were calculated to hit Nixon right where he lived, and they did. As time went
on, he began to waver; he was no longer so firm in his commitment
to principle. ("Churning" would later become the favorite word
around the White House to describe Nixon's dramatic shift on both
the China question and the economic front.)

By midsummer, the economic problems at home were aggravated by a major monetary crisis abroad, as the dollar came under severe attack in foreign money markets. In the meantime, Connally kept up the pressure, boring in on Nixon, making more vivid than ever the specter of his Presidency going down in flames before the onslaught of Ed Muskie or, far worse, Ted Kennedy. (Connally, in private, was an intense Kennedyphobe, which is another reason why Haldeman and the others liked him.) Nixon's resistance finally collapsed, and in August, 1971—one month to the day after the China announcement—the President again went on television, this time to tell the country he was imposing a ninety-day freeze on wages and prices, and that it would be followed by a "Phase Two" program of controls to be extended over an indefinite period.

The wage-and-price decision was just one of several economic changes Nixon announced that Sunday evening in August. To meet the monetary crisis, the President liberated the dollar from the gold standard, thus permitting it to "float" and find its natural level of value in relation to other currencies. Other moves included clamping a 10 percent surtax on imports, and proposing a $4.7 billion cut in federal spending. Taken as a whole, it was the most sweeping set of economic decisions to be made by an American President since the New Deal reforms of the Roosevelt years. And Connally had a direct hand in every one of them. But, in terms of domestic politics and the bread-and-butter issue that had given the Democrats such heavy ammunition in the 1970 campaign, the most critical step was the one to freeze and control wages and prices. For that took some of the steam out of inflation momentum that had been building since the U.S. economy became a casualty of the Johnson buildup in Vietnam.

So all of a sudden John Connally was the new hero of the Nixon administration. Not since Pat Moynihan had one man, through sheer force of personality, been able to steer Nixon into adopting such a bold course of action. But, whereas Moynihan had used the con man's arts of guile and flattery to seduce the President, Connally employed the more primitive tactic of raw terror. He simply scared the living hell out of Nixon by drawing lurid pictures of the political grave that awaited him if he didn't follow his, Connally's, advice. A popular saying around the White House at the time was: "Kissinger is Nixon's brains; Connally is his balls." ("Disgusting and untrue" was the comeback of Nixon loyalists, who added, "And don't forget that the President was smart enough to hire both of them.")

It was during the weeks following the August economic decisions that the reports about Connally replacing Agnew on the 1972 ticket began to filter through Washington. Connally himself encouraged this speculation and, as already noted, so did Haldeman. For by the fall of 1971 Haldeman was adopting the view that Agnew had become a liability, who, in the end, would only bring discredit to the Nixon White House. (At the time it was assumed that Haldeman's concern centered on Agnew's friendship with Sinatra, but given his extensive intelligence network, it is possible that even at this early date he was picking up an odor from Baltimore County of Spiro's misdeeds.) It is also possible he was reflecting the President's own disenchantment with Agnew. The problem, however, was that the White House strategists had created a Frankenstein. As the "dump Agnew" rumors picked up steam, conservative Republicans rushed to the Veep's defense and persuaded the White House that such a move would not be worth the commotion it would cause within the party. So Nixon had to abandon even any consideration of running for re-election on a pseudo-coalition ticket (part of the theoretical strategy was for Connally to remain a nominal Democrat), and in January, 1972, the President confirmed, in a nation-wide television interview, that Agnew would again be his running mate.

But, if Connally had powerful friends inside the White House, he had powerful enemies there as well. Shultz fought bitterly against the wage-price controls right down to the end, and after losing the battle, he was more determined than ever not to lose the war. Nor did Kissinger appreciate the role Connally had carved out for himself. Insofar as he influenced decisions dealing with foreign trade and other international money matters, Connally was pushing into Kissinger's territory and threatening him on his most vulnerable flank —economics. So between them the two professors, Shultz and Kissinger, moved quietly but effectively to cut the rambunctious Texan down to size. By early 1972 Connally sensed he was getting caught in a power squeeze; while he was confident he could win a head-to-head struggle with Shultz, the combination of Shultz *and* Kissinger pitted against him was something else again. So he decided, rather abruptly, to quit while he was ahead. In the spring of '72, after a little more than a year in the Treasury post, Connally stepped down from the Nixon Cabinet to devote all his energies to drumming up Democratic support for the President's re-election.

Connally's brief but dazzling career as Treasury Secretary plus the good-soldier labors he performed on the President's behalf in the '72 campaign put him on a course that many, including Connally, believed would carry him straight to the White House—as Nixon's successor in 1976. Shortly after the second term began, Nixon strongly intimated, in a private interview, that Connally was his personal choice for the Republican Presidential nomination in '76. And, in the spring of 1973, the Connally drive appeared to be proceeding on schedule when he announced he was switching his party affiliation from Democrat to Republican. But then, all of a sudden, things began to go awry.

In May of 1973, when he was summoned to Washington to become a Presidential adviser in the post-Watergate shakeup, Connally soon discovered that his blunt and aggressive style was no longer to Nixon's liking. In particular, the President resented Connally's telling him, in no uncertain terms, that people simply didn't believe the President; that whatever had happened, Nixon should make it public and trust in the public's willingness to forgive, and that he must clean out the remains of Haldeman's group still at the White House.

After a few weeks, it became evident that the President really didn't want him around; so once again Connally turned in his badge and went back to Texas. Then, as the year wore on and the web of interlocking scandals grew to monstrous proportions, Connally himself came under suspicion and intense investigation by federal authorities. He stood accused of direct involvement in Nixon's 1971 decision to raise the price of milk, and the subsequent decision, on the part of the dairy industry, to pledge two million dollars to the President's re-election campaign. By the end of 1973, there were federal investigations into the possibility that the poison which had spread through the Nixon White House had infected John Connally as well.

By then, the bold economic policies he initiated had long since perished. In badgering Nixon into setting up wage and price controls, Connally had made his hard-sell pitch on political grounds, and Nixon had acted on those grounds. The tipoff that his strong anti-inflationary measures were, in reality, little more than a re-election maneuver came in May of 1972 when George Shultz was named to replace Connally as Treasury Secretary. Whatever Shultz's failings were as an economist, he was, at all times, a man of conscience. Hence, there was no way he would have accepted the Treasury post if he had not received private assurances from Nixon that, once the election was out of the way, there would be a return to conservative economic principles.

Sure enough: just two months after the 1972 election, the Phase Two controls were lifted; and within a matter of weeks, as Nixon moved into his second term, the country once again found itself in the grip of a virulent inflation as the price of food and fuel, in particular, soared to unprecedented heights, and unemployment again began rising. But the wage-price freeze and the Phase Two controls that followed had served their purpose. During the months leading up to the '72 election, the forces of recession and inflation both had subsided to the point where they were no longer of paramount concern to the voters. Thus Democrats were deprived of the Economic Issue, which they had been able to exploit so successfully two years earlier.

Between them, the foreign-policy initiatives and the economic decisions of 1971–72 were probably enough to assure Nixon's reelection. But none of that could be predicted with certainty back in the dark and dismal days of November, 1970. All that the President and his top political advisers knew for certain then was that "to be thus is nothing." And over the next two years, while Nixon was being "Presidential" in foreign capitals and temporarily changing economic policy at home, others would pursue their own methods to make him "safely thus."

Twenty-three

Ultimately, the most critical decisions to come out of the post-election gloom of 1970 were the ones Richard Nixon did *not* make. In assessing the first two years of his Presidency and the judgment returned by the voters in the midterm election, Nixon was quick to recognize his need for foreign-policy accomplishments and a new economic approach. And, as we've just seen, he acted accordingly by turning to men—Kissinger and Connally—who would spur the necessary changes. The dramatic moves that followed the Connally appointment and the decision to conduct global diplomacy through Kissinger, rather than through Rogers and the State Department, revealed Nixon at the top of his political form. Indeed, his public performance in 1971–72 could serve as a textbook case study of how a President, sensing himself to be in deep political trouble, can maneuver adroitly, on a large scale, to rally the electorate back to his banner. Yet, in the weeks following the '70 election, when so many major changes were being planned, Nixon did nothing to correct the fundamental weaknesses in his domestic policy and the political strategy that was so closely allied to it. In the end, his failure to act in those areas would bring about his undoing.

For example, with all his political savvy, Nixon might well have concluded, by the end of 1970, that John Ehrlichman just wasn't working out well as the man in charge of domestic affairs. The enmity Ehrlichman had aroused on Capitol Hill alone was enough to justify a change there. Similarly, in the case of John Mitchell. By the fall of 1970, even Republicans were complaining about the blunders Mitchell had committed as Attorney General. Conservatives were especially rankled by the slipshod screening methods that resulted in the Haynsworth and Carswell nominations since, as they were quick to point out, there were many Southern jurists who met the ideological requirements and yet whose judicial credentials were impeccable; hence, unlike Haynsworth and Carswell, they would not have been so vulnerable to broadside attack by the Senate liberals. As for Mitchell's reputed political wisdom, the cherished Southern Strategy had been put to the test in the midterm campaign with results that were not entirely encouraging. The White House had staked much of its prestige on Senatorial races in three key Southern states—Texas, Florida, and Tennessee—and the Republicans wound up losing two of them. Nixon had ample reason, by this time, to take a fresh and critical look at John Mitchell as well, but here too he failed to act.

Finally, of course, there was Haldeman, the reputed super-efficient manager and media genius. More than any of the President's other advisers, Haldeman had been responsible for triggering the most controversial actions of the 1970 campaign: the heavy-handed

Agnew blitz . . . the abrupt decision to follow up with an all-out Nixon effort . . . and, most damaging of all, the election-eve telecast of the strident Phoenix speech. This was the third Nixon campaign in which Haldeman had played a major role. As campaign manager in the 1962 California race, he had helped to bring on that disaster. In 1968, he had isolated Nixon to a degree which contributed greatly to the inflexibility and superficiality of the campaign. It was a campaign based on form, not substance, and nearly resulted in losing the election to Humphrey. And then, in 1970, his decision to turn the Phoenix speech into a nation-wide media event had succeeded in drawing such an unfavorable contrast between the President and Ed Muskie that the Senator from Maine was soon to surge ahead of Nixon in the national polls. Thus, by the end of 1970, a man of Nixon's political acumen might also have entertained serious second thoughts about the vast power and authority he had delegated to Haldeman.

But during this period, when he was reassessing and groping for ways to improve his Presidential accomplishments, Richard Nixon's otherwise keen political antennae did not alert him to the shortcomings of Haldeman, Ehrlichman, and Mitchell. What this basically reveals is that by the end of his second year in office he already had become the victim of his deep-seated yearning for isolation. Having chosen to seal himself off from regular contact with his Cabinet officers and any others who might offer dissenting views, he was now utterly dependent on the small circle of men he had designated to stand between him and the outside world. At a time when it was easily apparent to others that there were serious deficiencies in his approach to domestic policy and politics, the President had come to rely, in these areas, almost exclusively on advisers who were hardly in a position to recommend new solutions. In fact, by the end of 1970, they themselves had become the problem.

Yet, during these weeks after the midterm elections, and as the troops geared up for the struggle to make Nixon "safely thus," one man—Chuck Colson—did manage to penetrate the tight inner circle and nail down a commanding position. In fact, in a few months' time, he would go on to challenge the authority of all the others: first Mitchell, then Ehrlichman, and finally, by the summer and fall of 1972, he would even loom as a threat to Haldeman, the master empire builder himself. But Colson's sudden rise to power did not alleviate the problem inherent in so much authority concentrated in the hands of political hard-liners operating from a dangerously narrow point of view. On the contrary, he helped to aggravate the situation, and later was even instrumental in turning it into a total disaster.

Of all the Kennedy haters at the Nixon White House, none was more impassioned than Chuck Colson. This was one of the things that most impressed Haldeman when he and Ehrlichman first brought him into the White House in late 1969. Not only did Colson despise the Kennedys, but he was a *Bostonian* who despised them. That, in fact, was no small part of it. As a Republican, he had fought against the Kennedys back in the days when they were clawing their way to power in Massachusetts politics, a world that bore little resemblance to the later elegance of Camelot. The scars from those early local battles stayed with Colson all through the years that followed in much the same way that California liberals who worked for Helen Gahagan Douglas back in 1950 have never been able to rise above their gut loathing of Nixon. So there was a visceral, even menacing quality to Colson's anti-Kennedy fervor. This came to the surface in the aftermath of the 1970 campaign. Ted Kennedy had sharply criticized Nixon's performance in that campaign, and Colson said at the time that if the Senator had crossed his path after that, "I might have attacked him physically."

Such a remark was entirely in character. Colson prided himself on being tough and ruthless in the best knee-to-the-groin fashion. His general view of the world during his White House years can be summed up by the Green Beret slogan he proudly displayed over the bar in his den: "If you've got 'em by the balls, their hearts and minds will follow." Colson himself had been a Marine officer in his youth, and although his horn-rimmed glasses and pudgy cheeks softened his facial features a bit in later years, he still managed to convey the "cold steel" manner of a Parris Island platoon leader. He once confided that two of his three all-time heroes were Lieutenant General Lewis "Chesty" Puller ("the greatest blood-and-guts Marine who ever walked") and John Wayne. The third name on his list was Richard Nixon. Those who knew him well around the White House were hardly surprised when, in 1972, he uttered his famous line "I would walk over my grandmother if necessary" to get Nixon re-elected. After all, they had heard him say often enough, in private, that he liked to be thought of as a "flag-waving, kick-'em-in-the-nuts, anti-press, anti-liberal Nixon fanatic."

This, then, was Colson. Yet, for all his flair, he had only been able to nip around the edges of power at the Nixon White House during his first year of service there. As noted, he was one of the middle-echelon political operatives working under Haldeman in the planning for the 1970 campaign, sharing duties in that area with, among others, Murray Chotiner and Harry Dent. Chotiner and Dent did not improve their standing in that campaign, and once it was over they gradually faded out of the picture. But Colson made the most of the opportunity, impressing Haldeman and others with his knowledge of politics on the nitty-gritty precinct level (he had learned plenty from his struggles in the hard Irish ward politics of Boston), and by the end of the midterm campaign, he already was making his big move.

Colson was one of the select few summoned to the critical strategy meeting at Key Biscayne four days after the '70 election. In addition to the three top advisers—Haldeman, Ehrlichman, and Mitchell—the men who gathered around Nixon in his Florida home that Saturday morning in November were Colson, Bob Finch, Donald Rumsfeld, and Bryce Harlow.

Harlow's presence was, perhaps, the least significant, for he was planning to leave the White House staff. Since the first day of the Nixon administration, he had served as the President's top liaison man with Congress, an assignment he had previously undertaken for the Eisenhower White House back in the fifties. But, by the fall of 1970, Harlow had grown weary of trying to instruct Haldeman and Ehrlichman in the basic proprieties needed to get along on Capitol Hill and was preparing to return to his lucrative career as Washington's number-one lobbyist for Procter and Gamble. So, at the Key Biscayne meeting that November, Harlow was in a lame-duck position. His counsel was sought and welcomed, as always (almost everyone at the White House respected Harlow's political savvy), but he and the others were aware that he would not be an in-house participant in the long-range planning for the 1972 campaign.

Finch's presence at the Key Biscayne meeting also was perhaps not deeply significant. He had been openly critical of the Agnew blitz and the whole basic thrust of the midterm campaign, and at this post-election meeting, he once again argued for the need to broaden the base and sound a more positive, conciliatory note. So did Rumsfeld, the former Illinois Congressman whom Nixon had appointed in 1969 to head the Office of Economic Opportunity. He believed it was particularly short-sighted for Nixon and the Republican party not to do more to appeal to young voters. In the early months of the administration, Rumsfeld had been an ally of Finch and Moynihan in the battles for welfare reform and other progressive policies; and now, in the fall of 1970, he and Finch represented the last chance for a possible alliance that might serve as a counter to the Haldeman-Ehrlichman axis. Indeed, if they had emerged from the Key Biscayne meeting in a strong enough position to establish a foothold in the inner circle, Finch and Rumsfeld just might have been able to provide enough checks and balances to alter the course of strategy for the 1972 campaign, even to the point of preventing the Watergate disasters themselves. But, even though they were called on to take part in this high-level meeting, both men by then had too much going against them, not the least of which was the opposition of Haldeman and Ehrlichman.

Colson, on the other hand, had no such problem. He was, in a sense, a Haldeman disciple, and beyond that, he did not have any strong reservations about the strategy that had been employed in the recent campaign. He thought the Agnew stuff had been terrific (blistering attacks on "radiclibs" was right down his alley) and he made a special point of praising the President's own performance on the stump. The heart of Colson's message at Key Biscayne that day was that in 1972 the heavy concentration of effort should be directed toward the Northern Flank of the Southern Strategy: the ethnic groups and blue-collar workers who, in recent years, had been shifting away from traditional Democratic candidates and toward George Wallace. In Colson's view, these voters were even more important than Wallace's constituency in the South because they were clustered in and around the major cities in the larger states, the ones with big electoral votes. These disgruntled Democrats could be had, Colson insisted, "but we have to *want* them. We have to go *after* them."

Colson himself had gone "after them" once before. Back in 1960, when John Kennedy carried Massachusetts by a landslide margin in the Presidential race, Colson had managed the re-election campaign of Senator Leverett Saltonstall—and had saved that Republican seat precisely by cutting into blue-collar Democratic strongholds in Boston and Springfield. Ten years later, he still licked his chops over the

sweet memory of that nose-thumbing, home-state embarrassment to
the Kennedys on the night of their greatest triumph. And now, as the
focus began to center on Nixon's re-election campaign, Colson was
itching to apply the same strategy, this time on a national scale. For
one thing, Colson believed it was possible to attack AFL-CIO President George Meany *and* get him going for Nixon, both at the same
time. It would take some doing, it wouldn't be easy, Colson argued,
but he had a plan for trying and he insisted (correctly as things turned
out) that it could be done.

Nixon was deeply impressed. Not only did he agree with Colson's
analysis, but his own adrenaline was charged by the hard, combative
edge of Colson's style. At a time when so many Republicans around
the country were singing the blues because of the '70 midterm results, here was this tough ex-Marine talking not only about winning
in 1972, but about winning big—and in a way that would humiliate
the Democrats. So, coming out of the Key Biscayne meeting, Chuck
Colson was the new star in the Nixon firmament. Later that month,
a more secret political strategy meeting was held, and this time, as
far as could be determined, only four men were present: Nixon,
Haldeman, Mitchell, and Colson. Finch and Rumsfeld—and others
like them—had been consigned to the background. They may not
have been aware of it, but there they were, and there they would
remain. Thus, in the uncertain aftermath of the 1970 election, the
inner circle around Nixon had opened just a crack, enough to allow
Chuck Colson to squeeze in. But then, just as quickly, it closed tight
again.

Colson's swift rise to power would not have been possible without
the subtle sponsorship of Haldeman, who had his own reasons for
bringing the Boston lawyer so deeply into the mix. The fact is that
Haldeman himself may have been feeling just a bit insecure at this
point. He was aware that all the criticisms of the Phoenix speech
decision and other aspects of the midterm campaign were essentially
criticisms of him; and while most of the people who were complaining had no way of knowing that, there were others who *did* know
it. John Mitchell, for one. Haldeman was incensed by Mitchell's own
crack that the President had campaigned like a man "running for
sheriff," and now, as the attention began to shift to plans for 1972,
he became extremely wary of Mitchell. For it was Haldeman's firm

intention to orchestrate the '72 campaign from within the White House, and he knew that Mitchell was determined to run the campaign himself. Foreseeing the inevitable power struggle, Haldeman wanted to have at his side an ally with enough moxie to stand up to Mitchell. Thus Colson. In other words, he could use Colson as a buffer against Mitchell in much the same way that Mitchell had served as a buffer in the earlier White House moves against Hickel and Finch.

Colson, for his part, was more than willing to take on that role. He didn't like or trust Mitchell, mainly because he didn't think the Attorney General was very smart, at least not "politics smart" in the hard, driving, street-corner way that he, Colson, felt one had to be if one wanted to be sure of winning. But, in addition to joining forces with Haldeman for a later power move against Mitchell, Colson seized every opportunity, over the winter months of 1970–71, to strengthen his position in other ways, especially in terms of his personal relationship with the President.

Building on the favorable impression he had made at the Key Biscayne meeting, Colson continued to talk politics in the kind of hard and uncompromising language that blended in so well with Nixon's own mood during this period. For these were bleak days, the rock-bottom point of the first term as far as White House morale was concerned. The President was trailing in the polls. The economic situation was going from bad to worse. There was a somber, oppressive sense that it was all slipping away, and that perhaps there wasn't anything that could be done to prevent it from happening. (At that time, no one at the White House, including Nixon, could predict with confidence the big breakthrough moves on China and the economy, and the positive impact they would have.) The President was said to be in foul spirits most of the time. The word around the White House was that he was brooding a great deal about the real possibility that he could be headed for another painful defeat, one that would make him an object of ridicule again, this time as the first President since the scorned Herbert Hoover to be repudiated in his bid for a second term.

A high-ranking member of the White House staff at that time, who worked just outside the inner circle and was familiar with the deepening anxiety that prevailed in and around the Oval Office, would later recall:

"To understand this man, you have to bear in mind the deep and terrible wounds he brought with him into the Presidency. He was never able to forget what others had done to him in the past. That is, he so believed in his heart that *he* had been done dirty so many times, that once he was on top he was determined not to have it happen again—ever—to him. One of the major goals of his administration, although it was never articulated publicly, was to make sure that never again would he be humiliated, not by the Kennedys nor by anyone else. So, during that period in early 1971, when everything looked so bad, he was in the Oval Office saying to himself: 'Look, I'm a good guy. I've always *wanted* to be a good guy. But I know—better than most, because after all I've been through the worst possible fires—that there is a dirty, bad, dark side to this business, and by God, I'm not going to get beat again. I'm not going to get kicked around anymore by people who profess to be goody-goody but then go around knocking my brains out, and defeating what I think is important for the country.'

"That's where Colson came in," this first-hand observer went on to say. "He played to Nixon's dark and bitter side, even more than Haldeman did, if you can imagine that. He sensed the desperate mood that was sinking in during those first months after the '70 election, and he saw that as his opening. So Colson came on. He came on tough as rail spikes, blunt and nasty and snarling—and willing to do *any*thing. And in that mood the President decided he was just the man he needed. Nobody else around him—not even Haldeman—was hard enough or mean enough to do the job he thought had to be done."

So it was that by tone and attitude, if not by direct order, the message came out of the Oval Office: Get them before they get us. Hurt them before they hurt us. Don't let them take it away. Do whatever is necessary. But do it! No one was more eager to translate that message into action than Chuck Colson.

By the spring of 1971, the grand strategy for the 1972 campaign had been charted. It was decided that the re-election effort would move forward on three distinct levels. First, Nixon himself would be "Presidential," and concentrate all his attention on the pursuit of "monuments" and the cultivation of an above-the-battle image. Whatever he might have to say to someone like Colson in private, there would be no more partisan, Phoenix-style speeches to give the Democrats ammunition. Second, there would be a special out-front campaign organization, to be headed by John Mitchell. It would function independently of the Republican National Committee, for its sole purpose, its one and only *raison d'être*, would be to re-elect one man: Richard Nixon. Thus the origin of the Committee to Re-elect the President—or CREEP, as it would later be called. And third, there would be a clandestine campaign operation, with Colson the point man for that. The Colson group would be given the task of organizing efforts on the precinct level to transform the blue-collar Wallace voters on the Northern Flank into a solid base of support for Nixon; and beyond that, to harass the media, gather political intelligence, monitor all enemy activities, and devise ways of keeping potential Democratic rivals off balance.

Haldeman, it was understood, would be involved on all three levels. He was responsible for making sure that any and all "Presidential" successes received the full media treatment (e.g., the China trip). Then, to maintain coordination between Mitchell's group and the White House, he would have his own people—first Jeb Magruder and later Gordon Strachan—prominently placed at the Committee to Re-elect. And, finally, the Colson operation would proceed from within the White House, always in communication with Haldeman and under his general if not specific supervision. Thus Haldeman had maneuvered himself into perfect position. By seeing to it that Magruder was designated Mitchell's deputy over at the Committee, he would be able to keep close tabs on all developments there. Yet, at the same time, much of the thrust of the campaign strategy would come from the "media and muscle" combination set up at the White House—his media and Colson's muscle.

By the summer of '71, the tri-level push was under way. Kissinger had sold Chou En-lai on the wisdom of an election-year visit by Nixon to China. The CREEP office had been secretly open since April, and once the shop's existence became known publicly that summer, Magruder moved in to run it until early 1972, when Mitchell would take over full-time command. And Chuck Colson was finding more than enough to keep him busy.

The intelligence operation Colson helped develop was not exactly a new idea. Its origins could be traced to the early weeks of the Nixon Presidency. In March, 1969, John Ehrlichman, who was then still working as White House counsel and had not yet made his move

toward the center of power, hired two New York City policemen—
John Caulfield and Tony Ulasewicz—to work as undercover investigators for the White House. For the most part, their assignments
seemed to be checking out job candidates. As far as is known, their
work did not amount to much—until Chappaquiddick. But, for
weeks after that, Caulfield and Ulasewicz investigated young woman
friends of Mary Jo Kopechne (some of whom believed they were
wiretapped in the process) in an effort to find out all they could about
"that night."

Then, in June of 1970, there occurred the first White House attempt to establish a secret police force. This was the infamous "Huston Plan," named after Tom Huston, a young White House staffer
who worked under Haldeman. The plan, which Huston researched
and wrote, called for the formation of a "new, dynamic" domestic-
security group, made up of representatives from the White House,
the FBI, the CIA, and other government agencies, military and civil-
ian. In essence, the group would have been authorized to wiretap,
commit burglary, and violate other laws in the interest of tightening
domestic security. As the proposal itself specifically spelled out: "Use
of this technique [burglary] is clearly illegal. . . . It is also highly risky
and could result in great embarrassment if exposed. However, it is
also the most fruitful tool and can produce the type of intelligence
which cannot be obtained in any other fashion."

Another attractive feature of the plan, from the Nixonmen's point
of view, was that it would have placed the White House in a position
to exert direct control over the FBI and CIA, two agencies which,
over the years, have been able to maintain a large measure of political independence. That point, apparently, was not lost on Nixon, who
gave the plan his wholehearted approval, and sent memos ordering
it into effect to all the appropriate agencies. Five days later, he
recalled the memos, a move which ostensibly, at least, killed the
project, although no record has been produced proving that he formally, officially, and definitely rescinded his approval. The problem
was that J. Edgar Hoover, of all people, refused to go along with what
the memos ordered unless the President gave him specific written
consent to break the law. Part of Hoover's objections may well have
been a concern over civil liberties, although the tough old cop had
never previously been known for excessive sensitivity in that area;
but he was definitely determined—to his everlasting credit—to pre-

vent the FBI from becoming any less independent than it was from unchecked control by Presidents. He no more wanted to be an out-and-out adjunct of Nixon's administration than he had wanted to be of Kennedy's or Johnson's. But the White House learned a valuable lesson from its experience with the "Huston Plan." The next time it decided to set up a secret police force there would be no attempt to work out an arrangement with the statutory agencies.

"The next time" was one year later. More than any other single event, it was the publication of the Pentagon Papers in June, 1971, that put the Nixon White House squarely on the road to Watergate. Even under normal conditions, the President and his top advisers were almost morbidly obsessed with the problem of news "leaks." And in the early summer of 1971 conditions were far from normal. These were the weeks when Kissinger's negotiations with the Chinese through intermediaries in Pakistan were in their most delicate phase; a leak in that area could have wiped out months of intricate statecraft. So Kissinger and Nixon were understandably concerned when the Pentagon Papers—classified documents dealing with the U.S. involvement in Vietnam—were leaked to the *New York Times*. But understandable, even justifiable concerns do not always give birth to justifiable actions.

Less than a week after publication of the Pentagon Papers, Nixon secretly ordered the establishment of a Special Investigations Unit within the White House. Its mission, as he later put it, was to "stop security leaks and to investigate other sensitive security matters." Henry Kissinger already had a miniature special investigations unit of his own working to plug leaks out of his office. A White House aide in a position to know (with no special ties to either Kissinger or Haldeman) said: "Kissinger was perhaps even more concerned about the loyalty of his staff than Haldeman was about everybody's loyalty to Nixon. Kissinger was deeply concerned about news-story leaks, not just because of what he considered national security but also for what it seemed to say about his staff's loyalty to him. Kissinger got furious any time he felt he could not absolutely control information—about himself, personally, about national-security matters, about *any*thing out of his shop." Two other high-ranking former White House aides agreed that this was true. Nixon, they said, admired Kissinger's little leak-finding and -plugging operation.

One of Kissinger's most loyal aides, David Young, was in charge of the group, and in 1971 he became an original member of the President's larger Special Investigations Unit. Nixon assigned Ehrlichman to supervise the project, and Ehrlichman, in turn, appointed his protégé from the Seattle law firm, Egil "Bud" Krogh, to head the unit. The next step was to find the right people, who would be willing to get their hands dirty plugging up the "leaks"—i.e., the actual "Plumbers."

Chuck Colson was helpful in that area. He was overjoyed by the decision to form the Plumbers Unit, a move he felt was long overdue. Moving fast, Colson now went to Ehrlichman and Krogh and said he had just the man for their new group: E. Howard Hunt, a former CIA agent and fellow alumnus of Brown University, whom he, Colson, had come to know quite well in recent years. So Hunt, the moody romantic who wrote lurid spy novels in his spare time, was Colson's contribution to the Plumbers Unit. The other Plumber who went on to acquire no small measure of renown was G. Gordon Liddy. The dubious credit for bringing him into the group belonged to Egil Krogh. A former FBI agent who specialized in breaking and entering, Liddy also had been a deputy prosecutor in Dutchess County, New York. On one occasion, while arguing a case in court there, he fired off a pistol with blanks in an effort to impress the jury, a performance that earned him the nickname "Rainmaker." Such behavior was, unfortunately, all too characteristic. Emotional stability was not one of Gordon Liddy's strong points.

Thus by 1971 the White House view of its investigative needs had escalated considerably. Two years earlier, a couple of New York cops had been deemed sufficient. Now on the payroll were veterans of the CIA and FBI. The original gumshoes, Caulfield and Ulasewicz, were still around, but even before the Plumbers Unit was put together, they weren't getting many assignments. "For some reason," a White House aide would later recall, "it was decided that Caulfield couldn't handle the really heavy stuff." In the aftermath of the Pentagon Papers leak, Hunt and Liddy were brought in to take care of the "heavy stuff."

Colson, apparently, had his own reasons for wanting Hunt at the White House "at that point in time." As a matter of fact, when Hunt was hired on as a $100-a-day "consultant," he was assigned to Colson's staff, and he did not officially move over to the Plumbers squad until late in the summer of 1971. Colson would later say that was strictly for "internal budget" reasons, but Hunt insists that he worked almost exclusively for Colson during his first weeks at the White House, and that he continued to carry out assignments for him even after he joined the Plumbers. In any event, Hunt's activities that summer had little to do with plugging up "security" leaks. Instead, most of his time was spent trying to discredit the Kennedys, whom he abhorred almost as much as Colson did.

Two years after Chappaquiddick, Ted Kennedy had once again become a prime source of anxiety within the Nixon White House, polls indicating he was the favorite for the Democratic nomination for 1972. At one point, donning a disguise he had acquired from the CIA , Hunt tracked down Kennedy watchers in New England in an effort to get some dirt on the Senator's personal life. Still another assignment centered on Kennedy's brother, the late President. Hunt has said it was Colson who told him to forge the State Department cable to indicate President Kennedy's complicity in the 1963 murder of South Vietnam's President Ngo Dinh Diem. Later, after the forgery, Colson would try to sell the story of Kennedy's complicity to a reporter for *Life* Magazine.

But, if Kennedy was regarded as White House Enemy Number One, there were plenty of other American citizens who, for one reason or another, were marked for secret wrath from their government. The intention was to attempt to ruin their reputations, and in some cases their livelihoods, through the power of the executive branch. For it was during this period that Colson and others were compiling the famous White House Enemies List and considering various ways of dealing with those on it. In August, 1971, John Dean, who worked closely with Colson on this project, wrote his vivid memo to Haldeman and Ehrlichman suggesting that certain weapons available within the federal machinery—such as the Internal Revenue Service—could be used "to screw our political enemies."

The "Huston Plan," the formation of the Plumbers Unit, Hunt's forgery of the Kennedy cable, and the Enemies List were all part of what John Mitchell would later describe, in his testimony at the Senate Watergate hearings, as "the White House horrors." Yet apparently the "horrors" could have been much worse than they were. Later on, after the Watergate scandal broke, a high-ranking White

House official, expressing a view he shared with many of his colleagues, would tell a reporter: "If you think what Colson *did* was bad, you should have heard what he *wanted* to do, what he was *kept* from doing."

One of the more elaborate of the "White House horrors" took place in Los Angeles in September of 1971. Shortly after the *New York Times* began publishing the Pentagon Papers, a young scholar who worked for the Defense Department during the Johnson years came forward and admitted that he was the source of the leak. From that moment on, Daniel Ellsberg would rank second, just behind Kennedy, on the Enemies List. He became the target of the Plumbers' first full-scale secret investigation, and by September that effort was focused on the office of Dr. Lewis Fielding in Los Angeles, where Ellsberg had recently been undergoing psychoanalysis. The Plumbers were convinced that Fielding's private files could provide a rich harvest of material for their anti-Ellsberg campaign. At no time was any evidence produced that the physician had any connection whatever with leaks. It was conceivable (and ostensibly the reason for the break-in) that his files contained leads on what the Nixonmen would consider useful information about Ellsberg's personal life, the kind Hunt had been trying to dig up on Kennedy. So the decision was made to burglarize Fielding's office—a "bag job," as Liddy and Hunt phrased it—and by early morning of September 4 the deed was done.

The entire anti-Ellsberg operation was set in motion by general orders from Nixon and proceeded under Ehrlichman's overall supervision. But Egil Krogh was responsible for the detailed planning and specifics of the burglary itself. Ehrlichman later claimed he did not know about the precise plans to commit burglary beforehand, but admitted that he was told about it shortly afterward. This was the critical moment for Ehrlichman: had he acted then to fire Krogh and Hunt and Liddy and blown the whistle on them and the crime they had committed, he would have prevented the disasters that were soon to follow—the Watergate break-in and cover-up. What's more, he would have saved himself as well. Instead, Ehrlichman merely allowed as how he "did not agree with this method of investigation" and instructed the Plumbers "not to do this again." By acting to conceal the crime, Ehrlichman left himself open for later charges that he had been a lot more involved in the planning of the break-in

than he cared to admit. And in the summer of 1974, he was convicted
of conspiracy and perjury for his role in the Ellsberg burglary. So the
critical moment passed, and Hunt and Liddy were free to move on
to other pursuits.

Not long after the Ellsberg burglary, Liddy was transferred, on
Krogh's recommendation, over to CREEP to set up a security and
intelligence operation there. That decision led directly to that fateful
day in January, 1972, when Liddy went to John Mitchell's office at
the Justice Department to make what he called his "presentation."
There to meet him were Mitchell, Jeb Magruder, and John Dean, and
before this small but attentive audience Liddy unveiled his master
plan. It included the following proposals: the kidnaping of known
leaders of radical groups to be detained "in a place like Mexico"
during the week of the Republican convention, the hiring of "mug-
ging squads" to "rough up" those demonstrators who were not ab-
ducted, the use of call girls to infiltrate the Democratic convention
and extract information from unsuspecting delegates and officials.
(The girls, Liddy assured the group, would all be "high class, the best
in the business.")

For Mitchell this was the critical moment. Bear in mind, he was
still, at this point, the Attorney General of the United States, and this
bizarre scheme was being proposed in his office at the Justice Department, the seat of law and order. Mitchell's only legitimate course of
action was to fire Liddy on the spot and launch an immediate investigation to determine if others were involved in these criminal proposals. Instead, as Magruder later described it, Mitchell simply indicated
"in an understated way that this was not an acceptable project
. . . and that Liddy should go back to the drawing boards and come
up with a more realistic plan." Even more than Ehrlichman, then,
Mitchell all but invited the disasters to come.

Liddy, for his part, was deeply disappointed. He had spent a great
deal of time on the plan, drawing up detailed charts to give his
"presentation" maximum effect; moreover, he thought the means,
while a bit unorthodox, were thoroughly justified by the end: the
re-election of Richard Nixon. Yet, even after he scaled everything
down to the point where all that was left of his grandiose vision was
a plan calling for a few break-in and bugging operations—even *then*
Liddy had trouble getting a green light. So one evening in early
March he and Hunt went to see Colson and asked him to intervene

on their behalf. Shortly thereafter, Magruder received a call from Colson, in which, as Magruder remembers it, Colson told him to "get off the stick and get the budget approved for Liddy's plans." Colson later acknowledged making the call, but he said he did not know what Liddy's plans entailed. Whatever the case, his phone call helped tip the balance. By April, "Operation Gemstone," as it was called, had moved into its tactical phase. Now there would be no turning back.

The supreme irony, of course, is that by the time the "third-rate burglary" occurred, early on the morning of June 17, Nixon had the election all wrapped up; indeed, by then all signs pointed to a proba- ble landslide. The China trip and the economic decisions of the previous summer had succeeded in reversing the trend that had been rising against him in early 1971; by the early spring of '72, he once again was leading all Democratic challengers. The President's prospects were further enhanced by the unexpected rise that spring of George McGovern, whom the White House viewed—correctly— as their weakest possible opponent. Nevertheless, through those weeks of April and early May, the Nixon strategists did have one nagging problem that promised to make the election too close for comfort—and the name of that problem was George Wallace.

The flash-point issue all across the country that spring was school busing, and that was like throwing a chicken to a fox: Wallace pro- ceeded to pick it clean. Running hard in the Democratic primaries, he swept to a big victory in Florida and followed that up with impres- sive showings in several Northern primaries. And, while it was obvi- ous that he had no chance for the Democratic nomination, it was just as obvious that as a third-party candidate in the fall he would be far more formidable than he had been four years earlier. What this meant was that even if Nixon held on to his lead there was a real chance he would remain a minority President with a narrow man- date. But on May 15—more than a month before the Watergate break-in—Nixon was suddenly assured of an easy victory when Ar- thur Bremer, a disturbed loner in the Oswald-Sirhan tradition, shot Wallace and eliminated him from the campaign. (The President him- self later cited the Wallace shooting as the most significant factor in his re-election, ahead of the trip to Peking, which he ranked second.) After May 15, the only question left was whether Nixon could swell his lead into a landslide. George McGovern and Thomas Eagleton provided the answer to that.

In fact, Nixon scarcely bothered to become a candidate in the customary sense. Having established himself as "Presidential," he intimated that to indulge in a campaign was beneath the dignity of his high office. So the Richard Nixon Presidential ship glided serenely across the summer and fall to its overwhelming re-election victory. Except for a nervous deviation here and there, in response to storm warnings issuing from the Washington *Post*, it gave no outward sign of the corrosion beneath the surface that had spread all through the hold.

Twenty-four

THE night of his greatest triumph, Richard Nixon—the solitary man, the compulsive loner—chose to remain in seclusion. As returns came streaming in on Election Night, 1972, the President sequestered himself alone in the Lincoln Bedroom on the third and most private floor of the White House. His family and most intimate associates were gathered in a nearby hallway (the third-floor reception room), to watch the landslide take shape on television. Every now and then, one of them would step quietly into the President's inner sanctum to exchange a brief word of cheer. But for the most part Nixon sat by himself in front of the fireplace in the Lincoln Bedroom, alone with his thoughts, his "Victory at Sea" music, and his yellow legal pads. It had often been his habit in the past to seek solitude when under pressure, when the sense of crisis weighed heavily on him; and now, as this evening carried him to the supreme moment of his long political career, he preferred to rejoice—as he had preferred to suffer—in private.

On the surface, at least, Nixon had much to rejoice over that evening. His towering victory was of a magnitude comparable with the great Presidential landslides of this century: Harding's in 1920, FDR's in 1936, and Lyndon Johnson's in 1964. His percentage of the total vote, 60.7, was exceeded only by LBJ's record-breaking 61.1 figure; and in winning forty-nine out of fifty states, he even surpassed Roosevelt's near-sweep of the electoral vote, when he carried everything except Maine and Vermont. Finally, in the last election of his career, Richard Nixon was able to exorcise, once and for all, the "loser's" tag that had so cruelly mocked him in earlier years. Actually, as the impact of his re-election victory set in, people began to recognize that, in fact, it was his record as a winner that enabled him to stand now, unchallenged, as the dominant political figure of his time. Over the past twenty years, Nixon had run for national office five times, emerging victorious in four of those races. Only one other man in American history—Franklin D. Roosevelt—could make the same claim. Like Roosevelt, Nixon had been able to outlast his enemies and to endure as a political force long after they had been driven from the field of combat.

There was, nevertheless, a hollowness to the President's landslide, for it differed significantly from those of his predecessors. Harding, Roosevelt, and Johnson had scored great victories for their parties as well as for themselves, sweeping in on their coattails huge Congressional majorities. But the Nixon triumph in 1972 was oddly limited in that respect. The Committee to Re-elect and all the other forces that had been set in motion to assure him a second term in the White House had certainly succeeded in stunning fashion in the achievement of their principal objective: the re-election of one man, Richard Nixon. But there was a price to be paid for the strategic decision to run the President's re-election campaign as a separate entity, independent of the Republican National Committee and the party organizations on the state and local levels. For, even as McGovern was being buried in the Presidential contest, his fellow Democrats successfully resisted the Nixon landslide in the House and Senate races. The Republicans were able to gain only thirteen seats in the House and, far more astonishing, they actually suffered a net *loss* of two seats in the Senate. Despite the enormous scope of the President's personal victory, the opposition party remained in firm control of Congress. More than anything else, then, the story that unfolded Election Night, 1972, only re-emphasized Richard Nixon's peculiar status as the solitary man, the political loner, who sat by himself in the Lincoln Bedroom, sealed off from even the rest of his own party.

In the weeks immediately ahead, events of passing historical interest were to underscore further the uniqueness of Nixon's position
in American politics. Early in December, 1972, the aged and frail
Harry Truman was taken to a hospital in Kansas City, and there, the
day after Christmas, he died. Less than a month later—just two days
after the start of Nixon's second term—Lyndon Johnson's failing
heart gave out during an afternoon nap on his ranch in Texas. Their
deaths left the country without a surviving ex-President for the first
time since the Theodore Roosevelt era. What is often referred to as
the most exclusive club in the world was now reduced to a member-
ship of one: Richard Nixon.

More importantly, the deaths of Truman and Johnson symbolized
the passing of the long legacy left from FDR's reign in the White
House. Truman, of course, had been the direct inheritor of Roosevelt's philosophy and programs, and had carried them forward with
his own Fair Deal policies. Johnson too had been a Roosevelt protégé,
who first came to Washington in the late 1930s as a young Congressman deeply committed to the measures FDR had taken to steer
America out of the depression. In later years, his own Great Society
legislation was recognized as a robust descendant of the New Deal.
The deaths of Truman and Johnson seemed to add a solemn, funereal
note to McGovern's defeat, which itself was being interpreted as a
final and definitive repudiation of the Roosevelt-Democratic approach to governmental action.

Then, just a few days after Johnson's death, the Vietnam ceasefire
accord was formally signed in Paris. With that agreement, Nixon was
able, at last, to remove from his shoulders the war burden he had
inherited from LBJ. Now the President could press forward with
more tactical and strategic freedom toward the long-range foreign-
policy goals he had begun to pursue in his first term. Thus, during
these weeks of January, 1973, it seemed as if, almost by cosmic design, events were falling into place to dramatize the idea that America had come to the end of one era and had crossed over into another
—the Age of Nixon.

There were a number of immediate signs to indicate what the
tone and direction of Richard Nixon's second term in the White
House would be like. One of them occurred just a few days before
the Second Inaugural when Senate Minority Leader Hugh Scott re-

ceived a telephone call from Bob Haldeman. The message was brief: the White House, Haldeman said, wanted to replace Scott as minority leader on the grounds that he wasn't measuring up to the job. Scott could hardly believe his ears. As one of the more-seasoned politicians on the Washington scene, the Pennsylvania Senator had no illusions about the level of political sophistication at the Nixon White House. Nevertheless, he was astounded by the brazenness and arrogance of this attempt to cut him ruthlessly down and, at the same time, dictate to Republicans in Congress. Scott was furious at the personal insult, *and* at what he considered to be interference with the prerogatives of Congress, a violation of the separation-of-powers doctrine. Therefore, his first response was to demand to know if this was the President's personal decision.

Nearly three years earlier, at the time Wally Hickel wrote his famous letter and Haldeman telephoned the Interior Secretary to disinvite him to the White House religious service, Hickel had asked almost precisely the same question. At that time, Haldeman's reply had been cryptic and tantalizing. "The President was in the room when the decision was made," he told Hickel. Now, however, in response to Scott's query, Haldeman didn't even bother to suggest tacit Presidential approval. Instead, he merely informed the Senator that John Ehrlichman had concurred in the decision. Scott icily noted that Ehrlichman had not been elected to anything, and a few days later, he accepted without hesitation when his Republican colleagues in the Senate re-elected him Minority Leader.

Haldeman and Ehrlichman were more successful with other calls at about the same time, calls which cost many loyal Nixon Republicans their jobs in various government agencies. Shock set in as Under Secretaries and their aides in one department after another were curtly informed, "Your services are no longer needed." Little or no effort was made to find other work for them. In some cases even "Thank yous" for past service came late and perfunctorily, if at all. When these Republicans began asking why, they usually found that the answer was: Being a member of the party was not enough. Nor was having worked faithfully and loyally for Nixon. The new requirements called for loyalty to Haldeman and Ehrlichman as well.

Such actions demonstrated how far Haldeman and Ehrlichman were prepared to go by this time to bring the entire federal government under their firm command. Their power had become awesome, and frightening. They had extended their personal authority over the far reaches of the executive branch, and their control—as well as the hard-line philosophy that came with it—was reflected in the men who, by the start of the second term, were installed as heads of the various departments and agencies.

The Attorney General now was Richard Kleindienst, the Arizona politico, once described as being "a notch or two to the right of Barry Goldwater." Kleindienst had passed the litmus test of loyalty during his confirmation hearings in March, 1972, when he denied any knowledge of Presidential involvement in the ITT antitrust case, and the heavy campaign contributions that were related to it. (For that exercise in deception he would later plead guilty in federal court to a misdemeanor charge just short of perjury.) As the first term came to an end, the decent but docile Elliot Richardson was shifted over to Defense to replace the departing Mel Laird there. Chosen to succeed Richardson as HEW Secretary was Caspar Weinberger, who, as state Republican chairman in California in 1962, had worked closely with Haldeman on the Nixon campaign for Governor. In more recent years, Weinberger had been associated with Ronald Reagan, and it was understood that his primary mission, as HEW Secretary, would be to preside over the dismantling of the Great Society and other social-welfare programs, some of which had been on the books since New Deal years. The new man at HUD was James Lynn, an obscure Indiana businessman who had served as Under Secretary of Commerce during the first term. Moving into Volpe's job at Transportation was Claude Brinegar, an oil-company executive. From now on, there would be no pushy Governors around trying to sell independent ideas drawn from their own political experience. Those days were over.

Still other Cabinet appointments reflected the complete dominance of the Haldeman-Ehrlichman hard line. Ever since late 1971, Agriculture had been in the hands of Earl Butz, who, by the early weeks of the second term, had distinguished himself in a number of ways. In the spring of 1973, when consumers were hit by a meat shortage and soaring food prices, Butz showed his concern by observing that Americans were eating too much anyway, a remark that may have entitled him to permanently retire the Marie Antoinette Memorial Award. The new Labor Secretary, appointed in the last days of the first term, was Peter Brennan, the construction-union

leader from New York. Brennan had been a big favorite at the Nixon
White House ever since the spring of 1970, when a group of New
York construction workers, calling themselves "hard hats," attacked
and beat up antiwar demonstrators who were protesting the President's decision to invade Cambodia. Now, two and a half years later,
the head of the "hard hats" was rewarded with a Cabinet post. He
demanded and got his own personal squad of bodyguards to "protect" him in Washington (in addition to the usual Government Services Agency protection afforded Cabinet officers). He also literally
wore a pistol in his belt, becoming the first known Cabinet member
since at least Andrew Jackson's time—and the first Nixon official since
Gordon Liddy—regularly to wear a sidearm while performing official
duties.

In addition to the malleable yes men named to the Cabinet, the
White House had taken steps by the end of 1972 to bring the two
most sensitive government agencies—the CIA and FBI—directly
under its political control. Throughout most of the first term, the
Nixonmen had waited for an opportune moment to get rid of CIA
Director Richard Helms, whom they distrusted on two counts: (a)
appointed by Johnson, he was a Democratic holdover, and (b) even
worse, perhaps, he was a former newspaperman. So in the early
weeks of the second term they quietly eased Helms out and replaced
him with their own man, James Schlesinger.

Even more crucial was the FBI situation. Ever since putting the
kibosh on the Huston Plan, J. Edgar Hoover had been a prime target
of the Nixon White House. Neither Haldeman nor Ehrlichman—nor
even the President—could move overtly against Hoover the way
they could against the likes of a Wally Hickel or even a Richard
Helms. J. Edgar Hoover, after all, was an American institution, and
therefore, if he so chose, he could remain FBI Director until the day
he died. Which he did. But Hoover's death in May, 1972, gave the
White House the opening it needed to put the FBI in its pocket, and
the instrument it selected for that purpose was L. Patrick Gray. Gray
(whom Nixon himself called "dumb") had no particular qualifications
for the critical FBI post except the most important one of all as far
as the White House was concerned: he had been, over the years, a
dedicated Nixon loyalist. In the end, his appointment would bring
disgrace on himself, the bureau, and ultimately on the White House
itself. As Acting FBI Director, Gray had become enmeshed in the

Watergate coverup during the summer of 1972, and in March, 1973, when he went before the Senate to win confirmation as Hoover's permanent successor, his blundering performance exposed the outer edges of the coverup and triggered the wave of panic that soon spread through the Nixon White House.

Yet, even before the Watergate story erupted, the tight concentration of power that had coalesced within the White House by the start of the second term had aroused, in some thoughtful observers, a rising sense of concern and apprehension. Early in March, 1973, the *New York Times* published a series of articles in which a number of historians and other scholars argued that, in its systematic push to expand its own powers, the Nixon White House was usurping the constitutional authority of both Congress and the courts. The President's refusal to spend funds specifically appropriated by Congress was cited as just one example in which, according to his critics, Nixon had gone further than any previous President in undermining Congressional authority. And, in his attacks on school busing and other court decisions, Nixon was accused of trying to violate the constitutional prerogative of judicial authority.

Some of the men interviewed by the *Times* focused their attention on the phenomenon that has been a central theme in this book: the drastic shift of power within the executive branch itself. Thus, political scientist Thomas Cronin was quoted as saying that the White House "has become a powerful inner sanctum of government, isolated from traditional, Constitutional checks and balances." He went on to contend that it was now common practice for "anonymous, unelected and unratified aides" to make important decisions in both foreign and domestic policy "with no semblance of public scrutiny."

From the historian Arthur Schlesinger, Jr.: "In his first term, President Nixon kept his Cabinet at arm's length; and in his second term he has put together what, with one or two exceptions, is the most anonymous Cabinet within memory, a Cabinet of clerks, of compliant and faceless men who stand for nothing, have no independent national position and are guaranteed not to defy Presidential whim."

Finally, there was this comment by the historian and biographer James MacGregor Burns: "We know almost everything about Presidents, but we know all too little about the vast gray executive establishment that expands, proliferates, and partly devours the decision-

making apparatus of the rest of the government behind the pleasantly deceptive 'low profile' of the White House."

The argument was being made, even among some of his friends,
that for an overwhelmingly elected Richard Nixon to mount a determined effort toward becoming a "Franklin Roosevelt of the Right"
was one thing—perhaps overdue and beneficial—but a lack of sensitivity to constitutional limits was quite another.

The President and the men to whom he had delegated so much
authority, however, were impervious to these arguments. They dismissed such questioning as unjustified and unfair, and considered it
to be motivated strictly by political partisanship. "Our revolution,"
as Nixon and those around him thought of it, was ready—and backed
by a smashing election victory.

It did not stay ready long. The White House power structure,
which seemed so impregnable to those outside the fortress, already
was starting to crack. Soon even the "pleasantly deceptive 'low profile' " would fall apart.

In 1610, ten years before the Pilgrims landed at Plymouth Rock,
177 years before the framing of the U.S. Constitution, and 362 years
before the Watergate break-in, Sir Francis Bacon wrote a letter to his
friend George Villiers, who was about to become an intimate adviser
at the court of King James I. Bacon wanted to be sure his friend knew
exactly what he was getting into, and his letter included these words
of warning: "Remember then what your true condition is: the king
himself is above the reach of his people, but cannot be above their
censures; and you are his shadow, if either he commit an error, and
is loth to avow it, but excuses it upon his ministers, of which you are
the first in the eye; or you commit the fault or have willingly permitted it, and must suffer for it: and so perhaps you may be offered as
a sacrifice to appease the multitude."

Francis Bacon might not have been able to comprehend the
rationale behind the Watergate burglary (he would not have been
alone), but he would have had no trouble understanding why those
in power were "loth to avow" any connection with the men who
committed the crime. Elaborate coverups and court intrigues were
not unknown in Jacobean England.

The simple facts behind the "third-rate burglary" at the Watergate apartments were not the reason the White House coverup was deemed so vital. If that had been the only problem, then it is entirely possible that the decision would have been made at the time of the burglary to clear the air and get it over with; there would have been a brief uproar, no doubt, but it is unlikely it would have been severe enough to affect the President's re-election prospects. But, as those involved knew and as later proved to be the case, once any disclosures began, there would have been no stopping them. The danger was clear: to tell all there was to tell about the Watergate break-in inevitably would lead to full-scale revelations about the Ellsberg burglary . . . the Huston Plan . . . the formation of the Plumbers Unit . . . the forged Kennedy cable . . . Howard Hunt's other activities, complete with CIA-furnished disguise, on behalf of the White House . . . Chuck Colson's undercover operation . . . the campaign "dirty tricks" carried out by the Dwight Chapin–Donald Segretti group . . . the ITT case . . . the dairy industry's heavy campaign pledge . . . and so on. Given all that to "avow," it is no wonder they were "loth" to do so. In the summer of 1972, with an election coming up, "Operation Candor" was not an especially inviting option.

Pressure on the White House, however, quickly began to build, with the arrests of Liddy and Hunt a few days after the Watergate break-in. By that time, the two burglars were in a position to make things extremely uncomfortable for three of Nixon's top advisers: Mitchell, Ehrlichman, and Colson. Liddy could have given damaging testimony about his meetings with Mitchell during the period leading up to the break-in. Both Liddy and Hunt could have blown the cover on the Ellsberg burglary, thus implicating Ehrlichman as the man in overall charge of the Plumbers Unit and the one who, at the very least, gave general consent to a covert operation against Ellsberg's psychiatrist. And Hunt could have chosen to reveal that some of the assignments he later claimed he carried out were under orders from Colson. So in terms of concealing their own associations with Liddy and/or Hunt, Mitchell, Ehrlichman, and Colson had a personal stake in the cover-up.

Haldeman, on the other hand, was in a more advantageous position. With characteristic finesse, he had insulated himself from direct contact with Liddy and Hunt. At the very worst, if Liddy and Hunt cracked, their testimony, based on personal knowledge, could reach only as far as the Mitchell-Ehrlichman-Colson level. Poised above this trio was Haldeman, just out of reach. He had what the White House liked to call invulnerable "deniability." And this itself was a critical factor, for Haldeman stood as the final layer of protection around the "deniability" that mattered most—that of the President himself.

But once the coverup was under way, Haldeman's deniability began to erode, perhaps not conclusively, but the process of erosion began to set in. For now the main action had moved away from fringe players, like Liddy and Hunt, and was moving into the very center of the White House, where the principal player was John Dean, the President's counsel, who not incidentally worked directly under Haldeman. This was the situation that carried over into the early spring of 1973, when Dean suddenly became fearful he was being set up as the sacrifice to "appease the multitude," as Bacon put it. When Dean broke ranks and took his story to the Watergate prosecutors, he implicated not only Mitchell and Ehrlichman and to some extent Colson—but also Haldeman, and by inference, at least, the President as well. In essence, then, the coverup succeeded over the short run—i.e., getting past the election—but at the cost of es- calating the stakes to the point where Nixon himself became the target of criminal investigation. For, once the investigation pene- trated to the Haldeman level—the last barrier to the Oval Office— the central Watergate question was destined to become the one Senator Howard Baker, in particular, would fixate on at the Ervin Committee hearings that summer: "What did the President know, and when did he know it?"

The problem was that by the spring of 1973 Nixon's fate was so firmly riveted to the fate of his top aides that there was no way he could smoothly extricate himself from their downfall. By allowing so much power and authority to concentrate in the hands of Haldeman and Ehrlichman, he had made them an intrinsic part of his Presi- dency. In the process, Nixon had planted the seeds of his own grief. This is what John Dean meant when he observed that there was "a cancer growing" on the Nixon Presidency. A main purpose of this book has been to suggest that the cancer had been growing there long before the Watergate crimes began to unfold. By the time Dean offered his diagnosis, it already had entered a critical, if not quite terminal, stage.

So it was that in the final days of April, 1973, headlines across the country were black with the sordid details of Dean's disclosures. But the event of greatest moment was that, by the end of the month, Haldeman and Ehrlichman were gone from the White House. With their departure, virtually all the great dreams of the Nixon Presidency perished. From that moment on, there would be no more talk around the White House about "our revolution" or the lofty pursuits that would bring to fruition the Age of Nixon. Within a matter of weeks it became apparent the Nixon White House no longer had the power or will to govern in the aggressive, supremely confident way that it had the first weeks and months following the 1972 election. Whatever energies it still retained had to be conserved for the increasingly desperate struggle merely to survive. Thus, on the last day of April, 1973, when Haldeman and Ehrlichman walked out of the White House, they took with them the high hopes of the Nixon second term, leaving behind a Presidency in wreckage.

Nor was that all Haldeman left behind. For he was the one who in 1970 had persuaded Nixon to install the elaborate taping system in the White House. Convinced as he was that Richard Nixon deserved to be thought of as the greatest President of the century, he envisioned the taping of each and every Nixon conversation in and around the White House as the ultimate PR job: the selling of the President before the bar of history. Haldeman's idea was that, after Nixon completed his time in office, the tapes would be carefully edited—the expletives and all other "image defects" being deleted —and the selected conversations would be left to stand as a towering monument to Richard Nixon and his Presidency—a sort of electronic answer to Mount Rushmore.

In the meantime, the potential was there for the tapes to be used as a secret weapon, one more way to keep in line those who claimed to be friends and to hurt those who were or who might become enemies. Exact quotes from conversations with the President would be on secret file, instantly available, should the need arise. Haldeman took great pains to make certain that hardly anyone knew about the taping system. Even Ehrlichman was kept in the dark as to the full extent of the operation until Watergate broke full.

But ironically, instead of serving as a weapon against others, the tapes became the ultimate weapon against Nixon himself. More than any other single event, it was the sudden discovery of the White

House taping system that put Nixon on the road to impeachment. (Part of the terrible irony is that it was Haldeman's protégé Alexander Butterfield—another fellow Eagle Scout and UCLA alumnus whom Haldeman had brought into the White House—who revealed the existence of the tapes to the Ervin Committee in July, 1973.) If the taping system had not existed or had remained undiscovered, the Watergate storm perhaps would have blown itself out by the late summer or early fall of 1973. At the time of the Butterfield disclosure, the Ervin Committee was floundering. It had taken its best shot with John Dean's testimony, but efforts to come up with corroboration were proving futile. The Mitchell-Haldeman-Ehrlichman line of defense was holding firm. The discovery of the tapes breathed new life into the Watergate investigation and soon the storm raged with more fury than ever. The attempt by Special Prosecutor Archibald Cox to obtain the tapes by subpoena led to the bitter court battles between his office and the White House, which, in turn, brought on the "Saturday Night Massacre" in October, 1973: the firing of Cox and the protest resignations of Attorney General Elliot Richardson and his deputy William Ruckelshaus. The events of that weekend caused something to snap in the country. Some fragile membrane of patience and tolerance broke and Washington was deluged with telegrams of outrage and demands for impeachment. It was in reaction to that "firestorm," as White House aides called it, that the hitherto reluctant House Judiciary Committee began to crank up the complicated machinery for impeachment proceedings.

Thus the final irony—that it should have been Haldeman, the super loyalist and stern sentinel whose job it had been to guard and protect his President, who had ordered into existence the instrument that, in the end, plunged Richard Nixon into his crisis of impeachment.

INDEX